The
Rantings
of a Single Male

Losing Patience with Feminism Political Correctness, ...

and Basically Everything

Thomas Ellis

Rannenberg Publishing – Austin

Published in the United States of America

Rannenberg Publishing
P.O. Box 202232
Austin, TX 78720-2232

www.rannenbergpubs.com

First limited printing, January 2005

Second revised printing, August 2005

Cover photo by Michael McIntyre

Interior Design by Place 4 Russ
(e-mail: place4russ@earthlink.net)

ISBN
0-9762613-1-6
Converted ISBN
978-0-9762613-1-5

Library of Congress Control Number:
2005907237

I know I'm supposed to say that the events and people in this book are fictitious, except that they aren't. The interpretations of events are my own and completely subjective. In addition, all events are described the way I remember them, and my memory is selective. Names of people in personal encounters have been changed to protect, well, me. Easily offended females should avoid prolonged contact with this book. If you think I'm talking about you, I probably am. Just not specifically. If you think I've defamed you, please get over yourself and on with your life.

Thanks to my brother Bob and my friend Andy for their encouragement. I would also like to express my gratitude to the numerous people who provided me with feedback concerning this work during the last two years.
And kudos to Mac, who originally told me in a bar after a few beers,
"Hey, you ought to write that stuff down!"

CONTENTS

Disclaimers and Motivation

I've got years of feminism, political correctness, and male-bashing clogging my arteries. So do most men, though they pretend not to notice. I wasn't aware of the extent of the damage until I began some serious self-examination. From the beginning I thought feminism was a toxin that only afflicted women. Now I understand that it's our problem too. Most men I've talked to have only a vague awareness of the impact three decades of unrestrained feminism has had on public policy and relationships. The anti-male onslaught has succeeded in part because men have neglected to actively oppose it.

It's time to end our polite tolerance of injustices committed against us. As men we must make a serious effort to educate ourselves about the ideas feminist literature is cultivating in the minds of women. We must become aware of the extremely negative portrayal of men and "masculinities" in women's studies courses, which are attended by tens of thousands of women each year. We must learn about the huge feminist organizations that are systematically dismantling the rights of men. We must acknowledge the scope of the problem and that we have failed to act. We must also expel the residue of feminist misinformation from our own systems. As it turns out, this book is my own process of detox as I come up to speed on the thirty-year ideological assault on my gender.

Although women are always welcome in my world, I expect these writings will be a challenge even for those of you who consider yourselves "open-minded." If you are capable of reading something that does not simply force-feed you the standard validation and inspiration, read on. For the rest of you, bail now before your heads explode. There are a thousand other books written just for you.

I am not restricted from saying anything by the culture of political correctness that is so rampant in universities and the media. There are professionals who spend their whole lives doing scientific studies of gender characteristics but are constrained by the herd mentality when it comes to presenting their findings. The few who stray from the pack remain cautious and civilized, even apologetic. They have their careers and their respectability to worry about. Not me. I'll say what I please, thank you.

This is opinion, not science. At least I'm not pretending it is, like all the pop psychologists out there. There are hordes of books by "experts" on the subject of men and women. I see most of them as either manipulation strategy books for women, angry woman books, or books about ways men can change to make women like them. I can't figure out why being who I am is not good enough, at least not in my own culture. A lot of syrupy self-help books are marketed to women asserting that men are dumb and women are right—yeah, we're the primitive men who need to go brood and sulk in our caves—and since they all have "Ph.D." on the cover they must be true. I'd say my views have at least as much validity as a follower of Maharishi Mahesh Yogi with a phony Ph.D. who exploits our neighboring planets metaphorically.

Who am I to write anything? I'm just another laid-off software engineer—a novice writer with a word processor. I have no training, qualifications, grant money, nor data of my own. Not even a TV show. But I have something just as valid. I've got years of my own personal wreckage to draw upon. What the hell happened? I have some thoughts on that topic.

As it turns out, feminism inspired this book. My thirty-year sporadic involvement with a German feminist raised my awareness about what the "women's movement" has been up to all this time. I watched as feminism dictated her life decisions and destroyed her relationships. My wake-up call came early. Even for me, it still took several wake-up calls before I realized the magnitude of the feminist disaster. I barely noticed the erosion of respect for men, the ridicule of our sexuality, and the assault on our rights. Most of my male friends don't understand how widespread the anti-male culture has become. They laugh at the stupid guys on TV shows and commercials. So what if most movies now glorify men getting kicked in the groin? That's just good fun. They think affirmative action is a benign program that corrects inequities, and that there is still a "wage gap." And even though every woman they meet considers herself smarter and morally superior to men, they think the next one will be different. How many wake-up calls will it take?

In the last four decades, men in Western society have actually changed as a result of women's nagging, persistence, emotional out-bursts, and most of all, because women have had some genuinely valid points. I must also say that men have had to sort through all the completely bogus studies and angry demands that women have thrown at us in order to find those points with merit. Feminism's valid points were exhausted long ago. All that's left is narcissism and anger masquerading as empowerment. I'm tired of nonsense. That must be why I am so profoundly tired.

But if women thought it was a long rough ride getting men to change their attitudes, it will be far more difficult to get them to admit that the attitudes in need of changing are now their own. Women have always seen themselves as the molders of men, and are not used to being challenged on issues concerning gender. I'm not sure how to convince women of anything, since they are more responsive to emo-tional outbursts than to reason. And what can men do to apply pres-sure, withhold sex? At the end of the day, men just give in to anything if getting laid is on the line. Women react angrily to any criticism, and they can stay angry a long, long time, holding out for that male apolo-gy. Lots of women now automatically disregard any male viewpoints, since they believe criticism of women is a form of verbal abuse. They will rip apart a relationship if they are offended, even if they are wrong. Women are in really deep.

I also doubt whether women are willing to consider change even if it's laid out in terms of why and how, and even if they decide to try. They enthusiastically avoid responsibility for their actions with trendy denial therapies and philosophies. The only things women are willing to change are their hair, their clothes, and their breast size. And a lot of times not even their hair.

Though I believe women have as much innate intelligence as men, I'm tired of the fiction that women have no limitations other than those imposed upon them by male society. If women don't excel at some-thing, it must be because of male oppression, and damn it, they de-serve some compensation. At least dinner and some new shoes. And even if their specific misery can't be traced back to the patriarchy, men should feel at least as bad as they do.

Disclaimers and Motivation

The Rantings

This book is not an attempt to deny women any rights they should have as people, nor is it an attempt to deny that women are treated in substandard ways in many parts of the world. But why are men always excluded from such statements? Why is it acceptable to ignore the suffering of men? I support many women's rights. I do not support more and more women's privileges. I know men have some female allies out there who accept us as we are and believe in us. There *are* a few women who understand that equality does not simply mean getting their way all the time. Very few. Neither do I blame women for all our problems. Men and women both possess amazing talent when it comes to screwing up a good thing. In that sense I truly believe in equality.

When I began writing, I was concerned that I would upset female readers. I got over it. What is so abhorrent about offending women? They take full liberty in offending us. In fact, I would like to dedicate this book to all the men who have ever been told to "shut up," "get out of the way," or "take it like a man" when challenging the validity of feminism and standing up for their rights. Why do men put up with that? As a man who brushed it aside for many years, I'd say it's because we have been taught it is our responsibility to please women. But there's a difference between pleasing women and appeasing them.

I should not have to compromise my rights as a man to make anyone feel equal. I can make compromises, but not on things like maintaining my own identity, being able to express my own ideas without female approval, or refusing to tell rhetorical lies to maintain a relationship. After many years of being unable to conform to the female vision of men as docile servants, I just want to be myself and speak my mind.

Consider these writings a male catharsis. I'd say the main reason I felt compelled to write an entire book is that I've rarely been listened to by women. At least not for more than about 15 seconds at a time. I have no problem with women expressing anger or whatever they want, but I'm really tired of it now. I'm tired of hearing only the feminist viewpoint of every issue concerning gender. I'm tired of tolerance for female sexism and double standards. I'm tired of the exaggerated consideration given to all females at the expense of males. I've heard it day after day and year after year without any real chance to respond. So finally and without interruption, here is an unobscured look at the world from the male point of view. I'm sure most women will summarily dismiss it as the rantings of a single male. The male voice must be disregarded, ridiculed and silenced. Let's burn that lace curtain. I hope others will help light the fire. Let there be rant.

The Learning of Ignorance

I am a free man. I've stopped caring what women think of me. The endless quest for female approval is over. No longer will I strain myself trying to divine what a woman's expectations are so I can meet them. Getting to this point took most of my life.

I remember the exact moment it all started. There was a girl named Sally with long, soft hair, who showed up wearing a little sailor dress one day. She was adorable beyond words. Her smile was simply stunning. I found myself wondering how anything on earth could be so cute. Impossible. It was the first time I was completely captivated by a female. It was also the precise moment I became a complete sucker. I was five.

Even at age six, I already had a strong sense of desire for the neighborhood girls. It was not a desire to perform any kind of sexual act, but I knew I wanted their clothes off. It went beyond mere curiosity. A girl with her pants down was like Christmas. Only better. Susie from down the street was a willing participant. We got caught and punished several times for showing ourselves to each other. It never stopped us. I always initiated. The foreplay was minimal. "Hey, let's pull down our pants." "Okay." Achieving a similar result would be far more complex in real life.

We had a playroom together where I had a pretend job building bridges and railroads. Susie had a pretend house set up and she was my pretend girlfriend who would pull down her pants for me whenever I wanted. At age six we already knew what we were supposed to do, so why do adults step in and mess everything up?

The Rantings

I believe childhood foreshadows events in our adult lives. Susie moved away, leaving me alone in the playroom. Without her, my pretend life collapsed. I asked a girl down the street named Mindi to pull down her pants, but she declined. That is, until I offered her a nickel. Suddenly she thought it was a great idea. She didn't want to get in trouble, so she took me behind her house by some bushes and fulfilled my request. I told another boy from the neighborhood about Mindi, and we gave her nickels on several occasions. She never asked us to show ourselves in return, though we would have done it for free. When we didn't have nickels, Mindi would accept little gifts like Tootsie Rolls. It wasn't what I had with Susie, but it was something.

Years later I was sitting in a strip joint when it struck me how nothing had changed except the price. Or had it? Let's see, I paid Mindi five cents to pull down her pants for a second or two. That comes to $3 to $6 per minute. And now dancers charge $10 to $20 for a three to five minute dance. Nope, same price!

Why would I want to see a girl with her clothes off before I even knew what sex was about? I don't know, ask God or a psychologist. See if you get the same answer. All I know is that anyone who tries to suppress their nature runs into some serious inner conflicts. The planet is rife with these people.

A Glance at Pre-Feminist America

I've heard men say that feminism is responsible for the decline of relationships between men and women. Though I find validity in that statement, pre-feminist America was no paradise. Women were angry at men as they always have been. They just hadn't refined man-hating into a science yet. I remember how religion was taught in public schools run by the old matriarchs. Sexual repression was the norm for both boys and girls. As children we were taught shame for our bodies and for our natural interest in the opposite sex.

I can remember they way girls were before they had the concept of guilt drilled into them. It was the first day of Bible school, and one of the kids discovered a private bathroom upstairs. When no one was looking, all the boys and girls went in to check it out. Right away two boys demonstrated their technique of peeing while the girls watched. Fascinated and amused, a couple of girls then reciprocated by demonstrating their method of peeing for the boys. This was terribly enlightening for us. But then the grown-ups came and caught one of the girls

on the toilet, and she got yelled at in front of everyone. We were separated from the girls and scolded for looking. The next day all the boys
were ready to try it again, but the girls screamed when they saw us
and slammed the bathroom door. It was a prime example of learned
behavior. A day earlier the girls had responded according to their true
nature, but they would never be the same. One dose of guilt had shut
them down. I couldn't understand why one day the girls thought it
was okay, but the next day it was wrong. Besides, it was too late. We'd
already seen them do it. They had totally bought into the indoctrination. I think that was when I got my first clue. Girls are different, and
it's not just the way they pee.

Why were we taught to *not* learn something? All the critical information about gender was deliberately withheld from us. How about
some of the basics? How about explaining why there are boys and why
there are girls? This attitude of shame about our bodies must be a left-
over from the Victorian era. Even now that dead 19th century queen
haunts us, whispering in our ears that curiosity is bad. Our natural instincts are evil and must be suppressed. We just can't seem to keep that
bitch's coffin nailed shut.

Typical for the times, my mother taught me that my attraction to females was wrong. Like mothers everywhere, she thought she could
shape me into the perfect little boy—religious, obedient, subservient
to women, and willfully postponing my sexual desire until I was married. God apparently overruled her. I would rebel, think for myself,
and become a devout agnostic. I would morph into a depraved, drunk-
en single male, a true product of my culture.

And how did the girls turn out? They were given all the necessary
skills to cultivate dysfunctional relationships. They seemed to embrace
their own sexual suppression. Just like they were taught, they grew up
to regard sex as deviant and abnormal unless within the confines of
commitment. They also learned that containment of the male libido
forces men to respect women. I suppose it works. If respect means not
having to pay for stuff. If respect means getting your way all the time.
If respect means having sex-starved guys pander to you. They were
taught that respect is something you demand, not reciprocate.

Regardless of what they are taught, respect is not something girls
find exciting. Polite guys take forever to make a move. That's why
girls seek out the most aggressive alpha males they can find. Females
see constant displays of respect as a submissive trait in males, and respond to them with acts of humiliation. Me? I've always sucked up to

girls I find attractive. I'm nice and try to please them. I show them too much respect, and they don't respect that. If you want a girlfriend, you'd better show her minimal respect. Aretha Franklin has been telling us that for years. Women want respect, but "Just a little bit, just a little bit."

Girls yearn for that challenge. They want to show they can tame even the most dominant, uncontrollable male and put him back beneath her where he belongs. Confuse him. Make the bastard grovel and show some respect. Sweet. But now he's useless and pathetic. Dump him.

The high school culture has been etched upon us forever. Guys have to try, girls do not. We have to approach them, they have to reject us. We have to impress them, and they have to remain unimpressed. Women are more desirable to men than men to women. They don't return our calls. They don't have time for us until next week. Then they cancel or don't show up. They can be late to meet us because their time is more valuable than ours. We have to pay. In a daily ritual we are called upon to sacrifice our own self-worth for theirs. How many girls are sitting around alone right now waiting for the phone to ring so they can say they've already got plans?

It was in high school that I learned I was not interesting enough to converse with females. You can't just talk about boring everyday life. You need to be able to keep girls excited and make them laugh. You have to spend money, fight with other guys, excel at a sport, defy an authority, break some rules, something. Then, if you get a girlfriend, what are you supposed do with her? Apparently, you have to torment her. She has to tease and taunt you. Then comes the power struggle. You have a big fight over nothing. Break up with her. Get back together. Who invented this system?

Girls are conditioned to take all they can because men are bastards. As boys we're conditioned to suck it up and take it like men. The high school environment is an exercise in conformity rather than learning. Our personal development is not the acquisition of knowledge so much as it is the learning of ignorance. That was true long before the onslaught of feminism.

Most women never get out of high school. They remain grown-up girls forever, spending years honing their rejection skills. They still use the "hard to get" philosophy in their adult lives. "Hard to get" is the fundamental way the concept of inadequacy is sold to boys and men. It starts out as hard to get attention from a girl in school. Then it's hard to get a date, a kiss, a kind word. It's hard to get sex. And it continues into relationships. What happens after you "get" the hard-to-get girl? "Hard to get" becomes "hard to get appreciation," or "hard to get a point across." "Hard to get" becomes "impossible to please."

A lot of guys try really hard to be liked by women. Before long they become manservants. And when being a nice guy doesn't work, they'll try being a jerk. Either way, you may as well forget about women actually liking you. They want our attention and they want our money, but actually liking us is not something women deem necessary. Men have come to regard it as a success merely to be tolerated by women. We are very willing to degrade ourselves if it makes women happy. We practice self-deprecating humor because it always gets a positive response from them. We use it so much we don't notice that everyone believes it.

No matter how much we humble ourselves before them, women are in constant need of more worship. They must remain elevated above us mere males. If women suspect men aren't viewing them as goddesses, they panic and develop a neurosis around it. Why is it part of the male job description to constantly prop up the self-confidence of women? Whenever women have their recurring crisis, men are expected to rush in and grovel in a demeaning and stupid manner. It always seems to work. Sure, it helps women feel confident, but there's a difference between being confident and being totally into yourself. At least there should be.

I want women to be confident, but if that requires the ritual sacrifice of my self-esteem or the metaphorical removal of my penis, I must object. We're constantly pressured to meet female expectations, but in this culture it's an unattainable goal. We always fall short. We forgot something. Something wasn't perfect. Whatever we said wasn't exactly what she wanted to hear. We have to try again. It is our role to remain unconditionally and permanently inadequate.

The Prophesies of Petra

After 21 years in the American culture, the concept of male inadequacy was firmly engrained within my sense of self. Women don't like men, they just want us to pay for their stuff. Women don't like sex either, they just use it to taunt us. Women don't desire men, they tolerate us. I was incapable of ever pleasing them or even knowing how to please them. I would have to leave the U.S. to learn otherwise. I had a place to stay in Germany, so I decided to take a year off from school and live in Europe.

The Fairy Tale Summer

I was in a dismal state of mind when I met Petra in Munich in 1974. She was only 19, and very French looking for a German girl. She was slender, with short hair and breasts much larger than necessary for attracting me. Since I couldn't speak German and Petra didn't speak English, someone had to translate for us that day. All I did was mention I was planning on driving to Spain, and Petra volunteered to go, on the spot, without so much as an invitation. Up to this point, girls wouldn't even go to a movie with me, let alone Spain. She also wanted to bring along her friend Ursula. Two teenage girls? Gee, let me think about it.

I was so used to rejection I wasn't sure what to do. I thought I should at least meet Petra again before the trip since we had only spent an hour together. Through Ursula I arranged to go over to Petra's house. Besides, her parents wanted to meet this American guy who would be driving their teenage daughter to Spain. I was sure Petra would cancel.

I met Petra's parents; they looked worried but somehow granted approval for her to come with me. To my surprise, a few days later the three of us set out for Spain in my VW as planned. We had hardly any money, enough for gas, some cheap food from markets, and not much else. We wouldn't be able to stay in hotels very often. None of us even had a credit card. We would mostly sleep in fields and on beaches, getting up early before anyone noticed us. If the car broke down, I wouldn't have the money to fix it, and we would have to leave it there and hitchhike back. That was fine with Petra and Ursula.

Ursula could speak some basic English in case Petra and I really needed to say anything to each other. Usually we didn't. It was the stuff of fantasy, driving off with two girls I didn't even know. When we arrived in Switzerland, they had the idea to ask farmers if we could sleep in their barns. So we pulled up to a farmhouse, and within minutes the girls got permission to sleep in the loft for free. The family even made us dinner and laid out some fresh straw for us to roll out our sleeping bags in.

Since we couldn't talk, Petra and I created fantasy versions of each other. I watched her as we walked through the wheat fields together. She was so happy she was glowing. I wanted her more than anything, and for the first time in my life I had a girl who would not disappoint. Once in the loft, the sex began almost immediately. The fact that we couldn't talk to each other eliminated the need for any verbal seduction. It also allowed our pure fantasies to survive intact. I did manage to ask her why she liked me. She replied that I was "not so manlike." That threw me. Okay, enough talking. Back to sex.

We were completely oblivious to Ursula, who was right beside us pretending to sleep. If you're hoping to hear that I did Ursula next, sorry. That didn't happen. I was totally taken with Petra, and she kept me plenty busy. We couldn't sleep, so we went at it off and on for most of the night. I went from never having a girl to having a girl who never said "no."

The next day we pulled up to a beach at St. Tropez and Petra immediately had her top off. So did all the girls. Topless volleyball. Could it get any better? Yes. Coed public showers. Petra was an exhibitionist, and became popular very quickly. I couldn't believe this incredibly cute naked girl was with me. After her shower, she walked into a beach restaurant topless for a couple minutes to ask directions. The hostess scowled her disapproval. You don't do that even in St. Tropez.

In the early evening the three of us drove around and found a rocky field on a hill where we rolled out our sleeping bags. Petra and I were going at it again when a farmer herding several cows came through and saw us. He began swearing at us in French before switching over to English, as if his thoughts on the matter needed any clarification. Apparently, English is the international obscene language.

I was amazed how Petra agreed to sex anytime and anywhere. She was like a grown-up version of Susie. "Hey, let's pull down our pants." "Okay." We did it in fields, on beaches, in a public shower, in a church. One time in Southern France we ended up pulling off onto a small back road late at night. We were so tired we just rolled out our bags right there beside the car in some soft grass. Early in the morning, roused by the sunrise, we went at it again. When some people walked by on their way to work, we looked up and realized we were in a ditch in someone's front yard. We just waited until everyone had gone past and then continued with our mission. As always, Ursula was right there observing us in all our splendor.

Our exercise of unrestrained lust continued throughout Spain. I remember driving down the road with Petra giving me head and poor Ursula sitting calmly in the back seat, as if it was completely normal. We were terrible. It was wonderful. We actually saw a lot of Spain, but that's not what I remember about the trip. No matter what the future held, there would always be something compelling about Petra. There was an undeniable warmth between us. Nothing could take away those two weeks. She had given herself to me completely. At the time, I didn't know why. Only later would I realize it was because she imagined she had found her soulmate. But reality can never keep up with fantasy. Our fantasies survived only because we couldn't talk. My simplistic sex fairy tale was also coming to an end, and I was about to be jerked harshly back into reality.

While all this was going on Petra was learning a few words of English and kept saying she couldn't get pregnant "right now." I offered to get some condoms after the first night but she said not to bother. I figured she knew more about her body than I did. Even so, I upset her several times by pulling out while climaxing. She would insist it was not necessary because it was "safe" right then. When we got back to Munich, suddenly Petra started exclaiming that she was "sure" she must be pregnant. Welcome to the world of female logic. It was a stressful several days. Fortunately, she was not. On the trip she had just "hoped" she couldn't get pregnant while leaving it for fate to decide. From this experience I learned that you *cannot* trust women to take responsibility for their own bodies. They prefer to wait until responsibility is thrust upon them. No one had ever mentioned this to me. Unlike lots of men who learn it the hard way, I was lucky. It was the end of summer and I returned to the U.S. free and clear.

The Gulag Summer

A few weeks later Petra came to the U.S. to live with relatives in Connecticut. I was finishing my last year of school in Ohio. Having studied English in high school, she became completely fluent after just a few months. We couldn't wait to see each other again. She asked if she could come live with me for the summer and, of course, she was welcome. We both expected fairy tales, but reality immediately reared its ugly head. We could talk.

Incredibly, Petra was a radical feminist. While living with her relatives, she had been sitting around all day reading the latest books by American feminist writers. My only impressions of feminism from the early '70s were a few women calling men "male chauvinist pigs," or bursting into rage when someone used the word "girl." None of my teachers were feminists. Neither were any of the girls I knew. Feminists were a few angry women from Berkeley or somewhere. Suddenly, I found myself living with one.

We tried to cling to our fantasy images of each other. She expected me to live up to her "soulmate" expectations. In Europe she had seen me as a non-aggressive man who would completely agree with all her feminist views. That's what she meant back in Switzerland when she said I was not so "manlike," as in macho. She was obsessed with feminism and regarded it as her mission to teach me everything about it. Did I mention I don't respond well to indoctrination? She was quickly disappointed when I didn't agree with everything she said. I was not the feminized man of her dreams. Apparently, to *not* know me is to love me.

I also tried to cling onto my vision of Petra as a sexual fairy tale, but it too collapsed. The first thing I learned is that if you disagree with a woman, you don't get sex. Even from a girl who never says "no." Of course, she was not withholding sex "deliberately," she just never "felt like it" if I disagreed with her on any feminist issues. At the time I didn't understand that her opinions were emotionally grounded, and I tried to apply my male logic to her ideological assertions. I wanted to teach her how to analyze and reason. She would have none of it. I never told her what to think or believe, I just challenged her. That only infuriated her.

My summer with Petra was like a sexual re-education camp. My house became a feminist gulag. She waged psychological warfare in an attempt to get her feminist ideology into my head. Sex, guilt, crying, anger, tenderness, no sex. She tried everything. Her big aspiration was to be a feminist writer so that she could convince men to change and stop oppressing women. I didn't realize it, but I had become a rat in her lab. She was determined to transform me using any means necessary.

The onslaught was relentless. I really tried to find things to agree with her about. It was not easy. She said women should be granted jobs in fields in which they are underrepresented. It didn't matter if they weren't qualified. They could be trained on the job. Yes, and women should make at least as much as men in all lines of work. How about men that are more qualified and have more experience? That's all because of oppression. That's right, women have been oppressed by men for thousands of years and now women deserve to be compensated for it. And furthermore, women are not just sex objects, they want to be respected by men. Wait a minute, isn't this the same girl who fucked me in a ditch by the side of the road with people walking by?

She was especially emphatic about rape issues. For example, if a woman identifies a man as her assailant, he should be immediately sent to prison on her word alone. Doesn't that mean that any woman could single out any man and accuse him of rape and send him to jail, even if he was innocent? Oh, but women would never do that! Women don't lie about that, and they never misidentify rapists. In fact, Petra claimed that a husband who does anything sexual to his wife without consent is a rapist and should be treated the same as any other rapist. She should be able to call the police and have him arrested on the spot. I had some problems with that, but I wasn't worried it would ever happen. Obviously, Petra was foreign and didn't understand the American legal system. We have the constitution and the justice system to protect our rights. The accused are always presumed innocent until proven guilty. People can't be arrested on allegations alone, thank God. That feminist crap would never make it through the courts. Would it?

While I was in class, Petra had all day to plan whatever feminist wisdom she intended to convey to me that night. Each feminist issue I expressed doubt or disagreement over was a crisis to her that needed immediate resolution. But the resulting arguments were driving me away, so sometimes she would sit around nude reading a book to distract me from studying. Once she had my attention, it was right back to her feminist obsessions: sexism, equality, oppression, empowerment. I never expected her to agree with me on any point, yet she demanded agreement from me.

I remember agreeing with Petra that perhaps female artists suffer from oppression because they are just as talented as men but get no recognition. She was so delighted that she immediately undressed and rewarded me with sex. It was certainly during this period of indoctrination that it was drilled into me that women want to be treated as equals. It took me years to realize this is absolutely false.

Petra also enforced femspeak on me. There were to be no more sexist terms like "chairman" or "freshman." Women had to be treated with respect, but somehow it was still okay to refer to men as "assholes." She caught me using the "girl" word so many times it was funny, except that she didn't think so. Though it was trivial to me, it was imperative to Petra that I use the word "woman." As soon as a girl menstruates she is a woman and must be addressed as such. "So, when a boy reaches puberty and is capable of impregnating females, should we call him a man?" I asked. "No, that's different." She was going to such lengths just so I wouldn't turn into a pig like all those other guys. Whatever. I just wanted her to be like she was in Spain.

By the end of summer Petra had become completely bipolar, being tender and caring one moment and making my life hell the next. Feminism was her religion, and she actually thought she could convert me. It was her version of salvation. But I don't think a man's role in a relationship is simply to validate the views of a woman. Why does it always come to that?

In the end, even the sex wasn't enough to make it worth it for me. I asked Petra to return to Connecticut so I could finish school without constant ideological outbursts. Disillusioned with me, she complied. On the one hand, I felt a sense of closeness to her for opening up to me. At the same time I felt that Petra and I remained strangers to each other, and that our whole relationship was based on a big misunderstanding. But then, I suppose that's nothing unusual.

Even with all the torment, my gulag summer with Petra was not a complete waste. Had it not been for her endless stream of irritating drivel, I would still have only a vague awareness of feminism. I had just been presented with a vision of the future insanity of women. Little did I know Petra's irritating drivel would turn out to be prophecy. The prophecies of Petra were a look into the darkness looming ahead.

There would be many more encounters with Petra, but none better than the time in Spain when we couldn't speak to each other at all. I still had a lot to learn about women. This knowledge would be painfully acquired. There is no simplicity in relationships. Fairy tales are few and far between. Spain was already long ago and far away.

The New Equality

By the time I began taking German and Spanish language courses in 1976, the university was choking with feminism. Female students deliberately saturated the discussion with the same brand of feminist propaganda I'd heard from Petra a year earlier. Women are victims who just want equality. Men are oppressors who think they are superior to women. Yes, we live in an oppressive environment all right. Not oppression of women, but oppression of thought and ideas.

One thing I gained from that gulag summer with Petra was an ability to confront attempts at feminist indoctrination. I remember sitting in a German class full of girls pressuring male students to repeat feminist dogma as part of a conversation exercise. The guys were unprepared for the ideological assault, so they just regurgitated everything to avoid getting pounced on. *"Ja, Frauen sind unterdrückt."* I was asked, "Why is it always a *Putzfrau,* and never a *Putzmann*?" I was supposed to say it was another example of oppression. Instead I said, "I don't know, why is it always a garbage *man*?" Collective female gasp. The guys perked up. "Wow, you can say that?"

Even so, I still viewed feminism as a harmless fad. I thought most feminists were nice women trying to expand their participation in the male world. Given time, they would grow out of the negativity. To prove to a couple of female classmates that I wasn't anti-woman, I agreed to help set up the stage for a women's conference sponsored by the university. That is, until I noticed they were using a man's face with a pig nose for the "o" on their "Welcome" sign. I showed it to a couple of other guys, and we asked a coordinator about it. "Oh, that's just for fun," she said. We walked out. At that moment I understood that I wasn't the one with something to prove.

A Defining Moment

In the meantime, Petra had moved to Montreal. She was enrolled in a new curriculum called "Women's Studies." There were only a few such courses offered at universities in Germany, but she wanted to major in it. Canada was the only place she could find a school that actually offered a Women's Studies degree program.

I hadn't seen Petra in over a year, so I called and offered to make the trek up to Montreal. To give you an idea of how naïve I was at 24, Petra told me on the phone she thought of me as her "special friend," and I thought that was really good. I also thought her curriculum of "Women's and Third World Studies" sounded pretty benign. I was encouraged because she wasn't just studying feminism, she was learning about different cultures of the world, too. It was a little eccentric, but so what? Besides, I was ready to sell my soul for ten minutes of sex. I was prepared to agree with any feminist bullshit she could throw at me. What harm could come from some stupid ideology?

Petra unenthusiastically told me, "You can come up if you want to," and my male brain interpreted that as, "You can come up if you want to fuck me." At the time I didn't understand the difference between sex and love. I would learn the difference on this trip. Montreal didn't sound so far from Ohio when I thought of all the easy sex I would be getting in exchange for my "enlightenment." And now Petra was working as a nude model in an art class. This was going to be good. It didn't matter to me that it would be January, so much the better. Got to keep her warm in bed with me.

The bus/train connection took me all day to get to Montreal. I couldn't afford a plane ticket on my restaurant wages. When I finally got to Petra's apartment, I found her strangely dispassionate. She didn't feel like sex, but this time I wasn't disagreeing with her about anything. She might feel like it tomorrow. This continued for three days. It wasn't even the dreaded female issues. When I asked her again if she felt like it, she told me, "If you want sex, why don't you just go to a prostitute?" Where did that come from? So, sex was just a service that women provide? She had always been very willing to pull me from the depths of deprivation before. Now I was denigrated for my sexual needs. I was stunned.

Since we weren't having sex I had plenty of time, so Petra gave me a bunch of her feminist books as assignments to transform me. I no longer remember all the titles, but some of them seemed predicated on the notion that hating men was well justified. Don't feel bad about that, they deserve it. We must fight the patriarchy and male domination. Be a lesbian, it's very progressive.

Most of her books were just bland, boring and forgettable, like Kate Millett's *Sexual Politics*. I only made it through a few pages before realizing I wasn't shocked to the degree expected by the book. Oh, some male authors have written about fucking and controlling women? The horror. I'm supposed to continue through another 400 pages? No thanks.

Petra had a copy of *Ordeal*, the book describing how porn actress Linda Lovelace of *Deep Throat* fame had been kidnapped, beaten, and forced to make the film, as if no woman would ever engage in such sex voluntarily. But more importantly, Ms. Lovelace complained she wasn't paid nearly enough for doing the film. I'm down with her on that one. I found *Ordeal* an unconvincing attempt at victimhood. At least it wasn't boring. I'd already seen *Deep Throat* in a theater (since it was released before the time of VCRs), and the most perverse thing I remember about it was how I qualified for a discount because I had a student ID.

One of the books in Petra's collection was supposedly written by a man. It talked about how the elimination of gender roles and the re-definition of masculinity would be a wonderful change for men. This women's liberation stuff was going to be great! All we have to do is auto-lobotomize ourselves and supplant feminism into our brains. Then men will be liberated too! Woo-hoo! I was sure the book had been written by a female writer using a pseudonym. That is, until I just recently discovered the book was *The Liberated Man* (1974) by none other than Warren Farrell, the guy who used to sit on the board of N.O.W. It took him several years to extricate his nose from the warm rectum of feminism and begin producing incredible men's rights books like *Why Men Are The Way They Are*, *The Myth of Male Power*, *Women Can't Hear What Men Don't Say*, and *Father and Child Reunion*.

Petra had another book that explained how women are equal to men in every way. Its intention was to reprogram all us ignorant males in accordance with the newest feminist thought. One section compared the strength and height of men and women. Bar charts clearly showed how men were on average taller and stronger than women, but the new way to think about this was that the tallest men were taller than the tallest women—otherwise the vast majority of men and women were equal in height and strength. It's our perception of equality itself that is wrong. We needed to redefine equality.

After going through her stack of books, I realized it wasn't just Petra's illogical babblings I had a problem with. The whole women's movement had something bogus about it. I also realized I couldn't pretend to agree with this bullshit even for sex. In any case, it didn't look like sex was going to happen, so the point was moot. As it turned out, Petra was already screwing some guy named Jorge from Peru, but then, why tell me beforehand? And this wasn't just any boyfriend, this was a third world boyfriend. I didn't understand at the time that as a white male, I had become politically incorrect as an oppressor of women, minorities, and people throughout the world. Jorge made jewelry for a living, and probably earned about what I made at my restaurant job, but he was "oppressed." I'm sure it was all explained in her Third World Studies classes. I found myself inadequate again, but this time in an ideological sense.

A minority boyfriend is like a political statement and proof of a certain set of values. The only challenge for a "liberated" woman is to put up with the oppressive nature of such a man while believing that through her involvement with him she is rejecting male oppression in her own society. Petra's Peruvian boyfriend never had to be reprogrammed like she tried with me. She never assigned him feminist books to read. She never required him to agree with her political views. He was exempt from that as a minority.

It didn't matter to Petra what her oppressed lover was like. He stopped in that evening carrying a black bottle of ouzo shaped like an Incan artifact and downed the whole thing himself. He'd found enough money for *that*. I'm sure he was in Canada illegally. He was staying in someone's unheated attic for free, and it would drop below freezing at night. None of it mattered. Petra announced she would be leaving to spend the night with this oppressed third-world drunk in his freezing attic. Since I was Petra's special friend, it would have been inconsiderate for her to have him there in the same apartment with me. But I'd show Petra who loved her. I'd show her what tolerance was. I told them to stay in Petra's room and I'd sleep on the couch. Love triumphs in the end. At least that's what I'd heard.

For the first time that visit Petra seemed delighted and gave me a big hug, which disgusted me. From the couch I could clearly hear the sounds of sex through the wall. I would have walked back to the train station right then but my coat and suitcase were still in her bedroom. They didn't come out until 3:00 p.m. the next afternoon, which gave me plenty of time to reflect. I didn't learn was love was, but I learned what it was not. Love is not simply a feeling of gratitude for good sex. Love is not the tolerance of selfishness. Love is not the infliction of agony upon yourself for the pleasure of another.

It was a defining moment. On the train ride back I swore I would never let a woman walk on me again. Wishful thinking perhaps. But that has defined me as deeply as Vivian Leigh swearing never to go hungry again. Sure, I've been walked on by women since then, but I have refused to lay myself down for them. It's my choice, and probably the main reason I am single. I will not tolerate mistreatment by women. I continue to watch as married men get trampled by unappreciative, demanding wives. It will not happen to me.

It would be years before I saw Petra again. She felt no need to repair any damage she had done. Nor will she ever. As a white male I deserve no consideration from her. She didn't destroy my ability to love, but she did destroy my ability to love *her.* They say time heals all wounds, but I disagree. Over time we just learn to disregard our wounds, and that's not really healing. Time doesn't heal, it just makes us numb.

The Expectation of Male Superiority

Women think it is men who insist on being recognized as superior. Using male oppression as justification, feminists have counterattacked with an unending salvo of female supremacy. Women are emotionally and morally superior. Women are more caring, sensitive, and nurturing. Women are not ruled by their hormones like men. Women have superior verbal skills. Tests suggesting that men might be better at anything demonstrate the need for remedial action to overcome discrimination.

In spite of all the female supremacy propaganda thrown at them, women still require men to be superior to themselves as a condition of acceptance and respect, and for consideration as sex partners. Women still demand men who are superior to themselves in strength, knowledge, skill, height, success, determination, aggression, and just about everything. Men who are less capable or powerful than women are summarily dismissed by them. We are all supposed to pretend this is not true.

I'm sure there were evolutionary reasons for this. Stronger, taller, smarter men were better able to protect and provide for females. Women still want men to be all that, but there's no need now in our complicated modern times. The biology hasn't caught up. Regardless of all their talk of equality, women scorn and ridicule men they view as physically weak. It's the same with any skill requiring eye-hand co-ordination. But smarter? Give us a few years' head start. That's why women go for men a few years older. But you've been told it's a "fact" that women mature faster than men. I'd say men need more time to grasp the level of responsibility demanded of them, and to pull to-gether the resources they need. Girls are viewed as "mature" as soon as they develop basic social skills and wear bras. Teenage boys don't gain immediate approval because of their looks. If they want to be men, they must assume responsibilities.

Even though women seek out men they perceive as superior, they've been conditioned to demand the appearance of equality. If they need something fixed on their car or their house, you have to jump in and help. But it's not because women don't know what the fuck they're doing, it's because you really enjoy using power tools and getting dirty and oily. We must interact with women as equals except when they choose to break protocol.

One time I picked up a girl from the airport, and she had a big heavy suitcase. "I'll get that," I offered. "No, I can get it," she snapped. "No, I'm getting it," I insisted. "And it's not because you can't. It's sim-ply an act of oppression on my part. As men we want to make you feel less capable than we are. It's part of our plan to keep women subju-gated. We're men, and that's just what we do!" She giggled with de-light and took my arm. She got her bags carried and got off the hook ideologically to boot. Obviously, she wasn't a true feminist. She had a sense of humor.

One girl pronounced to me that men are superior to women. I had just lifted something for her when she gave me a speech on how men can do everything better than women. "Men are more coordinated, smarter, and just better at everything. Why can't women accept that?" Huh? I had to disagree. "Come on, there's lots of smart women around," I told her. "Maybe we can lift more, but that's not every-thing." "No, all women think men are superior, they just won't say it," she said.

Apparently, I have more confidence in the abilities of women than women do in themselves. I've met enough highly intelligent women who can do complex math and write computer software that I have no doubts about women's innate abilities. Sure, women are flaky and vain, but that doesn't mean they're any less intelligent than men.

Different Equalities

Women are completely modern when they talk about equal rights. But when a scenario involving traditional female privilege comes up, suddenly we hear how they are "old fashioned." That doesn't mean they want to wash your clothes and clean your house. They become "modern" again in that case.

Women are now a confused mutation of old and new privilege. Old privilege is that of previous generations. Ladies first. Men are supposed to support women. Men are held responsible for the happiness of their wives. Men must risk their own safety to protect women. Men have to pay. Women don't have to register for the draft. Old privilege is females getting whatever they want cause they're so damn cute. New privilege is affirmative action. New privilege is hundreds of women's commissions promoting women's causes and expanding female entitlements. New privilege is an express lane to success for women. New privilege is women getting credit but no blame. New privilege is making it hazardous to your job to openly disagree with gender politics that favor women. Women want all the old and new privileges, and to call it equality.

Can there be such a thing as "selective equality"? Should women be able to pick and choose what they want to be equal with men about? If a woman does one "guy thing," does that exempt her from having to do any more "guy things" to confirm her equal status? Taking it even further, how about when a woman does some difficult "guy thing," like climbing Mount Everest? Why do all women get credit for that? Do men get collective credit for scientific discoveries? Were Einstein's achievements a victory for *men* everywhere? It was men who engineered and built the pyramids. Do I share credit for that? It's a male hand painted 35,000 years ago on a cave wall at Lascaux in Southern France, so do I get partial credit for inventing art? Apparently, everything done by men is an achievement for humanity, but things done by women are achievements for women. Sorry, but it's not making sense.

If it's not making sense, it's because men and women now think of equality itself differently. For men, it is a logical approach of applying an equal standard and measurement to something. To women, it is about being equally valued even if the method of valuation is different. Women want to *feel* equal. They don't grasp the concept of *being* equal. What does feeling equal mean? It means a measured equality does not apply. It means that role reversal as a test of equality is not relevant to women if it goes against them. It means women can choose what they want to be equal about. It means women only feel equal to men when they have more of everything.

An Utterance from Susan B. Anthony

I finally got some clarity concerning the equality issue, albeit indirect-ly. In 1984 I saw John Glenn on TV campaigning for president, and he was speaking to some women's group. Glenn quoted Susan B. Antho-ny, who said "Men, their rights and nothing more; women, their rights and nothing less." The women erupted in cheers. That was the first time I had heard the quote, and I thought, *What the hell did he just say?* Yeah, I remember how gutsy Glenn was when he risked his life atop that poorly tested Mercury Atlas 6 rocket, but those women turned him into a complete wuss. I'm not surprised he lost his presi-dential bid. In all fairness, it's not just John Glenn; women turn us all into wusses. It's their hobby. But that Susan B. Anthony quote accu-rately describes the contemporary female concept of equality. Maybe we should call it "the new equality." Women say men just don't get it. If they mean sex, they're right. And I don't get this "new equality" ei-ther. How about "to everyone their rights and nothing less?"

If feminism were really about equal rights, I'd be a feminist. When women speak of equal rights, they generally mean rights that *exceed* those of men. The suffragettes were quite passionate about gaining the right to vote, but not about being used as cannon fodder in World War I. They decried the fact that the male Negro slaves won the right to vote before white women, but they disregarded the fact that black men fought in the Civil War. Washington even used black soldiers in the Revolutionary War. So if you don't see me lining up to beatify the likes of Anthony and Stanton, you know why.

I'm not questioning the right of women to vote. I'm saying that be-cause women can vote on issues involving war and are also exempt from ever being forced to participate in actual combat, they have equal rights with fewer resposibilities than men. As of 1920, women have had no claim about being oppressed. In case you're wondering, no, I've never been to war. But I still have my collection of draft cards from the early 1970s. I don't know any women who do.

Whether we are talking about early or modern feminism, the women's movement has always been about winning rights as well as special privileges for women. The goal of modern feminism is to insti-

tutionalize female privileges as rights, and to shield women from responsibility. I can hear George Orwell laughing. Hey, I actually
learned something in high school. "All animals are equal, but some
animals are more equal than others."

Society is playing right along. Everything in feminism reeks of
"Men, their rights and nothing more; women, their rights and nothing
less." Anthony's distorted view of equality now permeates all aspects
of male/female relationships. We can say women are better than men,
but not that men are better than women. We accept limitations on men
as necessary, but women must be free of them. All achievements by
women are treated as more significant than male achievements. It is
acceptable for women to be paid more than men, but not for men to be
paid more than women. Women's opinions are automatically awarded
more merit than men's opinions. It's good for women to be controlling,
but not for men. Women have options, but men have obligations.
Women can have double standards because they're more complicated
and misunderstood than men. Men deserve to be criticized, but women
are above it because criticism of women is oppression.

So, what are the consequences of this redefinition of equality? It
means women do not care about being equal, they just want to be
considered equal. It means women can have rights without responsibilities, and men responsibilities without rights. It means that because
of all the supposed oppression women have suffered since the beginning of time, they feel justified in surpassing men in power, recognition, and wages. It means women still insist on superior men for their
personal relationships, but they want these men to affirm that women
are generally better and smarter than men.

The Final Challenge

I like it when women succeed, but I'm not interested in seeing a few
women in success roles simply to show all of us ignoramuses how
wrong we were. A female CEO, so what? Women flying F-16s? Whatever. A woman president? Women have led nations as queens for
centuries and can be just as brutal and oppressive as men, so why
does anything need to be proven here? Even Pakistan elected a female prime minister. I don't care about anyone's politically correct
agenda, and I'll vote against anyone who has one. If a woman wants
to be president just to make women feel empowered, it will be obvious to male voters. It doesn't prove anything to have a woman fuck-

ing up the country for four years instead of a man.

Why hasn't a woman been elected president of the United States? One reason is that women don't elect them. According to the U.S. Census Bureau, 59,284,000 women, as compared to 51,542,000 men, voted in the 2000 presidential election. That's *7.7 million* more female voters. The discrepancy increased to 8.8 million in the 2004 election, with 58,455,000 men voting compared to 67,281,000 women. Still there are drives to get more *women* to register to vote, driven by alarmed feminists who give the impression that far fewer women than men are voting and that women are underrepresented (see http://www.wvwv.org/). And I don't buy it that women have little influence during the nomination process. They've virtually assured that no bald men will ever again be presidential candidates.

Since so many more women vote than men, why don't women elect more women? I'd say it's because of the persistent cultural expectation that men be held to a higher level of responsibility than women. After all, who are the ones called upon to die for their country? Who rushes into burning buildings to save others? Who is held accountable if a family goes hungry?

But if men are still reluctant to vote for female candidates, I'd say it's because women in politics have never learned how to represent men. The problem isn't that they are women, it's that they are women-firsters. They will speak out on behalf of their own gender and children, but they actively disregard inequities suffered by men. They are oblivious to their own biases. Sure, women vote for male candidates all the time, but that's because male candidates pander to women and give them whatever they want. Just like in relationships. Besides, women don't really want to run the world—they'd rather sit back and tell their political sugar daddies how to do it, then bitch that they aren't doing it right. I will be willing to vote for a woman for president when she acknowledges the injustices against men and promises action to correct them. And she better have a record to back it up. Of course, that won't happen. The first woman president will go on a pro-feminist shopping spree.

No, the final challenge for women is not the election of a female president. I'm looking for something far less dramatic. The day I know women have stopped limiting themselves will be the day I walk around downtown Austin, on any given weekend, and see competent female musicians playing lead electric guitar. I don't want to hear crap like, "Men aren't ready to accept that." Men are totally ready for women who can actually play. Will someone please explain to girls that an electric guitar is not a fashion accessory? And no, strumming a few basic folk chords on a Stratocaster does not qualify one as a lead guitarist.

So why don't girls play electric guitars? It's not because they can't, it's because they don't need to. They realize they have better options for getting what they want, and none of them involve anything as complicated as becoming a lead guitarist in a rock band. They achieve that level of adoration simply by showing some skin. They understand their target audience. Wearing a short skirt is a lot easier than practicing. That's certainly why adult women never take up instruments. Better start teaching them early, before they get breasts.

I remember seeing fourteen-year-old female violin prodigy Leila Josefowicz perform live at the front of an orchestra. It came at a good time. I was just starting to have some doubts about women's abilities to master anything requiring at the high levels of coordination and complexity. I'd always assumed talent and intelligence were inherent to both genders. But after years of watching women giggle their way through various ineptitudes, I caught myself wondering if I was ignoring the obvious. Could that girl have been right that men are just more capable than women in lots of areas, including music? Was I suppressing this question because I was afraid it might be true? I was relieved to have my doubts removed when Leila played several highly complex classical pieces flawlessly, standing boldly front and center facing the crowd. I was in awe of her. It wasn't an exercise in activism. Her instrument and music were clearly paramount to her age and gender. I was reassured by Leila that women can do such things if they want to, but not that they ever will.

I want more of that experience. I want to be in awe of women for more than their ability to get me off. I want to see more accomplished female musicians. I don't care if they're performing on a stage or in their living room. If women want to convince me of how capable they are, they should stop spewing propaganda at me and show me some creative electric guitar technique. The will must come from within. I've had women say they don't need to convince me of anything. More denial. It's a huge goal of women's groups to make believers out of people like me, because maybe then women will finally start to believe in themselves.

So, what do women need to do if they want to achieve equality? They have to understand what equality really is, accept responsibility for their actions, become physically coordinated and develop dexterity, be willing to have sex with non-aggressive men who are less accomplished than them, play electric guitars, interact with men rationally and respectfully, give up their precious vanities, and surrender a lot of old privileges. But women don't want that. Why can't I get that through my head?

Much of the whole "equality" issue doesn't matter to women because even if men are physically stronger and have spent more time acquiring skills, women see men as easily controllable. Sure, let those dumb testosterone-saturated egomaniacs go off and prove themselves every day. Men are the worker bees, the disposable drones driven hormonally to serve the queen. Men are programmed to provide and protect, and we don't know anything else. Women drop the talk about eliminating gender roles whenever they find a man willing to buy them dinner. And flowers, and shoes, and a car, and a house, and furniture.

Women do a lot of things in the name of equality. It's become a license to do whatever they want. It means getting at least as much as someone else. It's getting their way *all* the time. It means not having to consider other points of view. In the name of equality some women want to tear down men. Others claim the right to control us and plunder our resources. Some women want to punish us for being who we are. But only a very few women are interested in anything resembling actual equality. They would have to give up a lot of gender privileges, take on more responsibilities, and even behave. Most women don't want equality that badly. Bless the women who understand what the hell I'm talking about.

The Perpetual Female Self-Worth Crisis

Even before the rise of feminism, women used a combination of male validation and male-bashing to boost their self-worth. Feminism has just emphasized the male-bashing part. Regardless of what feminism has done to diminish the importance of men, most women still crave traditional male validation. Oppressed or not, they still expect men to suck up and buy them diamonds. Inadequate as we are, women keep coming back for relief from their perpetual self-worth crisis.

Because of feminism, women are now hopelessly schizophrenic about how they want to be valued by men. If men respond to their sexuality, women will feel underappreciated for their inner qualities. In these moments women yearn to be seen as intelligent, creative and talented. But if women begin to think men do not desire them in a sexual way, they panic and start doing things to attract men. They flirt and wear sexy clothes, seeking male attention as reassurance that they are still desirable. Not that they want us pervs to actually respond to them sexually.

What Women Want

At some point most women arrive at the basic reality that they want to be desired by men, regardless of the influence of pop-feminism. A lot of them have simply given up on the whole idea that education and professional success are the means to fulfillment. They'd rather have a quick fix for their self-esteem, and right away they know what they want—implants.

So which is it that gives women the most confidence, is it being talented and intelligent or breast size? I'm afraid I already know the answer. Leave it to cable news to publicize one of those "studies." A bunch of high school girls were asked if they would rather be really smart and not very attractive, or really sexy and not very smart. Well, duh! Naturally they chose being sexy. You'd have to be pretty dumb to want to be smart. Not that being smart is bad, it's that attractive women have a much better shot at the pampered life. A plain-looking smart girl has to go out and earn everything, and where's the fun in that? American females are convinced looks and big breasts will make them more powerful than any knowledge can.

Sure, there are lots of men whose appreciation for women does not extend beyond breast size. Nevertheless, women crave approval from such men. Apparently, women think these men speak for all of us. It's probably because these men are the most vocal.

Women in general do not understand why breasts are attractive to men. They assume bigger is always better, which leads them to get cartoon-like implants or ridiculous foam enhancements. One time I was in a Hooter's, and the waitress was wearing some kind of obvious breast enhancement. When she leaned over even a little, we could clearly see some plastic devices pushing up her breasts. It was pathetic and sad. Oddly, these women seem absurdly confident.

The implant queens often do not listen to boyfriends or husbands who tell them their breasts are fine. Besides, all American women think there is something wrong with their breasts. If you tell a woman her breasts are great, it has almost no impact compared to whatever some dumb drunk guy said to her two years ago. Dumb drunk guys in bars wield enormous influence when they make careless and rude comments about a girl's breasts. Of course, it happens that some men encourage their girlfriends to get implants. Even dumb drunk guys get girlfriends. But listen, girls. If your boyfriend wants you to get implants and says he'll like you better if your breasts are bigger, I'd say there's something wrong here, and it's not your breasts. My advice is, if he likes plastic tits that much, why not go all the way with it? Hit the road and give him a plastic blow-up doll as a parting gift. There are plenty of men who will appreciate you if you are willing to meet them. Give the intelligent drunk guys a shot.

But it's the dumb drunk guys that women go under the knife for. I don't get it. I remember being in a strip club and noticing an incredibly cute young dancer. I waited an hour until it was finally her turn. She got up on stage and took off her top, revealing nasty surgery scars under each breast. It's insanity. She was absolutely gorgeous, and I can't imagine that she thought herself so unappealing as to undergo such a painful and expensive procedure. It has convinced me of something. Women are far more obsessed with their breasts than men ever were.

Conventional wisdom aside, there is no direct correlation between breast size and attractiveness. But there *is* a direct correlation between breast size and attitude. In fact, women who get breast implants are actually getting *attitude* implants. Women with smaller breasts seem to suffer from low self-esteem regardless of their intelligence or level of success. They can be drop-dead gorgeous but it doesn't matter. They may have men who love them, but that doesn't seem to matter either. They want an objective opinion. They want approval from the dumb drunk guys. I'll never understand it. There are plenty of men who know women are more than just the sum of their bosoms. I, for one, would never judge a woman by her breasts. I'm an ass man.

Ironically, the new attitude that comes with implants is *not* very attractive. There's a certain ugliness about artificially beautiful women. Real beauty is simplistic. Real beauty is not over-engineered clothes, extrusive breasts, excessive make-up and fake eyelashes. Once everything is in place these "beautiful" women become too good for me, even though I have no desire for them. But that *is* the target attitude women want to achieve. They think they've placed themselves above us all. They want drooling idiots lining up for rejection.

Emotional Validation

Besides the reassurance that they are still attractive to drunken, depraved derelicts, women also need to establish a sense of emotional self-worth. Women still want our unwavering approval, even if they don't really like us. We're supposed to rush in and validate their inner vanity with compliments, gifts, and male attention.

Women evaluate all gifts for that sense of emotional significance. Money itself has no emotional value. That's why flowers always work. But money spent on something frivolous becomes an emotional act. Even an expensive gift won't cut it if it has a practical use. That's why the best gifts for women are useless. Like a tiny box that holds nothing, or a shiny glass egg. Any practicality interferes with the emotional purity.

Women don't crave expensive restaurants for the food, they just feel more valued when taken there. All the little amenities and obsequious service are not so much indications of how good the restaurant is as how much she is valued by the man paying for it. They want assurance from us that they deserve everything by virtue of being female. But if women like money being spent on them, they *love* money being wasted on them. They'll order an expensive dinner when they aren't even hungry. And the more money the man is willing to waste, the more powerful he is perceived to be. He'd better not flinch, or it's ruined. That's an indication of his weakness, and she won't feel special. He must demonstrate that his money is worthless when compared to her feelings. It's a supreme act of sacrifice in her honor. Women know how much we like money. To us, money itself has value. To women, money has no value until it is spent. On them.

Romance has degenerated into a form of groveling. Do I have enough points yet? More dinners, flowers, fix your computer? Oh, I can come over to help power wash and paint your house? I don't think I could get away with "inviting" her over to do my housecleaning and laundry. "The dishes are in the sink and there's a six-pack of roses in the fridge, help yourself." Opening or holding a door for a female is no longer an act of respect, it is an act of submission. Romance is a void that sucks like a black hole. It's a one-way street I've gotten tired of going down. Tell me, when is the Valentine's Day when women come pick us up, tell us we're great, buy us a steak, get us drunk, and then fuck us in all the ways we want? Let's make "Steak and Blowjob Day" a reality. How about two days before Valentine's Day?

Even girls who want to be our "friends" expect all the traditional girl perks. We have to call. We have to drive. If they fuck up, we have to say it doesn't matter. Sure, they'll take our flowers, let us pay for dinners and bathe in our flattery, then think they're doing us a favor by hugging us good night. You can be a tit slave for years and years, but at some point you have to ask yourself, "What has a tit done for *me* lately?"

Diamonds and Whores

Can there be any question as to why diamonds are a woman's favorite gift? Diamonds are like emotional currency, and a woman takes on that emotional value whenever she wears them. Of course, diamonds are a complete waste of good money, which is also very exciting for women. It's not the beauty of the diamond that interests women so much. After all, women can't tell cubic zirconium from a real diamond. The size of the diamond certainly matters, but what's really important is the size of the sacrifice the man made when he bought it. How much did it hurt when he plunked down the cash? Was it really, really, *really* painful? Wow, a guy who's willing to be completely miserable for her? That's true love.

Women don't like cash so much; it can be dirty with germs from other peoples' grubby hands. Besides, cash is what whores get. But diamonds are all sparkly and clean. Never mind the very diamond she's wearing may have been mined in Sierra Leone using slave labor, stolen by Colombian jewel thieves, or used as payment for international crimes. Or smuggled in someone's rectum. Women vaguely know about that, but they don't care. They may have given up mink coats, but don't fuck with their diamonds.

In relationships as in sex, women always seem to be on the receiving end. If I ever wanted to get married, I know I'd have to go out and buy a damn diamond, and never question it. Diamonds symbolize eternity. How about a nice fossil instead? And I guess big diamonds are more eternal than small ones. The female diamond fetish has become a cultural attribute of American women who've been bombarded with those sappy commercials all their lives. They now see diamonds as an expression of passion, just like they've been programmed. Diamonds are forever. Or at least until her next upgrade.

I don't think anything will ever change how women view diamonds as an indication of self-worth. They will always be pursued by these demons. Just like garlic keeps vampires away, diamonds protect women from being called whores. It's an archaic concept that's still ingrained in the female brain, that married women can't be whores— and, of course, married women get diamonds. Diamonds are just very expensive garlic.

Women don't want to be perceived as exchanging cash and favors for sex, but they don't want to just "give it away" either. How do they resolve this? As a general rule, women won't have sex until you've spent at least as much money on them as you would on a whore. But even after that threshold is met, women do not consider themselves obligated to actually have sex because, after all, they're not whores. In fact, it's another reason men should spend lots of money on women—to prove they are not whores. A diamond as a gift from a man has become the ultimate expression that a woman is not a whore, because a diamond costs so much more than a whore. The more expensive the gift, the less whore-like she becomes. That might be a good marketing slogan: "Come on, buy her diamonds; she's not a whore!" Or maybe "Only whores wear moissanite!"

The Commitment Orgasm

In the female reality, commitment itself is far more important than whatever arbitrary commitment they make. Committing to something means it's "forever," which is a magical word for women. Most women think committing to something is a sign of success. Sure, she gets her "commitment orgasm." Then what? What will it take to make her happy next week?

Commitment is different for men. Men commit to a woman. Women don't commit to a man, they commit to a lifestyle. Women see a relationship as an entity that exists on a higher plane than the random man they actually marry. The man is just an unpleasant necessity of life, a requirement by nature for her to live within that higher plane. That's why the specific man is usually not important. It's the concept of commitment itself that women love, not men.

Women go into commitment mode for lots of reasons. Why are women so anxious to get commitments? Because commitment implies that you are finished debating the merits of something. You are ready to cut off any more logical challenges to it. Women like that. No more analyzing. A wedding, besides being her coronation, is also a commitment ceremony. The commitment in this case is a promise to curtail debate on whether the marriage is really a good idea. For men, commitment itself is a bad idea. We don't like to shut down our logic. We want an out. Commitment doesn't make any sense. What if the reasons for the commitment are no longer valid? What if the original decision was based on wrong information? Are we to have no recourse? What are we committing to exactly? How long is forever?

Women who harp on about "commitment phobic" men are missing the point. Men don't fear commitment, men fear ambiguity. Men fear the dysfunctional relationship we can't get out of. When men hear women talk about commitment, it sounds like they're saying, "Promise you'll never leave no matter how bad it gets." Tell us, please. How bad *can* it get?

Commitment phobia? How about "not having any time for myself" phobia? How about "her demands are out of control" phobia? How about "I have to spend more and more money to keep her happy" phobia? How about "she never wants sex" phobia? How about "what if she gains a hundred pounds" phobia? How about "expensive divorce attorney" phobia? How about "she might accuse me of sexual assault" phobia? How about "she could get a restraining order and kick me out of my own home" phobia? Didn't I read that women now file for 75 percent of all divorces? Or maybe we should call it "cashing out." Although I agree with the concept of reasonable child support, having to pay alimony strikes me as absurd as requiring a woman to continue having sex with a man after she has divorced him. If I quit my job, they don't keep paying me.

I don't care how extravagant the ceremony is, a commitment cannot guarantee anything. Neither can a big diamond. So why do women associate diamonds with commitment, love, and self-worth? A diamond can't transform anyone into a better person. Perhaps it makes a woman feel worthy of her own vanity.

The Czech Border Girl

In 1999, I was driving back at night from Dresden into the Czech Republic. Just after I crossed the border, there were all kinds of women standing along the road. At first I thought they were waiting for a bus. Then I realized they were all roadside prostitutes. I'd seen a few in Italy. They were usually overweight African women wearing disgustingly bright dresses in an attempt to lure truck drivers to pull over. But here in this stretch of seven or eight miles there must have been a hundred or more women of all kinds. A lot of them were repulsive, and probably ended up standing there for hours without managing to stop a single car. There were so many, I felt compelled to talk with one.

I pulled up by one girl who looked different than the others. She had on formal black dress pants and a white blouse with ruffles, an outfit she should have been wearing to work in an office or mall, probably her best clothes. She was attractive, probably in her mid-twenties, and offered me sex in my car. When I declined, she thought I was bargaining and reduced the price to anything I wanted for 20 German marks. At the time that was the equivalent of eight dollars. In German I asked her where she was from. It was one of those war-torn Balkan republics. I think it was Croatia, or maybe Kosovo. I could only imagine what devastating set of circumstances had brought her to this place, offering herself up to strangers in cars. I couldn't help thinking how often we sit around complaining that *our* lives suck while a waitress brings us more drinks.

I wish I could tell you that I at least gave her the 20 marks before driving off and leaving her to her cruel fate. Besides, how much difference would a couple of dollars make to her situation? Not much. It occurred to me as I drove away, that's probably what people thought as they walked past Beethoven when he was homeless and in the street. What's eight dollars to me? Nothing. And who am I to pass judgment on the value of anyone? I got about two miles down the road before I actually turned the car around and went back to find her—so I could hand her 20 marks. She was gone. Busy in one of the many parked cars no doubt. I still think about her from time to time. Was she able to work her way out of that place? Or has something more awful befallen her? No, I don't think the women back home are better than her. They're just more fortunate. That's about all a diamond means.

It's Different in Other Places

There used to be just one basic type of American princess, modeled after the high school prom queen. Now we have another variety— the angry feminist princess. The two princesses have a lot in common. They both have a superiority complex, they both think they should get their way all the time, and they both expect men to be their servants. The only difference is how they justify it. Princesses of the old high school variety feel they deserve everything because of their appearance, whereas feminist princesses have an entire ideology to justify and politicize their self-worship.

Many American women alternate between princess types depending on the situation at hand. They're a lethal mixture of narcissism and feminism. They expect men to both idolize and obey them. They regard anything less as anti-woman. They feel more validated by demeaning men than by bonding with them. Their promises typically amount to superficial courtesies or forgettable intentions. I don't trust them to do anything they say they will do. Be reliable and responsible? Why should women agree to such silly restraints? They're beyond spoiled. They're ruined.

Sure, I've met responsible American women. They have the "me first" attitude well in check. They're respectful and haven't done anything wrong. Yet. But given my experience with women in general, they have a hard time convincing me that they aren't going to have a princess relapse and retaliate if something isn't perfect. The nice girls are nice as long as we meet their expectations. After delivering more than my fair share of sucking-up, I began to notice my acts of servitude were rarely reciprocated in any significant way.

To really understand how difficult most American women have become, you need to meet women from cultures where female supremacy and feminist hostility do not form the basis of the female psyche. It's shocking. It's simply amazing to be in a place where women openly express appreciation and affection for men. Yes, they would be happy to meet you again. They don't have to check their calendar. They offer their number without being asked. They return calls. They show up. They respond. They reciprocate. They initiate. They don't act like they're doing you a favor. They don't judge you by your car. They don't treat you like a potential stalker. Even the most attractive women don't consider themselves above us. Being attractive is *not* something they use to torment and exploit us—it's something they use to, well, attract us.

Daniella From Italy

In the early '90s I had a travel voucher that was ready to expire, so I decided to check out a Caribbean island. But I couldn't persuade any of the women I knew to go with me. I offered to get them a ticket using frequent flier miles and cover the hotel and car. No takers. One even asked me to promise not to expect sex from her. I assured her sex was not a requirement. She still declined. So I went to St. Maarten alone and hung out with some cute European barmaids.

I decided to take a day trip to St. Barts, and when I got on the boat I noticed a cute young blonde sitting on the deck. There was one empty seat next to her so I took it. I found it odd she wasn't flanked by four male bodyguards protecting her from guys trying to say "Hello." Oh yeah, I forgot. This wasn't the States.

I didn't expect any acknowledgement from her at all, since that's what I had gotten used to from women in the U.S. So I was surprised when she turned to me and just started talking. This was Daniella from Italy. In charmingly broken English she introduced me to the group of Italians she was traveling with. They invited me to join them, so we all rode around St. Barts in a minivan. Daniella graciously offered me her address near Modena, Italy, in case I was ever in the area. "It's near Milano," she said.

As luck would have it I got sent to Europe on business a few months later, so before I left I sent Daniella a card saying I would be in Milan for a day and maybe we could meet for dinner. I would call from my hotel. At some point I looked up Modena on a map and discovered it was about 80 miles from Milan. Obviously a beautiful girl I met briefly was not going to drive 80 miles to meet me for dinner. That just doesn't happen. Besides, she was in her early twenties, and I was forty. And I hadn't talked to her since the Caribbean. I decided not to call and spare myself the rejection. Big mistake. When I got home from my trip there was a letter requiring my signature at the post office. It was from Daniella, and she had sent it express to try to reach me in time. She wrote that she only lived 120 kilometers from Milan, so she would be able to drive and meet me there. Gasp.

The American rules had been so deeply ingrained within me that I blew it. I assumed that as a man, I would have to do all the work in providing the arrangements. I assumed that unless I drove to Modena, she would not be interested in meeting me. I assumed that her original offer to meet had been a superficial courtesy. I assumed that because I was out of her league, she would not bother with me. All my cultural assumptions were wrong. I called and apologized profusely. Contrary to my expectations, she wasn't upset at all, and repeated her offer to meet next time I was in Italy. It crystallized for me at that moment. There was no concept of not being worthy to Daniella. There were no "leagues" where she lived.

I continued to get postcards from her saying things like, "You must come back to Italy and visit me as soon as possible!" You don't usually get second chances, but a year later I got sent back to Milan. Sure, I've done plenty of things in my life that would give that *Dumb and Dumber* movie a run for its money, but I was determined not to let this visit turn into a sequel. Although Daniella repeated her offer to pick me up in Milan, I took the train to Modena to save her the time and effort. I hadn't seen her in over a year, so I was hoping I'd recognize her. Outside the station I spotted a stunning young blonde waving in my direction. I fought the impulse to turn around to make sure there wasn't someone else behind me. Sure enough, it was her. Suit jacket, short skirt, long blonde hair, black stockings, heels. Daniella was like a supermodel without the attitude. I met her family, we enjoyed some pasta, I did shots of something with her father, then she showed me photos of herself wearing various bikinis. Incredible. A girl who doesn't treat me like a perv for finding her attractive? Why isn't it like this where I'm from?

The next day she asked me if I wanted to fly to London with her. London? She wanted to check out a business school and flights were cheap. So the following day I accompanied Daniella to London as if I had known her for years. Trafalgar Square, British Museum, pubs, Camden Lock flea market. With her bright red skirt and jacket she was an infusion of color among the Londoners in their drab browns and grays.

I wish I could report that we had a torrid affair, but that isn't what happened. She stayed in a student dorm while in London, and I was in a hotel. In any case, I don't think that's what it was about. I didn't feel that sense of urgency to be sexually validated by her. Neither did I feel teased by her. And I certainly wasn't expected to pay her way. In fact, she offered to pay for *my* hotel. Daniella was one woman who totally backed up her words. At the end of our time together, I realized I had just experienced what it was like to be treated as an equal.

I went back to visit Daniella and her family again the next year, and we all drove down to Naples together. Beaches, islands, antipasti, wine, castles, Daniella in her bikini. The year after that, I met her and the Italians at a ski resort near Grenoble. And all this happened because there weren't any American women who would come with me to the Caribbean. The world needs more Daniellas.

A Romanian Barmaid Named Alexandra

It was 1977; Petra was in Montreal working on her degree in Women's Studies. I wanted to live in Europe again and become fluent in German, so I ended up in my brother's dorm room in Bonn, Germany, where he was an exchange student. I got bored one night, so I took a long walk into the city center and ended up at a bar called "zum Elephanten." I took a seat at the bar and noticed a sultry young barmaid in a tight short skirt keeping the place lively. *"Sie kommt aus Romanien,"* said the old man beside me. She poured me a beer and introduced herself as Alexandra. She was especially flirty with me. I'd seen this before. Teasing for tips. She seemed thrilled I was American. Very unusual. I had three beers and asked to pay. *"Ein Moment bitte,"* she said. Five minutes later I asked again to pay. She tore up my beer *deckel*, indicating the beer was free, poured me another, and asked me if I would please stay. She was getting off in half an hour. Could this be happening? I had never been picked up by a barmaid. The old man sitting next to me kept grinning at me, and shook my hand as if to say, "You lucky bastard." This was going to be a very different night.

I waited another half-hour at the bar while she closed up. At the time I could barely speak German, so I sat quietly with my beer watching Alexandra work. She was beautiful and had those exotic Eastern European eyes and wavy brunette hair. She locked up the bar, then we walked hand in hand across the Rhine to her apartment. It was heavy on female décor. There were a couple hundred dolls propped up on a custom shelf that went all around the living room. Little stickers of pink hearts lined the doorways and baseboards throughout the apartment. She showed me a photo album of Romania, and we began kissing. Within minutes, she led me into her bedroom.

Things were happening quickly. Before she undressed, Alexandra had a special request—a fantasy for me to act out. She asked me in German, but I didn't understand the word *vergewaltigen*. So she described it for me.

If I were a soldier who had just invaded her city and discovered her hiding, what would I do? Or, if I were a criminal who had broken into her house and found her sleeping, what would I do? That made me uncomfortable, but she was very insistent. I should call her bad names in English and slap her and hold her down and *vergewaltigen* her. I hesitantly removed her top, then she suggested I rip off her panties. Whatever they were made out of, they wouldn't tear. I ended up mangling them a little before slipping them off. "Remember, you are a soldier," she said. "Now swear at me and slap me." Not wanting to disappoint, I called her a slut and gave her a light slap on the cheek. "Like that?" I asked. "No, it has to be harder," she said. Fine. I slapped her slightly harder. She was getting impatient. "No, no, you have to really slap me!" So I wound up and clocked her a good one across the mouth. "Ow!" she yelped. There was a little blood on her lip. "Oh, I'm sorry! I'm sorry!" I exclaimed. "Don't say that, you'll ruin it!" she said. Clearly I was not good at this. To my relief she gave up on her horrid fantasy and settled for some regular Ohio-style sex.

I woke up in the morning with this beautiful barmaid. I'll never forget the scent of her cigarette hair. As bizarre as it had been the night before, I felt comfortable with her. There was a sense of calm and warmth. Alexandra got up and tried on five or six outfits in front of me, starting over from nude each time. She had me select her outfit for the day, from bra and panties to skirt and blouse. Probably she'd never heard that guys can't coordinate colors. Finally we were ready to leave. I told her I was staying in a student dorm on the northwest side of town and would come back to the Elephant Bar sometime to look for her if she wanted. She wanted.

She took out an envelope full of German currency, handed it to me and said, "Take as much as you like." There was at least two thousand German marks in there, probably her entire savings. I asked her why she wanted to give me money. She said she wanted to give me a gift, and she always heard how Americans like money more than any-thing. I broke out laughing. When I handed the envelope back to her, she looked genuinely surprised. Next she offered me a "hero work-er" medal she received from the socialist Romanian government. It was one of several she got back in Romania as compensation for over-time in lieu of actual pay, as was common practice in the socialist states. I accepted.

A few days later I went looking for Alexandra in the bar, but she wasn't working. So I tried her apartment, but she wasn't home; so I left a note saying I had stopped by. Oddly enough, she didn't have a phone, probably because she took calls at the bar. That night at 1:00 a.m., she showed up at the front of the dorm and rang all the door-bells in the building, waking up everyone. At least a dozen grad stu-dents lumbered down to see who the hell it was. She told them she was looking for an American man. The irritated Germans knew who she was looking for and delivered her to my room.

It was then I realized Alexandra was insane. She had been going around in a taxi to the various dorms, ringing all the bells and waking up all the tenants. Insane or not, we went back to her place for more sex. The German girls in the dorm looked at me differently after that. Wow, a guy with a female stalker—impressive. They wanted to know all about it. So we swapped stalker stories.

Fun as that was, it certainly wasn't something I expected to devel-op into a relationship. What the hell did Alexandra want from me? Was this more than sex to her? What else was she capable of? That fear of ambiguity took over. I went to the Elephant Bar and told her I thought she should see other people. Rather than going psycho on me, she was fine with it and brought me out a huge dinner. She comped my tab again, and I realized that meant she had to pay for it herself. Here I meet a girl who is incredibly taken with me and is nice to me, so I assume she must be psychotic.

Days later I found myself thinking about her all the time, so I went back over to her place across the Rhine late one night and rang the bell. Hey, if she can stalk me I can stalk her right back. Alexandra an-swered the door completely nude. She was delighted to see me and invited me in. I sat there and watched as she rudely kicked *two* guys out of her bedroom, demanding they get dressed and leave immedi-ately. "Come on, hurry, get out! Get out!!" They looked terribly puz-zled, wondering what the hell had just happened, as they put on their shoes. Offering no sympathy, I simply shrugged my shoulders. Like I had any clue. When I told her she should see other people, I hadn't meant it literally in the *plural* sense.

For whatever reason, I was still the ruler of Alexandra's world. It occurred to me that I'd never had such sway over a woman before. I certainly didn't have that power for any perceptible reason. I also wasn't sure who was ruling whose world. I guess I didn't care. The sex was good. I decided to go with it.

I asked her if she normally had more than one guy at a time. She told me once in Romania she slept in a room with nine guys. She was willing to have sex with any and all of them, but the guys were jealous of one another; so whenever one guy would make a move on her, the other guys would turn on the lights and stop them from doing anything. So she gave up on them and went to sleep.

This was all very interesting, but I also noticed my stress level spiking again. Who was this girl, and what reason did she have to obsess over me? Could this all be chalked up to cultural differences? Did all Romanian women behave in such ways?

Before long, I learned that Alexandra also had a four-year-old son, and that her ex-husband had been awarded custody. She absolutely insisted that I meet her son, so we met up on one of the few days she had visitation. She was crazy about him, but wasn't allowed to see him very often. She commented on how we looked so much alike. He had light brown hair like mine. Alexandra went on to say that she hoped her son would grow up to be exactly like me. I never took psychology but was starting to get the picture. I had become Alexandra's surrogate son, and she had been searching for me in that taxi. Sex with me was a way for her to express her unrequited love for him. So it had all been some kind of bizarre reverse Oedipus complex. This was way past my threshold of strangeness. Once again, I had to get away.

I don't think I ever gained so much perspective on women of my own culture than I did from Alexandra. Never before had a woman relentlessly pursued me for sex. For the first time I understood the degree to which women of my own culture restrict their lascivious nature. Alexandra showed me that rules can be constructively broken. That women can crave sex as much men. That women can be the ones pushing the sexual envelope. From her I learned that women everywhere are out of their minds. But unlike so many women I've known, Alexandra did not exercise her sexuality in selfish, malicious ways. Of the many female insanities I've encountered, hers was the most enjoyable of all.

Alexandra Revisited

I returned to Bonn three years later and couldn't resist stopping by Alexandra's apartment. Sure enough there she was, surrounded by dolls, delighted as always to see me. She was directing a couple of German guys painting her kitchen ceiling with blue and white dabs of color to make it look like the sky. Since it was clear Alexandra liked me, I gained their immediate approval. I explained that I knew her from the Elephant Bar. She hadn't worked there in a long time, they said. "She's our close friend now," said one. "Yeah, too bad she's a lesbian," said the other. "Oh, I didn't know that," I said. "Such a waste!" they laughed. It looked like I might need to bail early on her this time.

Sure enough, Alexandra told me right away she had a girlfriend. But her personality had not changed. She was as beautiful and energetic as ever. It was early evening and the four of us went to dinner. When we returned to her apartment, she suddenly asked the German guys to leave, explaining that I would be staying with her that night. They were stunned. I'm sure they had been lusting after her for months, then in waltzes this American guy and snatches away their lesbian sweetie. Brings her back from the other side. They were awestruck. After three years, I still ruled Alexandra's world.

It was as if time had not passed. It was as if we had always been lovers. I suppose she still looked at me as her surrogate son. Not surprisingly, she never did get him back. In the morning she showed me a photo of her female lover, and asked if I would like to join the two of them sometime. She explained, we would have to meet first and get to know each other a little. It might take a couple of days. I know I'm supposed to jump at such an offer, but the other girl just didn't interest me. All I wanted was to be with Alexandra one more time, and I had that. I told her I didn't have time to stay longer. As always, she offered a gift. This time it was a silver chain. I fastened it around my neck, kissed her, held her, thanked her, and walked out of her life.

Someone's Fabio

I met Carmela in the opera in Buenos Aires. We flirted during the show, and I asked for her number right in front of her family. She picked me up at my hotel the next night and took me around the city. All I did was kiss her, and the next thing I know we're pulling into one of those by-the-hour hotel rooms with red velvet walls. She seemed far too innocent for that. A couple of days later her parents left town, and she invited me to stay with her in her family's condo. It turns out they owned a huge clothing manufacturing and distributing company. So for the next two weeks we had the entire floor of a high-rise complete with servants.

Carmela worked as an elementary schoolteacher. No free rides in this family. When she was 16, she had been kidnapped and held for ransom for several weeks. She couldn't remember much of anything prior to the kidnapping, such was the trauma. Unlike you see in the movies, no one rushed in to rescue her, and the family had to pay the ransom to get her back. Apparently, kidnapping is a big industry in Argentina. They lived in this condo because it was in a highly secured building. Carmela's brothers were concerned about the scruffy looking foreign backpacker their little sister had brought home, until they were satisfied I had no predatory interests in her.

I was Carmela's fairy tale romance. I was her Fabio—except for the hair, the body, and the good looks. See, there I go again. That cultural sense of inadequacy. But to Carmela, I was pure romantic adventure, an exotic foreign traveler with blonde hair. Since we only had two weeks together, we packed in all the intensity we could. We had deep discussions, candlelight dinners, and sex two or three times a day. If we had been living together long term, there would have been no need for that. Not even Fabio could keep up that level of performance. Two weeks was exactly right. More than that would have ruined the illusion that it could have gone on forever. She dropped me off at the train station on her way to the airport to pick up her parents. Although she's now married and has children, we still keep in touch.

Carmela considers those two weeks the romantic highlight of her life. It became a problem for her husband, who could never compete with the mythology. Years later she invited me back to Argentina to meet her family, who were curious about this guy she kept taking about. After some discussion, I flew back to Buenos Aires, where I was greeted like a celebrity. Her husband and I both understood that her image of me was more fantasy than reality. I tried to explain to Carmela that someone who is there for her every day is far more important than someone who was there for just two weeks, but she already knew that. I could have told her that it had all just been about the sex, but she would have seen right through it. I talked with her husband and we agreed there was no need to destroy her fairy tale image of me.

I still have a genuine sense of warmth for her. Through some dark times I've thought of her, this woman who holds me up as the man to measure all men against. Even today, it amazes me to think of it—*I am someone's Fabio.*

Brazilian Roads Not Traveled

American women would have me believe I'm doing something wrong. Brazilian women convinced me otherwise. They love men and have never been taught to conceal it. They are often the first to express interest. They come right up and introduce themselves. Romance is not a power game in Brazil. Why the hell did I ever leave?

My first encounter with a Brazilian girl was in a samba club in Manaus, near the Amazon. Jurema was young and gorgeous and on holiday. She kissed me and asked me to dance. I kept expecting her to tease me, but the concept was foreign to her. I think she was the first woman to ever tell *me* I was beautiful. She did so repeatedly. We were barely able to communicate, but it didn't matter. We spent two incredible days together before it was time for her to return to Rio. I asked for her address. Instead, she broke off some little shells from a strand she was wearing in her hair and gave them to me. "Remember me," she said in Portuguese, giving me a look that meant I would never see her again. Then she disappeared back into Brazil. I still have her little shells.

To say that Cecilia from São Paulo was stunning would be an understatement. You would have to see her. I was on the beach at an old Portuguese village called Parati when someone came up to me and said, "This girl would like to meet you." Something that never happens to me in the States. Amazing. We spent a couple of weeks together at the beaches of Parati and bars of São Paulo. We were kissing in one of those bars when she took me by the hands and asked me to stay in Brazil with her. But I was a traveler then. I had no career. I'd have to learn another language. We'd never even discussed religion. It would be complicated. I told her I couldn't and moved on.

I continued to write to Cecilia for the next two years until she got married. Eight years later I went back to Brazil looking for more of that magic. I was on the beach at Rio when a cute girl came right up and said hello. We spoke in English for 15 minutes, then she offered me her phone number. It's so easy in Brazil. I called her the next day and we met at a restaurant in Ipanema. She told me she worked at a bikini kiosk during the day and had a young daughter. After we ate she got impatient and said, "Listen, I am a working girl and we have to get started. I had to hire a babysitter to come here." Jesus fucking Christ. "You didn't make that clear before, that's not why I called you," I told her. "Come on, you want sex, and that's why you called. An intelligent man would know what to do." I asked the waiter for the check and she told him something in Portuguese. While we were waiting, she continued to bitch me out for wasting her time. She wanted cab fare. The waiter brought the check along with a pizza she had ordered to go. "That's your cab fare."

As I walked back to my hotel alone it was clear to me I would not be meeting another Cecilia. I had a new appreciation for her and the offer she had made me eight years before. Maybe we could have worked things out. I could have at least tried. It would have been better than this.

The Modern American Witch Hunt

Why don't we let the men who want sex and the women who want money get together without the pretext of a relationship? In places where sex can be freely purchased, men are less likely to seek relationships with women solely for sexual gratification. I also believe the availability of inexpensive prostitution is the reason European and South American women are not teases. They know they can't get away with it. Regardless of the whole morality argument, American women are against legalized prostitution because they know they wouldn't be able to sexually torment men as effectively. Women want sex to mean something, especially when they withhold it.

I read in Matthew Fitzgerald's *Sex-Ploytation* that American women are "dishonest whores." That strikes me as a bit harsh. Presenting themselves as sexual beings, taking our money, and then withholding sex doesn't make women whores. It makes them teases. And just because women can't decide if they want to love us or make our lives hell doesn't mean they're dishonest. It means they're psychotic. So in their defense, I must respectfully disagree with Fitzgerald that American women are dishonest whores. They're psychotic teases. Unlike whores, American women don't offer men sex, they only offer the possibility of sex. And they want a lot more than money in exchange for sex. They expect all their problems to be solved. They hold men accountable for any lack of bliss in their lives. The punishment is the revocation of sex and fulfillment. It's no wonder the U.S. is known worldwide for its unhappy, sexually deprived men.

I would agree with those who say that sex always has a price. But the money we pay to wives and girlfriends isn't exclusively for sex, it's also a bribe to encourage them to behave. That's right, American women have come to expect payment for *not* making your life hell. Paying women to *not* be psychotic can get expensive. That's why men flock to bars and restaurants featuring flirty young girls dressed in boxer shorts and hot pants. We want some interaction with attractive women who will be nice to us for a reasonable price. The money paid to a prostitute isn't exclusively for sex either. Besides clarifying the basis of the relationship, the real value is being able to walk away.

We've all seen those police shows where men are baited by under-cover agents posing as prostitutes. It's a modern day witch hunt, except the witches in this case are male. The police lecture the ensnarled prey like they've done something horribly wrong. They should be ashamed, like 14 year olds caught whacking off to a dirty magazine. It's hypocrisy for the camera. Probably the same cops have been with prostitutes, or would be if they could afford it. But now they're out enforcing part of the female power agenda. Yeah, punk, you shouldn't be fucking a girl if you don't love her. Now go home and think about what you've done, and jerk off like the rest of us miserable bastards.

That's right. It's illegal to hire a prostitute here in the United States. Unless you videotape your encounter and offer copies of it for sale to the general public. I believe people should have the right to take the risks of their choosing, then reap the rewards or suffer the consequences. Yes, the profession is dangerous; but then, so is construction. A lot more women than you might think are perfectly willing to have sex with several men per week to supplement their income. My main concern is that such encounters occur between consenting adults in a safe environment. Women take indirect payment for sex all the time, so shouldn't they be allowed to accept direct payment? Shouldn't men be able to satisfy their sexual cravings without having to become husbands or criminals?

Various witch hunts have been going on for a long time. It's amazing to think that within my lifetime it was actually *illegal* to have a venereal disease. Doctors reported it to the police. It was against the law to have an extra-marital affair. The local vice squad did investigations using VD as evidence. The children of unmarried parents were routinely called "bastard children." Fortunately, children conceived out of wedlock are no longer referred to as bastards. That term is now reserved for men.

The latest felony to hit the front pages is "improper photography."

This horrendous crime refers to men who attempt to take pictures up girls' skirts with their cell phone cameras. In Texas they can get *two years* in prison in for this terrible offense. A Hooters manager in L.A. who videotaped girls in a changing area got *five years*. Why can't these men get counseling instead of prison? I think I know. It's because counseling is for women—prison is for men.

The male libido needs to be decriminalized. Will psychologists ever be able to prescribe genuine "sex therapy" for patients? I'm aware that some recommend pornography to sex-starved male clients. Maybe someday psychologists will be able to say, "Sir, you don't need anti-depressants, you need to get laid." A "sex therapist" would be someone who actually treats a patient's sexual needs rather than talking about them. I imagine the hourly rate would be about the same.

A Tale of Two Parks

In Munich, there's a big park right downtown called the English Garden. A prominent section is recognized as the nude sunbathing area. On sunny summer weekends you can always find hundreds of naked people sunning themselves in public. People come from nearby offices in suits and strip down naked together over their lunch breaks. Cute girls bring bamboo mats, roll them out, and lie nude in the sun. Men leave them alone. In the mix are a few startled American tourists gawking at the unconcerned German girls.

Petra took me there to see if I would strip down in front of everyone. I think she was disappointed that I shed my clothes so casually. "People can still tell you're American," she taunted, looking at my private parts. It took a minute, then it hit me. I was the only circumcised male in the vicinity. It had never occurred to me that I had been sexually mutilated. What an odd cultural habit we have. If she was implying that I should be embarrassed, I wasn't. Have a look, everyone. I'm not ashamed to be an American.

I was lying there with Petra when she spotted a friend and waved her over. This attractive girl came up, undressed, and then introduced herself. "Nice to meet you." It was very nice to meet her indeed. And I didn't even have to tip her. Now I was with two attractive naked babes. A half hour later the three of us put on our clothes and had some beer in one of the park's *Biergartens*. Is it any wonder I like Munich?

There's also a clothing-optional public park outside Austin called "Hippie Hollow." It used to be a secluded section of Lake Travis until the county took it over and began charging a five dollar cover. With the popularity of the park, the cover charge has recently reached ten dollars. People drive in from Houston to check it out. The locals pull their boats up to get drunk and party naked. Several years ago I took a girlfriend there to see if she would get naked in public. She had her clothes off before I did. Impressive. We ignored the guy running around in an orange thong and the naked guy with a battery strapped to his back playing electric guitar. Then we noticed a guy with a telephoto lens taking pictures of us from some bushes. I stopped going to Hippie Hollow when it happened a second time. I never saw anyone sneaking around taking photos of nude sunbathers in the English Garden.

The U.S. is a nation full of guys in bushes. It's another consequence of the demonization of male sexuality. Is it any wonder so many men are uncomfortable initiating contact with women after being taught to suppress their sexuality? Suppression breeds deviance. The guys in bushes are there because they think that's the best they can do. They're attracted to women but want to keep a safe distance. They've been trained to be ashamed. It's that high school culture rearing its head. They're pervs unworthy of love and undeserving of sex. They don't want to risk any more rejection or humiliation. They've given up. But it doesn't have to be like that. Someone needs to tell them, it's different in other places.

Go Figure

I'm not as interested in what women think as I am in how they can possibly think it. A woman's head is filled with conflict. They're attracted to men who are controlling, but also want to control them. They expect us to be sensitive, then complain we lack backbone. They celebrate our fallibility, then express disappointment in us. They find us both fascinating and appalling. They hate us because we don't love them enough. We have to anticipate their every need and problem, and stop them before they fuck up. So, if they fuck up it's our fault, and we're supposed to make everything right. Fuck that. It's impossible for men to solve problems for women who don't know what they want. We can't just pull flowers and trinkets out of our butts every time a woman decides to have a personal crisis.

Women hone their irrationality skills thinking it makes them enigmatic to men. They're just so charmingly psychotic. It's their right not to make sense. Fucking up is another fun thing to do, like going to a movie. I guess we're supposed to obsess over them like a Rubik's cube that has no solution. Women feel no need to justify their behavior. But who needs justification if you're cute and pout a lot? It's like bad poetry sung very beautifully. We just keep buying it.

People tell me there are lots of wonderful available women. Maybe. Things are wonderful for the first few weeks. Then it all starts. Expectations. Demands for change. Bizarre secrets. Complaining. Crying. Men can't fix all the problems women lob at us. Nothing can. Not psychologists. Not flowers, not shopping, not eating, not crystals, not prayer, not even implants. Not really. Casey Jones couldn't keep this train on the tracks. But men are held responsible for the happiness of women, and so men get the blame. How many times are we supposed to pull the train out of the ditch? After a while you can spot a train wreck long before it happens. I learned something from Casey. Don't sacrifice yourself. Jump off the damn train.

Nicki, the Serial Train Wreck

I'd been trying for months to get something going with Nicki. She was a beautiful 19 year old with extremely long black hair. I was 23. I went out with her several times, yet she never seemed responsive. But I liked her, so I decided not to apply any pressure. One day she announced to everyone that she would be spelling her name "Nikki" instead of "Nicki." What the fuck ever. More eccentric, I suppose.

After one memorable rock concert, Nikki and another girl managed to get into the band's limo, ride back to their hotel and fuck a couple of the guys. She bragged about it to me the next day as if I should be excited for her. Jeez, she hadn't even fucked *me*. Fool that I was, I put up with it and went out with her again. I suppose I thought if she was willing to fuck some dude in a band, I had a shot. Apparently not. She used the "F" word on me. "Friend."

A month later Nikki slept with my housemate, a guy 22 years her senior who she had just met that night. When I refused to talk to her at that point, she thought I was being completely unreasonable. A few months later she called me from the suicide clinic of a local hospital. I was the only one she'd talk to outside of her immediate family. Why me? I'll never know. Maybe she was using the situation to compel me to speak to her. Maybe it was an apology. Maybe her psychologist thought I was the most harmless guy in her life. Was she implying I had something to do with this? In any case, she undoubtedly savored the drama of me visiting her there in the psychiatric ward. She seemed removed from the event, as if someone else had perpetrated this act of malice against her. When I asked her why she was there, she said she wasn't comfortable talking about it. I thought that odd, since she had just described how they had to pump her stomach and stick a tube up into her colon to suck the toxins out of her system. So we discussed the weather.

A few months later Nikki told me she was going to marry a divorced guy with five kids, and wanted to teach art to crippled children. Not just *any* old children, they had to be *crippled*. Oh, the drama. I lost track of her, but I doubt she ever changed. It's like asking someone to be taller. She'll always be an emotion junkie. A train wreck in a dress.

Petra and the Electric Blanket

Oh no, women aren't irrational, they're complex. Petra's whole life has been a quest for irrationalities. It's her way of transcending the ordinary. She believes she can see beyond reason into a world free of rational restraints. To her, an idea someone dreamed up is far more compelling than mathematics or science. The odd thing is, she considers her views scientific. But then, what can we expect from a girl who refuses to drink distilled water because "it doesn't have enough ions"?

Petra is against electric blankets. I didn't know that until she came to visit me one winter in the U.S. Apparently, she heard that electromagnetic fields are bad for you because they can "interfere" with the body's own electrical signals. Petra didn't know of any scientific studies, but those are for people with constricted rational minds. Certainly it made sense the electric fields created by the blanket could throw our personal auras out of balance. Wouldn't want to risk that!

Fine, so I turned the electric blanket off. That wasn't good enough for her. Maybe there was some residual electricity lingering in the blanket. It had to be completely removed from the bed. Fine. So I could heat up the bed and then remove the electric blanket, right? Wrong. Maybe the heat generated by electricity is "contaminated." Petra didn't want any "artificial" heat, she wanted "natural," healthy heat. Never mind that the electric range in her apartment in Germany emits far more electricity than my blanket, and the hot plates are right next to her ovaries! I didn't dare bring up to her that all the food cooked on her electric range has also been electrically "contaminated" with artificial heat. Not only that, but when she heats the water for her tea back in Germany, the electricity comes from a nuclear power plant. My electricity is from a coal plant, so I'd say my electricity is more "natural" and healthy than hers. I guess nuclear power is harmless when it's used to heat Chinese tea. But I kept quiet and threw the electric blanket in the closet. Damn, that girl has cold feet. If anything, it's her frozen toes throwing my aura out of balance.

Allison Buys a Stereo

I had a girlfriend named Allison who decided she needed a stereo. She made a lot of money at her high-tech job, but right away she started looking at all the cheapest pieces of crap available. She didn't care about the specs. Total harmonic distortion? Never heard of it. She just picked out a color she liked and bought it. She didn't even listen to it first. I don't think I've ever met a woman who insisted on a stereo with premium sound.

She asked me to come over to her apartment and set it up for her. Of course, in the "girl world" it's more important to hide a stereo than to listen to it. Aren't speakers already concealed in decorative cabinets? Whatever. Allison gave me that helpless look and asked, "You know how the speaker wires go?" The whole idea of cutting and pruning wires seemed to perplex her. I suppose none of this would have seemed unusual to me—or any guy for that matter—except that Allison had a *master's degree in electrical engineering*. That's right. A freaking master's degree. Shouldn't an EE major be able to prune her own damn wires? Hello?

Erika, Egg Shell Recycler

I had another German girlfriend for a while named Erika. Like all German women she was into natural everything. She was a recycling fanatic. She saved every scrap of paper, glass, plastic, and metal and meticulously sorted them before taking them to the recycle bins—by bicycle, so she wouldn't burn any gasoline. She hated to waste anything, she said. She even saved egg shells for months until she got a box full, then she would take them back to a farmer who would grind them up and feed them back to the chickens. That way he didn't have to buy so much feed.

But Erika's strict moratorium on waste got put on hold whenever I was paying for anything. One time we went to a lake near Munich called Starnbergersee, and she wanted pizza. It was available by the slice, but she ordered a whole pie. Sure enough, she ate one slice and was ready to throw out the rest. "Don't you want to save this?" I asked. "No, it won't be any good later." I gorged myself on the rest, but we still ended up throwing some away. She had no problem wasting anything I paid for.

Another time we were in a restaurant, and she ordered a second carafe of wine that I knew was more than she could drink. Sure enough, she drank half a glass. "See, now we have to waste all this wine," I said. "I'm sure they'll pour it into another carafe and serve it to someone else," she replied. Of course. Silly me. And I suppose she wasn't wasting my money, she was recycling it.

Go Figure

Diana Does Dallas

Women really are very warm and caring people. As long as you do what they want and agree with everything they say. I was planning on driving to a party in Dallas, and a girl I know named Diana wanted a ride. Fine. I'd taken her to dinner a couple times but nothing beyond that. Even so, that apparently gave her the right to tell me what to do.

On the way up she was giving me undue shit about everything, beginning with my soft canvas hat. She hated it and demanded I remove it. She didn't want people in other cars to see her sitting beside a man wearing such a hat. I mean, what the fuck? Of course I had to keep wearing it, which drove her into a verbal frenzy. It just wasn't worth it, so I removed the offending headwear. Her problem became apparent when she needed bathroom breaks every 40 minutes. Music failed to drown out the silence. It was a hellish three-hour ride.

When we arrived at the party, I decided to wear my hat. It was my way of saying she didn't control me. Now, whether she liked it or not, she would be seen making her grand entrance with a man wearing a soft canvas hat. That really set her off. She was so critical and insulting to me that everyone thought she was my girlfriend. Diana angrily declared in front of my friends that she would not speak to me as long as I wore "that hat." Fine by me. After ten stressful minutes, I removed it for the sake of the party, but it didn't help. She was rude and bitchy to all my friends the whole night. The food was not to her liking, and the music was all wrong. People kept asking me what the problem was. "Did you two have a fight?" I had to keep repeating, "She is *not* my girlfriend! I just gave her a fucking ride!"

Women can't help that. They have the right to "go ballistic" before or during that time, and men just have to take it. It's the original insanity defense. Oh, but this does not effect a woman's capacity to meet any of her personal or professional responsibilities. Just disregard it. But a strange thing happened. As soon as *Diana's* friends arrived at the party she was the perfect little sweetheart. These two guys could do no wrong. They could have been wearing the same damn canvas hats, and it would have been fine. Go figure.

The Bonfire Girls

A couple of years ago I met a girl named Daphne on Match.com. She was attractive, late thirties, had lots of interests, even a sense of humor. We were on our first date when she suddenly started telling me in graphic detail about the hysterectomy she'd undergone a few weeks earlier. It was a strange topic for a first date, but then, she'd had several drinks. It was strange how delighted she was, even though it had been non-elective surgery. She told me how great it was not having periods anymore. "We've been sold a bill of goods," she said. "Ha! No more of that PMS crap for me!" "They filleted me like a fish." "Should've had my plumbing ripped out years ago!"

To celebrate the purging of God's curse from her body, Daphne and some other women who'd also had their plumbing removed got together, built a bonfire, and threw all her tampons and pads into it. Then they joined hands and danced around the fire singing and chanting. Whoa. Very neo-pagan. She told me this story right before lunging at me and plunging her tongue down my throat. She was ready to jump my bones. So there she was, a girl who no longer had periods, couldn't get pregnant, and was ready to have sex immediately. Sounds like the perfect woman. She certainly thought so.

But there was something missing, and it was more than just her ovaries. Daphne assumed I would want her, even though she hadn't actually done anything to make me want her. The bonfire story was pretty whacked. Then there was all that repulsive surgery talk. And something else disturbed me. She seemed to think she was a *better* woman now that her "problem" was fixed. I didn't even want to kiss her. If she's going to kiss me, shouldn't it be because she actually likes me? Did I say that? Guess that means I have to surrender my claims of being a male slut. The next day I checked her profile again on Match.com. That's strange. Under "want kids" she put "undecided."

Olivia Makes Me an Offer

In college, I got involved with Olivia for occasional sex. At one point she shared with me that men's dicks "totally grossed her out." She told me how she went to see some male strippers with the girls one time, but she didn't realize they took everything off. It caught her by surprise when a guy whipped it out and dangled it in front of her face. She actually felt ill, she said. Obviously, she had never sucked a cock. Yes, as a matter of fact, she *is* Jewish. I think she liked having a dick inside her because at least that way she didn't have to look at God's most grotesque creation.

Olivia was sharing the downstairs of a house with a cute young blonde named Brandi who worked in a boutique. Brandi went out a couple of times with an older insurance salesman before deciding to dump him. The insurance guy knew Brandi was short on cash and offered to pay her for sex. Brandi was surprised but asked him how much he was willing to pay. When he offered $300 for an hour, she couldn't believe it. That was way more than the boutique. And to think, she'd almost slept with this guy for free! She was sold, but didn't want to be paid directly in cash—like a whore. Finally, they arrived at an arrangement in which they would go "shopping" and she would grab $300 worth of random merchandise which he put on his credit card. She would return it a day later with the receipt and have it credited to her own card.

After a few months Brandi wanted to quit the whole arrangement. The insurance guy was obsessed and started threatening her and demanding more sex. He had paid her several thousand dollars and thought that bought him some sort of relationship. Olivia and I monitored a couple of her phone calls in case she needed witnesses. We never heard him make any threats, and he eventually stopped calling.

The whole incident must have given Olivia some ideas, though. A couple of weeks later Olivia told me that for $500 she would perform any sexual act I wanted. She was serious. I thought that was quite unusual for a girlfriend, also quite expensive. And apparently, she considered herself worth $200 more than Brandi.

I told Olivia, "You've got to be ready to do some pretty kinky stuff for 500 dollars." "No problem," she said. "I'll do anything you can think of. You can have me all night." I couldn't believe it. My girlfriend wanted to whore herself out to me. What perversions did she have in mind? She didn't expect me to pay $500 for a stupid blow job, did she? What else could she be thinking of? Did she want it up her butt? That would be unbelievable for such a timid and mousy girl who gets ill at the sight of a cock.

What the hell was going on in that girl's head? Perhaps she was getting in touch with her inner whore. I found myself wishing I had $500 to throw away just to see how far she would really go. I also found myself coming up with more and more perverse stuff to try out on her. How about some sex toys? Maybe I could get Brandi in on it too for an extra $300. Was the money a vehicle for Olivia to try sexual acts beyond her limits? Did she just want to be ravaged? I know for a fact she didn't need the money. I told her I'd think about it. "Think about it and let me know," she said. We continued to have regular sex for a while before going our separate ways. Damn if I'm not still thinking about it. I wonder if the offer is still good? I've thought of a lot more stuff.

The Confessions of April

Then there was April, an American grad student who taught beginning German classes. She was a cute redhead with a pixielike face. We went out and always had a great time. We could switch over to German and talk about people for fun. I wanted her bad. I wanted her so bad I even wanted a relationship. *This could be it* I thought. But something was wrong. Whenever I dropped her off at the end of an evening, she would just about bail out of the car before it stopped. She would actually have the door open while the car was still moving. "Gotta go! Thanks, bye!"

It was obvious she was avoiding the kiss. You know, I'm not that bad. I'm not repulsive. I shower and brush my teeth. What was it? I suppose I should have taken it as a warning when she complained there was a guy in one of her women's studies classes. At the time, women's studies didn't register with me as a red flag. It's not unusual for campus girls to dabble in feminism. Besides, April was a total babe.

She went off to Germany for a few months, and I gave her a call when she got back. She was really happy to hear from me, so we went out again. This time she was pounding down the Long Island Iced Teas. *Keep 'em comin'*, I thought. Again, we had a great time. I was driving her home and asked, "Want to stop by my place?" "Sure," she said. How refreshing. She'd never been to my place. It was going unexpectedly well. She comes in and we start kissing immediately. Nice. Alcohol is a wonderful thing. After five minutes of my tongue in her mouth and my hand up her skirt she suddenly stops.

"Before we go on there's something I need to tell you," she says.

It can't be good. I already know it's over, it's just a matter of why.

"What's that?"

"No. No, I can't tell you."

Jesus, now I've got to drag it out of her.

"No, come on, what do you need to tell me?" I ask.

"I haven't been completely honest with you."

I think that's my favorite line of all time.

"I'm really upset right now because my fiancée just broke off our engagement."

"You've been engaged all this time? That explains a lot."

"I'm sorry, I should have told you, but I thought you wouldn't see me again if you knew, and besides, my fiancée lives in another state."

"Well, thanks for telling me. I wish you would have said something."

That wasn't too bad. In fact, I was ready to pick up where we left off. So what if she broke up with someone? I was in no position to care. With my hand still up her skirt I made an effort to continue when she interrupted.

"There's something else I need to tell you."

Somehow I knew there would be something else.

"My fiancée was another woman," she says, and starts sobbing.

Now I'm supposed to comfort her for the agony she's inflicting on me. She must feel awful.

"Why didn't you tell me all this before?"

"I was afraid you would reject me," she sniffled. "Besides, I don't really consider myself a lesbian."

There she was, ready to marry another woman and didn't think she was a lesbian. She must have learned that in one of her women's studies classes. I was willing to debate the point with her, but she was already in tears—the international female distress signal. At this point I'm supposed to figure out the right thing to say and say it. Not this time. April strung me along for over a year pretending to be available and straight, yet I was supposed to buy into how hard it was for her. She expected me to accept her for whoever she was, continue to date her and buy her dinners, and let her go off and fuck other girls and marry them behind my back. I removed my hand from under her dress and took her home. See ya.

Andrea's Complicated Life

I knew a 28-year-old blonde named Andrea from a small town in central Germany. She was beautiful and funny, and, of course, she was insane. Emotional wreckage was her forte. A few years before I met her, she supposedly fell in love with some guy; but at the same time she secretly took on both male and female sex partners. That is, until they all found out about each other. The whole thing blew up in a huge mess. She left that small town because all her friends thought she was psycho, but she still wanted that guy back. It became a long-term obsession. What? A guy who won't grovel and put up with her shit? Can't have that.

So Andrea started a new life in nearby Cologne. As part of her fresh start, she joined a local S&M club while trying to convince that guy she still loved him. Although she enjoyed the club, she confided in me that three strange men had raped her there. She seemed quite distraught just talking about it. Yeah, all she did was let a guy handcuff her naked to a bed, and then the others just came up and started having protected sex with her. Oh, the humanity! For some reason, she didn't call the police. Too bad. I was trying to imagine the police showing up and discovering that everyone was already in handcuffs.

Fortunately, Andrea was able to cope emotionally with her traumatic rape. I was surprised she didn't resign from the club or complain to management and try to get those guys banned. Neither did she feel any need to threaten the club with a lawsuit or try to get it closed down. She dealt with it in her own way, which was to dress up in her S&M gear and give a guided tour of the club for a documentary that was aired on German television. What a survivor.

The last time I saw Andrea she was studying witchcraft and casting spells trying to get that same guy back. She also took a lesbian lover as an expression of frustration with all the "unreasonable" men out there. They were studying Wicca together. The two aspiring witches were also into some kind of sexual yoga I'd never heard of. Hmm. Maybe I haven't given yoga a fair shot. As entertaining as that all was, it became apparent to me that Andrea was bragging about how screwed up and complicated her personal life was. Poor boring me.

Rant G

A
Control Thing

Women seem upset that they're stuck with men. Is that the best God could come up with? Since God obviously dropped the ball, it's now up to women to finish the job. Men must be controlled and improved by women, using manipulation, punishment, the withholding of sex, and suppression of men's animal desires. God did a lot better with women, of course, but dammit, couldn't he have given them just one more sphincter?

No, women don't need to change, but they need all the help they can get dealing with men; so thank God there's Valium. And Prozac, and Xanax, and Paxil, and Zoloft, and Serzone, and Lexipro, and Effexor and Luvox, and Celexa. I tend to prefer unbalanced, depressed, psychotic women who are still in possession of their libidos. Yes, as a matter of fact, I *do* have a lot of short-term relationships.

Many women think being psychotic is one of their many cute personality traits, but they still expect men to do all the changing. If only we hormone-driven males with our big dumb brains could comprehend women and their complexities, maybe we would finally realize the stress we cause them by being men. Maybe then we would understand that everything *really is* our fault, and that we need to change according to female values and sensitivities. After all, men are primitive and women are civilized.

It doesn't seem to matter if they have a Ph.D. in behavioral sciences, or if they just watched an episode of *Dr. Phil*, women are relationship experts. There's a problem with us, and women are determined to use their metaphysical wisdom to transform us. If women could only figure out what's wrong with us, then maybe they could be happy. What the hell is our problem? Maybe we're picking up some negative energy from somewhere. Maybe it's all that red meat we eat. Isn't there a new therapy or natural herb that can heal us? How about acupuncture? Aromatherapy? Meditation? Hypnosis? Anything show up in the dreamcatcher today? There must be a way for women to re-formulate us into the perfect men they so deserve. If we let them, they'll change us until we aren't us anymore. Sure, go ahead. See if you like us better after you turn us into a bunch of sick androgynous Frankensteins in skirts. Good luck finding your perfect dickless metrosexual shop-o-holic.

It's getting to be that men need advanced degrees in abnormal psychology and gynecology just to have a girlfriend. It's fucking complicated, I tell you. Are women asking so much of us? All they want is for us to love them every minute of every day, unconditionally and exclusively. Forever.

Call me crazy, but women have gone insane. And when I say insane, I don't mean it in the clinical sense where women need to be put into rubber rooms. Rubber dresses might be good. What's really scary is that women are not insane all the time. It's like they save it up. They can be really nice, then they hit you with all the cultural garbage they've internalized. Men are just not good enough for them. Men are losers who deserve to be treated like crap. And why do the bastards keep leaving?

Women seem eternally clueless as to why they keep getting dumped, rejected or divorced. Then they go out and try the exact same things again and again with different men. They're just a little angrier each time around. It often takes a disaster for anyone to accept change. So, maybe there *is* hope for change, since most relationships *are* disasters. But when you go through disaster after disaster without making any adjustments, that's insanity. It's the favorite insanity of many highly intelligent women.

Women are crazy about relationships. It's like a career to them. The problem is, women don't love us, they love the relationship entity itself. They love the issues to be resolved, the establishment of control, the emotional chaos. Men don't see a relationship as an entity. We don't want problems and chaos. To men, a relationship is just when the same woman starts showing up at our house every day telling us what to do.

If she doesn't get her way, she sees it as a violation of her civil rights. She retaliates by fucking up, and the guy has to fix it for her. She immediately becomes the one for him to please and make happy. A man is only permitted to be happy if she is happy. Suddenly, we are the ones who have to meet female expectations. How do they do that? Are we as stupid as they say we are?

Many men surrender because they know there isn't any hope. It's like those poor people during the French Revolution who got sent to the guillotine. Apparently, most of them walked right up and stuck their heads in the damn thing without a whimper. Their fate was sealed, so why fight it? I'm more the type who will bolt at any opportunity. Women want the men who will stick their heads right in. They want a man who will agree to anything. Struggling is pointless. No whimpering.

Women keep coming up with new demands. There's always more and more. We're like lions at the circus, trapped in a caged hell. Jesus, how many flaming fucking hoops do we have to jump through today? We're no longer taken seriously. We've become harmless entertainers doing tricks on queue. We know we have to do the stupid routine or our hell will get hotter.

Entering into the dreaded relationship brings on a whole new set of rules for men. We can't look at other women, but they can still be attractive to all men. Women start referring to the man as "my boyfriend" rather than using his name. Besides being a statement of domination, it also announces she has a relationship project she's working on, and that she is very busy and stressed. Most guys don't use the "girlfriend" title—we prefer her real name. But the most important rule is that the relationship is formed primarily for *her* benefit. A woman expects to be a man's highest priority in life. But she's still her own top priority.

Men want to be individuals but barely notice their identity and self-determination being stripped away. She will start to control his appearance, his clothes, his haircut, and oh—the beard definitely has to go. His name is now "Honey," and so is hers. He'd better not object to that. She starts to manage his free time. He starts doing her errands. He has to report in so she knows where he is at all times. All decisions he makes must be approved by her, including what he spends his own money on. He must have permission to do things that do not involve her. She will redecorate his place in a very effeminate way without consulting him. He was a man, now he's a cuddle toy, another doll in her collection. He has to know all the little details of her life and preferences, and if he forgets any of them he will incur the wrath of her choosing. Usually that will be the withholding of sex, until even that loses its effectiveness. Then they resort to something much crueler. They withhold happiness. Eventually, punishing men becomes more important to women than loving them. If women can't control their men, they engage in sabotage. Sometimes followed by looting.

A relationship isn't about love. It's a control thing. Love is merely a statement of that control. If you're in love, you're in someone's control. When a woman says, "I love you," it means "I control you." If a man says it, it means, "I surrender unto you." That's why women want to hear it. That's why men don't say it. We know women are not benign with power—they are merciless.

College-age girls have sex for the excitement. But adult women no longer engage in sex for pleasure, they do it for power. How good a fuck does he deserve? A blow job? What's the special occasion? He'd better start being more responsive to all her needs. Men think power is success and money. Women think power is a tight short skirt. Power is that perfect shade of blush. Power is a good set of implants. Power is the ability to control powerful men. Sexuality is the female hegemony.

Of course women want relationships. That's because a relationship isn't a partnership. It's not even a friendship. It's a dictatorship. If he is successful, he owes it all to her because she inspired and enabled his success. If he fails, what the hell is wrong with him? He will not be able to express his own views if they differ from hers, since that suggests rebellion against the relationship identity she's working so hard to create. He cannot challenge her on any of this, or she will go completely ballistic. She will fight and cry until he gives up or shuts up. To a woman, it is a non-negotiable requirement for her and a man to form a single entity, which she defines. Women refuse to let go of this relationship fascism until they find themselves divorced—for the second or third time. Maybe not even then.

A Few Memorable Disasters

Some women simply must maintain a level of emotional chaos in their lives. They embrace a dysfunctional relationship. They seek and create unsolvable problems. They think love means being able to fuck up over and over and over again, and to be granted unlimited second chances. They look down at the rest of us simpletons desperately clinging to our boring normality. It's that "more intense than thou" attitude. Or maybe it's really "more fucked up than thou." In relationships, these women stop short of accepting responsibility for the damage they do. They prefer denial, and maybe a trip to the spa. It's like they're waiting for that magic herb to be discovered in the rain forest, or for some healing crystal in a meteorite to drop out of the sky to create an aura of wellness within their chaos.

These women seek out controlling alpha males powerful enough to keep them from fucking up their lives—or to tell them exactly how they should be fucking up their lives. A woman may deliberately start to fuck up just to see if a man is alpha enough to intervene. The beta males go ahead and let her fuck up all she wants, after all it's her decision. Then they stick around to clean up. The alpha males know if women are not under control, women are out of control.

I continue to wonder if it is simply women's nature to fuck up, or if fucking up is an acquired skill they've perfected to achieve maximum drama. They think if they look good enough, personal credibility doesn't matter. Women have gotten away with it for so long it's become the norm. It might work for a while, but they can't hide behind mascara forever. We all have our nightmare stories. I have more than I care to write down. These are just a few memorable disasters.

Lindsey, Relationship Artist

Lindsey was a psych major in her late twenties when I met her. Like lots of psych majors, she had invested so much time figuring out her own issues that she decided to turn it into a profession. It's ironic how we take disturbed individuals and put them in positions of authority over other disturbed individuals. Lindsey had a whole collection of problems and was always looking for more. Of course, she had the mandatory female self-esteem problem. Otherwise, she dabbled in eating disorders, personality disorders, social anxiety, mood swings, hormonal imbalances, and emotional stress.

It sounded like a description of your typical American female. "Come on, is that all you got?" I asked. She offered that she occasionally took anti-depressants. "Pretty wimpy for a psych major," I responded. Well, she did work in a strip club as a waitress when she was 18. That caught my interest, and I bought her another drink. "Didn't you dance at all?" At first she'd claimed she just flashed her tits a couple times when a guy offered her $20, as if that made her more virtuous than those girls who earned it a dollar at a time. A drink later she finally fessed up that she had indeed danced topless for a short time. Perhaps for a year or so. In three different clubs. Okay, that's more like it. I had to agree that perhaps psychology was the appropriate field for her.

Lindsey had picked up some German from her time spent working at a bar in Heidelberg when she was 20. Cool. But she had a very specific preference in men. She was into oppressed minority boyfriends. Every boyfriend in her life since high school had been black. She couldn't explain it. Perhaps it was another case of diversity for its own sake, or maybe it added another degree of difficulty to the relationship. She adored problems. She lived for problems. In any case, it didn't sound like she was satisfied with her current black boyfriend. Who knows all what happened, but she did volunteer that he liked to bring his homies from da hood over to have a few drinks and watch him fuck her. It's hard to compete with romance like that.

She was deceptively intelligent for someone who enjoyed fucking up her life so much. We had deep conversations about all kinds of things. One time she told me about a guy in the psych department who had just gotten a new assignment. He had to teach a mentally retarded male teenager how to masturbate "properly." Apparently, after they reach puberty, they sit around and wank off all the time, and they can actually injure themselves if they do it wrong. So he had to demonstrate the

A Few Memorable Disasters

"correct" technique. I don't know exactly how he did that, but it got me wondering if my own technique could stand up to professional scrutiny. I've never been critiqued. Does my stroke need work? I wonder if there's a seminar? All I know is—I never want to be a psych major.

I'd say Lindsey was a balanced person. Her incredibly positive qualities were always balanced with destructive negative ones. She could be both incredibly sweet and brutally insensitive. She was one of the nicest and most unreliable people I've ever known. She never showed up for our first date. She didn't even remember making it, she said. Another time she called me up and asked me to a movie. I went to the theater and waited. Once again, she never showed up. Oh, she forgot, and couldn't get hold of me. Fuck up, make excuses, be incredibly charming and wonderful, repeat. That's Lindsey.

One night after drinks, she invited me into her apartment. She had broken up with the black guy. Cool, this was my shot. She put on some music. We were slow dancing and she invited me to take off my pants. She was wondering what color underwear I was wearing. I slowly took off my shoes. Then my pants. I went to her for some reciprocation. She said, "Oh, I don't want sex with you, I just wanted to see what color underwear you had on." A typical American taunt. I got angry, put my pants on, and walked out on her. She didn't stop me. I suppose I should have expressed my anger to give her an emotional rush. I should have thrown my pants in her face. I should have shouted at her and called her a bitch. No wait, I take that back. I can think of a better word.

A few weeks later she called and asked me to come over. No apology, she just wanted to see me. I was bored, so why not? As soon as I stepped into her apartment, she started French kissing me—I suppose to let me know she wasn't teasing this time. I was in no mood for it. "So, you think you can just snap your fingers at me and I'm yours. If you want me, you need to establish some credibility." "But I'm sure this time," she said. "I'm not," I replied, and walked out on her again.

Months had gone by when Lindsey called wanting to meet up again. She was seeing another guy, so there wouldn't be any old issues to resolve. After a few drinks, I brought up a standard question. How many people had she had sex with? She made me go first. I claimed 25 or so. Typical of my gender, I may have rounded up a little. I expected Lindsey to round down. Instead, she blurted out the truth. "Oh God, back when I was 20 I fucked more than a thousand guys." "What?" "I mean, just really a lot," she quickly backtracked. What interesting doors alcohol opens in a conversation. That coincided with the time she told me she had worked at the bar in Heidelberg. It was clear to me that this was her big secret. There's only one way she could fuck a thousand guys in a year. She must have been a prostitute. And probably a thousand was rounding down.

Am I imagining this? No, she told me about the first time. It went something like this:

She was with a student group touring Germany and got separated from them after staying in a bar too long. It was late, and she couldn't find the tour bus. She had no money and no place to stay. So she went home with a guy from the bar. He wanted sex, but she didn't. He offered to pay her. She asked how much he had. It was enough.

She said she returned to the tour group again the next day. That I doubt. I think she stayed in Heidelberg. She could have worked in Europe legally since she had dual citizenship. She'd found an easy way to make money and have sex all the time.

The problem with me is I know too much about Lindsey. She's alluded to it on occasion. She can't be involved with someone who knows her. Lindsey has been hiding from her past all her life. She nearly broke down and shared the whole truth with me, but withdrew at the last second. Too late. I already know, and she knows it. What she doesn't know is that it doesn't bother me that much. It bothers me that she minimizes me as a person. It bothers me that she won't return a fucking phone call. It bothers me far more that she so brazenly mocks me than that she fucked a thousand guys a long time ago. I have some of the answers she's been looking for in all that therapy and medication if she would just fucking listen.

Yes, Lindsey, I know the answer to your big question. It's the question you got a Ph.D. in psychology to try to figure out. It's the question you've been running from all these years. Let's go ahead and settle the issue right now. Can a whore be loved? The answer is "yes." What you did does not disqualify you from a rich and beautiful life. There are men who can accept you in your entirety, who understand both your strengths and vulnerabilities, your brilliance and your agony. There are men who will value you for who you are, not what you were.

My answer comes with some advice. Next time you find such a man, you must be willing to accept and value him at the same high level. You must be willing to reciprocate that sense of appreciation for who he is as a person. You have to honor him just as you expect to be honored. You have to be willing to treat him better than those thousand strangers you fucked all those years ago.

Lindsey has always been a struggling relationship artist. Each time she gets a new boyfriend she starts over with a big blank canvas, struggling to create a beautiful, tormented masterpiece. Her obsession is with the art itself, not the random subject she selects.

She's heavy into absorbing the identity of her subject as a means of artistic expression. Whatever he does, she has to experience it and feel it in order for her to express it emotionally on her relationship canvas. Her last subject was a mathematician. Lindsey asked for his advanced math books so she could see what he did all day. "Knock yourself out," he said. She spent hours studying advanced math formulas determined to understand the guy's mind. At some point she expects her obsession to be reciprocated. She's far more invested in the guys than they are in her. They don't want an intensive merging of their identities. They want something simple, like some company, some dinner, and some sex. They want some time alone. Lindsey demands more than that. She wants their undivided attention so she can share her deep sense of torment with them. But she'll never share the secrets of her torment, she'll only share the torment itself. She wants someone she can take for a pleasant walk through hell.

Time after time, they step out of her big painting, and it devastates her. Time after time, she rips up the unfinished masterpiece. But she mourns the loss of her art, not the subject itself. Even though she never likes the guys to begin with, she slips into separation anxiety mode. It's the relationship entity she can't let go of. She clings to the remaining shreds as if they might magically become whole again, like letting a plant die and then watering it heavily for the next year.

She expresses the loss of her relationship art by creating a tragic self-portrait. Lacking a canvas, her body becomes the medium. She captures that look of misery within her own eyes. She paints her face in shades of anorexia to express her deprivation of love. She has such a passion for suffering. It is her art.

You're lucky if you find a woman who paints a relationship like Rockwell, or maybe Monet. I don't mind a little creative abstraction. But Lindsey's relationships always turn out like a crude knock-off of Salvador Dali's *Premonition of Civil War*. She deliberately picks men who can offer her a long-term personal crisis to manage. She wants a guy she can count on for several years of therapy material. I was always an inadequate provider in that regard. In any case, I have no sense of loss that I never appeared on her canvas. It was always the artist that held my fascination, not the art.

Mandy's Favorite Song

I met an artist named Mandy in a bar. Not a weird artist, but an employed artist who made money. I liked how she was trying to impress *me*. I took her home that night and had some of that great immediate sex. I decided to get to know her, and she showed me some of her artwork. It wasn't just bar talk, she was actually a good artist. Really good. Her fashion drawings for newspaper ads were used once then thrown out. She was nice, talented, and liked sex. This could go somewhere. I hadn't respected a woman this much in a long time.

During our next encounter, I actually became the object of her art. On a dare, I posed nude for her while she sketched me. It was a creative prelude to sex. Someone told me women are perfectly normal until you fuck them. That was certainly the case with Mandy. After sex she cradled my head in her lap and started singing to me. She said it was the most beautiful song she knew. "Where is my lover? Neath the Pines," it went. I asked about it. She explained that it was about a white woman who takes a black man as her lover. When they are discovered, he gets dragged off and beheaded by all the angry white men in town. Then they take his head and bury it under a pine tree. So the girl sits under the pine tree and sings this song to her dead lover's buried head. "Isn't it beautiful?" she asks. Yuk! No, *not* beautiful! It's official, she's psycho. Get me out of this canvas! I wanted to grab my stuff and run like hell, but it was my apartment. Unfortunately, I didn't know any lyrics in which girlfriends are dismembered by gangs of crazy people. Unable to reciprocate the weirdness, I let the relationship die a quiet undramatic death.

Understanding Gertrude

When I was 28 I met a group of German backpackers in Washington, D.C. My brother and I let them crash in our apartment for a few days. One was a gorgeous 24-year-old girl from Osnabrück, Germany, named Gertrude. She was fun and energetic, and I was quite enamored with her. She gave me her address in case I was ever in that part of Germany.

A few months later I was planning a trip through Europe, so I wrote to Gertrude that I would stop by if it was all right with her. She didn't reply, but I was driving right by Osnabrück so I decided to look her up. I didn't have her phone number but by chance spotted her street, so I went right up and knocked on her door. Gertrude was astonished and delighted to see me. When I asked if she got my card, she dug it out. She had not actually read it. "I'm an idiot, it says exactly what day you will be here and that you will stop by!" I was going to continue on my way since she didn't expect me, but she insisted that I stay at her place. Cool.

I didn't know Gertrude's personal situation, but I figured it would become apparent soon enough. She already had plans with a friend, so the three of us met at a pizza place that evening. Her friend turned out to be an old woman in her late fifties with gray hair, so that was good. I had gone out of my way to see this girl again, and it was going well. Or so I thought. As soon as we finished the pizza, this cute 24-year-old girl suddenly starts deep kissing the old woman right in front of everyone. They went on like that for several minutes. It was devastating. Humiliating. She acted like it was nothing.

Now I was faced with the awkward situation of staying overnight in her one-room efficiency apartment. The old woman would be staying over as well. I suggested I find another place, but Gertrude insisted I stay. I don't know why, but I agreed. Maybe it was morbid curiosity, or maybe my own sense of reason had broken down. The two of them were in bed together as I lay on the carpet thinking of people and of places I'd rather be. I hardly slept. I was awake at 7:00 in the morning, so I gathered my stuff and said goodbye to Gertrude, who was in bed nude with the old woman. It was obvious I was distraught and wanted to bolt. Gertrude started explaining how she lost her mother when she was young and was looking for a new mother figure in her life. She needed maternal love, and people had to understand that about her. Although what I had witnessed between the two of them didn't look very maternal, I saw no point in confronting her. Instead, I responded that she needed to understand me too. With that she fell silent, looking perplexed. That had never occurred to her.

The Horse's Head Incident

I'm surprised at how my libido can take some serious hits and still rebound. Back in school again, I became casually involved with a girl named Caroline. It was one of those rare sexual friendships. Usually we would just meet for drinks, but sometimes she was ready for more. One Friday night she called me up at 11, and said she was drunk and wanted me to come over. Hey, from the male perspective that's pure romance. So I got there and caught up with a couple of quick beers, then we moved the action to the bedroom. After I got her clothes, off she informed me she was having her period. Perfect. Sure, get me started and then shut me down. But then she said if she put in her diaphragm, that would stop the blood and we could go at it. Well, I hadn't heard that about diaphragms, but fine, let's go with it. She usually wasn't interested in sex, but this time she was desperate, almost begging. There was a certain flattery about it. So we fucked around for a while and fell asleep.

I woke up as the sun hit the room. When I moved the sheets, the bed looked like that scene from *The Godfather*. There was blood everywhere, and I was hoping to God that someone had broken in and put a severed horse's head in bed with us. No such luck. Our faces and bodies were completely smeared with her dried blood. My stirring woke Caroline, and she shrieked as if I was that ax murderer women are all waiting for. She sprang to her feet and ran for the shower. I thought we would just rinse off together, but for some reason she locked me out. So I had to wait there naked, caked in her crusted blood for twenty minutes while she got completely cleaned up and dressed. It was an eternity, sitting there feeling like a used tampon. Finally I got in and had the best hot shower of my life. We never spoke of the "horse's head incident" again.

My Destiny

Does fate occasionally intervene in our lives? I've never believed in astrology, Tarot, or any other vintage superstitions—but I had an experience that challenged those assumptions and made me wonder if some people are deliberately placed before us for some vital reason.

In my late 20s I was backpacking through South America when I met two American girls in Bolivia. One of them was named Karen. She was from New Jersey, and the three of us talked and had dinner together. No big deal. I continued my travels, and a week later I ran into them again in Cuzco, Peru. We talked again for a few minutes because it's not too unusual to see the same people at popular tourist sites. Two weeks later I ran into Karen again on the street in downtown Lima, Peru. Lima is a huge city, and this was not at a tourist site. We were both amazed at our chance encounter and spent the afternoon together. Still, I didn't think much of it. I traveled for a few more months before returning to the U.S.

A year later in Manhattan, I stepped onto a subway car, and, lo, there was Karen again. That blew my mind. She invited me to visit her in New Jersey, gave me her business card, and hugged me as we reached her stop. I took the card out a couple of times to make sure I had really met her again. It was unbelievable.

It challenged my rational view of the world. What if all that fate stuff was true? Was Karen my destiny? I had to find out. I called her that day. She had the same thoughts, wondering what our many chance encounters could mean. She invited me to visit and stay at her place that night. Intense. I took a train over to the Jersey side. Rather than picking me up at the station, she told me about was a bus that went directly by her house. I kinda thought she should have picked me up, but I waited for the bus as instructed. Can you imagine telling a girl who may be your destiny to catch a bus?

Finally, after 20 minutes I saw the bus coming and walked out; but it just whisked by. Apparently, you have to be standing directly at the stop. But hey, if this girl was my destiny, a missed bus wasn't going to keep us apart. I called Karen again, and she said I should just catch the next bus, and if I missed that one she would come and get me. It was another 30 minutes before the next bus arrived. It turned out Karen's house was only five minutes away. Now I was in a foul mood. The magic had already worn off.

Even so, it was nice to see her, and I got over it. She had on some music that really sucked. I asked what it was. She explained that it was Holly Near, a lesbian singer popular with the women's movement. That set off some alarms. Karen had every album and insisted on playing more and more songs as if I should be interested. I patiently ignored it. Then she asked me if I could help unclog her bathtub, which still had dirty bath water from that morning. Fine. I headed upstairs plunger in hand. Alone in her bathroom I vigorously churned for 15 minutes to get the bath water to drain. It was pathetically Freudian. I think that was a far more accurate depiction of my destiny. Then Karen wanted to take a bath since the tub was empty. After she finished she invited me to plunge away that water too. She didn't offer to help. I guess as a guy it was my job. I don't think I would I invite a girl over and then ask her to do my laundry.

Besides wondering if Karen was yet another lesbian, I found myself developing some self-worth issues as I plunged on and on. Had fate intervened in my life just so I could help drain some girl's bath water? Was fate telling me I should become a plumber? It was late, and I was discreetly offered the couch. Fine with me. I also took a quick bath and then churned the tub for another 10 minutes. It was totally clogged. The only thing going down the drain was my fantasy that anything magical would happen with Karen. So much for fate. It's been more than 20 years since that visit, but I haven't run into Karen again. If I ever do, I guess I'll either marry her or tell her to call a damn plumber.

Beasts amid Beauty

I'm not sure if women like men at all. They are ambivalent in that regard. Women certainly like animals more than they like men. A lot more. Women are always very kind to animals. Not so with men. Women seem to have far more tolerance for the crude behavior and nature of animals than they do for that of men. Even vegans love their spoiled little carnivores. Women treat animals like people and men like beasts.

How did we as men fall to such a level? What terrible things have we done to irritate women? We don't wipe our bottoms on the carpet. We have more money than animals. Well, as long as you don't count debt. I think the answer must be that men are so much more difficult to train, and women can't simply lock us up to keep us from leaving. Animals are just more emotionally dependable.

We've all heard that women are like cats and men are like dogs. Or translated into psychobabble—women are "cat-identified" and men "dog-identified." Women are aloof, getting away with murder because they're so damned cute. Dogs are crude and will stick their noses anywhere to get a rush. Women train us like pet dogs, using little treats of affection for our good behavior and angry punishment when we're bad. Our sexual advances must seem like clumsy leg-humping. Women want to make it clear who the master is. Women will love us only if we obey. We just want to be petted and fed, but we keep getting punished for incomprehensible things. What did we do wrong? We don't understand, why are we bad dogs?

I've seen women with more office photos of their pets than of their husbands or boyfriends. For a lot of women, their cats and dogs are surrogate children, and they bond very strongly with them. This is especially true for women who have no children. To men, dogs and cats are like fun roommates, not children.

Watch out for cat-crazy women. Does her whole house look like a cat museum and reek of litter? Does she give her kitty-cats anti-depressants when they're moody? Does she take them in for acupuncture treatments? A woman's grip on reality decreases proportionally with the number of cats in her vicinity. No longer will I bother with women in violation of the two-cat limit. I've had women drop me immediately when they found out I was allergic. A couple of times they were blatantly rude about it. Who the hell do I think I am? If I'm allergic I can leave. I did.

Although cat-induced dementia in women is extremely common, dog-crazy women can be just as bad. A couple of years ago a girl invited me to a birthday party she was throwing for her collie. She didn't know the exact date of the dog's birthday, so she estimated it from the vet records—as if it made any damn difference. She said she wanted to make it really special and have some nice cuts of meat. For the dog, that is. As enticing as that was, I declined. Hope her dog didn't feel snubbed. Funny, she never asked me when *my* birthday was.

I went over to another girl's house once, and she greeted me at the door with a quick kiss on the lips. Nice. We went and sat on the couch, and her golden retriever jumped up on her lap. She grabbed it and gave it several big kisses right on the mouth. Oh yeah, I'm special. The dog was quite forward with the tongue action. Very tacky, I'd swear he was taunting me.

Dog Rape and Defenseless Monkeys

A popular female fantasy is bonding with wild animals and taming belligerent beasts. Women like to think they can gain immediate trust of all creatures because of their beauty and grace. It appears in our culture from animations like *Snow White* to movies like *Gorillas in the Mist*. Men who gain the trust of animals also gain the trust of women because women think animals can "sense" that kind of thing. Women like men who protect innocent animals, I suppose in the same way we are expected to protect females. I shielded a girl from an attacking dog once, so I know that instinct works—I just didn't know I was supposed to protect animals too.

I really blew it a couple of times. I was with a female backpacker named Liz in a park in Kathmandu, Nepal. We were sitting and writing in a remote area of the park when a group of about 30 wild monkeys passed through. We stayed very still as to not disturb or agitate them. The monkeys seemed to trust us completely, passing within a foot of us, their babies clinging to their backs. They lingered a few minutes, then headed into some nearby brush. We were very taken by the experience. A few minutes later, a local boy about 14 years old came over near the brush with some big rocks in his hand and started flinging them into the herd. A couple of monkeys were clearly hit and screeched loudly. Liz and I just looked at each other in disbelief. Otherwise we did not react. The boy walked off. Nothing was the same with Liz after that. We never discussed it, but I clearly picked up that I had failed in my role as animal protector. I had not intervened, even in a symbolic way. It didn't matter that she had also chosen not to intervene. Note to self: next time, you must defend the monkeys.

I guess I should have known by then, because I failed the same test a couple of years earlier. This was back in Ohio, and I was on my way to a class with a girl I knew named Greta. There were four or five loose dogs romping in someone's yard, and I was ignoring them. But Greta saw it differently. To her this was a dog rape in progress. There were three or four male dogs all trying to hump the female dog. Greta ran over and angrily chased off the bad male dogs, then held the female dog and comforted her for a minute. To me, they were dogs behaving the way all dogs do. I stood there, confused. What was I supposed to do, call the police and report a dog gang rape? But Greta was having her little bonding experience with the dog rape victim, and to her I was the insensitive male, probably on the male dogs' side. She was the heroine, I was the jerk. We continued on. I turned around to look, and the dogs were right back at it. I'm still confused.

Surrogate Men

I don't think there's any question that women prefer horses to men. Women seem to be in awe of horses the way they wish they could be in awe of men. Horses are large, muscular, and much stronger than women. And a horse will do whatever you want as long as you feed him—just like the ideal man. Climb on our backs and grab the reins. Women like that control. Horses don't smell very good and they drool a lot, so it's easy for women to visualize them as surrogate men. The difference is that women actually like horses.

Riding a horse for girls must be a very pleasurable experience, what with all the bouncing up and down with their legs spread. That must be why ladies used to ride side-saddle in the Victorian era. Horseback riding gives good girls that spanking they might otherwise be lacking. Combine that with all the unconditional animal love and it's no wonder horses are every girl's favorite animal. In fact, that's probably why women are willing to accept men into their lives at all— because most women can't afford horses.

I know what you're thinking. Women still need men to get them pregnant, right? Well, think again. I know two women who hooked up, got themselves a horse, then made a visit to the local sperm bank to pick out a catalog dad. They have twins. Who needs a father when you have two moms and a horse? "It's perfectly normal," proclaim all the lesbian psychologists.

Animal Victimhood

Women like cute animals the best because women relate to being cute and want people to value cuteness itself. Women don't want men to hurt bunnies or deer, but they don't care as much about cows, pigs, snakes, and other non-cute creatures. Women abhor the thought of baby seals getting hurt, but they want all the baby rats dead. Maybe they can get those guys who club baby seals to kill them. Men don't like to see baby seals get clubbed either, not so much because of the cute factor, but because they are defenseless and endangered. It's also extravagant waste. Don't forget who's going to be wearing the fur pelts. I'll take a dog kisser any day.

Men value animals that have the intelligence to work or play with us. Others run the risk of being eaten. Women value animals they can share emotions with, even if they only imagine that the animals are reciprocating such emotion. Women are more likely to become vegetarian for these emotional reasons than for the health reasons they claim. That, and of course, because it makes them morally superior.

The feminist concept of victimhood has been expanded to include animals, as described by Carol Adams in *The Sexual Politics of Meat* and *The Pornography of Meat*. Accordingly to Adams, women and animals are similarly exploited by the patriarchy-driven advertising industry. Oppressive males bent on validating their masculinity see both women and animals as pieces of meat. Another male tyranny.

I like how women are kind to animals. I think caged animals on farms could be treated more humanely. I've never understood the delight some men get at killing animals for sport, but I'm not against animals being killed for food. And I don't buy that eating meat is unnatural, or that the killing of animals is unusually cruel. If it is wrong to kill animals, then shouldn't all carnivores like lions and crocodiles be stopped from committing their barbarous acts against the peaceful herbivores? Carnivores often go after defenseless newborn animals and begin eating their prey while it is still alive. And right in front of their parents. Maybe we could use military intervention to stop the slaughter of these innocents. The cute ones, that is.

On this planet, everything eats everything else. I wonder how many trillion animals, insects, and fish devour each other alive every day? Killing something and eating it is the purest form of nature. We are not different than the hyenas in this regard. We just have better table manners. And hollandaise sauce. Becoming a vegetarian doesn't change the way nature works. But that's not the point. Killing animals conflicts with the female desire to bond with every living creature. Women also want to be morally superior beings. Women can only achieve that as vegetarians.

However, fish don't count. It's not that fish don't feel pain, it's that women just can't summon up any feelings for a carp. It would be different if fish could scream. Women want to remove themselves from the reality of how much suffering there is in the world, as if they can transform nature into something benign. They even pretend to bond with insects they consider attractive like butterflies, while hating those ugly insects like roaches. I've seen them talk affectionately to ladybugs as if they can understand.

Women don't like mean carnivorous insects such as spiders, except of course for the praying mantis, which comes up again and again for its unusual mating habits. Yes, for the 100th time, I know the female eats the male's head after mating. All women are absolutely delighted by that, vegetarian or not.

Oppression in Nature

Feminism has made its way into nature programs. We are told male animals are violent and pathological, especially when competing for mates. On the National Geographic channel, I've seen animal mating presented in the context of rape. Female narrators explain how the more nurturing female animals protect their young females from the hormonally spazzed-out males. Suddenly we're presented with themes of stalking, domestic violence, child molestation, incest, and polygamy. The male lions leave the pregnant lionesses to fend for themselves. What a struggle it is for the brave mothers fending for their offspring in such a hostile environment. If a lioness does the hunting for the pride, it isn't because she is aggressive and violent, it's because she's doing all the work while the male lions sleep. Just like "you know who." I thought this was supposed to be about animals.

Feminist dogma is infiltrating behavioral science. The same mentality of women being morally superior to men is now driving the effort to "prove" females are smarter than males. In April 2004, Professor Elizabeth Lonsdorf triumphantly announced the results of her observations of male and female chimpanzees in Tanzania. Female chimps learned how to catch termites using a stick sooner than male chimps. The patient mother chimps try futilely to teach the male chimps the technique, but they quickly lose interest and break away to play games. Of course, this is immediately applied as scientific evidence that girls learn more quickly than boys. In this latest version of junk science, Lonsdorf is not trying to determine if girls are smarter and learn faster than boys, that's already the assumption. She's just trying to determine *why*. CNN presented the new "findings" along with an interview of a female kindergarten teacher who confirmed that girls are quiet and mature and that boys really do act like chimps.

Noble beings that they are, women occasionally allow us in their vicinity in spite of our boorish behavior and lack of intelligence. As men we've come to understand that we are beasts amid beauty. We must be tamed and civilized by our gracious keepers. We're like the husband portrayed in a recent Honda advertisement. He is shown chasing other animals and catching a Frisbee in his mouth. The tolerant wife explains that he was raised by wolves. The theme even shows up in places like Dr. Laura Schlessinger's relatively pro-male book, *The Proper Care and Feeding of Husbands*. Women must be patient with our brutish ways. We are the ill-mannered chimps in need of training. We are the puppies to be petted, the ponies to be ridden, and the pigs for women to be disgusted by. And we will remain so as long as we continue to eat out of their hands.

The Overcoming of Obstacles

A lot of women measure success not in terms of what is accomplished but by the difficulty of the obstacles that must be overcome. Men pick goals to achieve a specific experience and to develop a set of skills. Women don't pick goals so much as they pick obstacles. Women often obsess over the obstacles themselves to the point that they lose sight of the overall goal.

Most women are more interested in achieving feelings than goals. In fact, most women think feelings *are* goals. Since everything must be translated into emotion before women can get really excited, women select obstacles that will drive them emotionally. Such obstacles might be fear of heights, fear of failure, or lack of confidence. When men jump out of airplanes, it is for the physical rush. The women who came along on my jump told me they wanted to overcome their fear and to feel good about themselves afterwards. One jump and they were done. The repeat jumpers are men.

Men by nature take all goals very seriously, even the goal of getting a ball into a little hole. Men value skill, dexterity and strategy, even if it is an arbitrary challenge. Women do not seem to value such skills because there's no emotional edge to them. Unless women can find a way to make motor skills emotional, they will never be interested in them. But they've discovered a way. Getting that little white ball into a hole becomes vital to women if it symbolizes overcoming male oppression. Suddenly it has meaning. Suddenly it's exciting. Trying to beat those stubborn men with their Neanderthal attitudes has lots of emotional potential.

Now we're getting to the point. To turn goals into something emotional, women assign an obstacle to each goal. That's why men have become the favorite obstacles of women. Either we're stopping them, or we don't believe in them. Now, any bland goal can become an emotional endeavor. The only way a woman will ever want to fix a carburetor is if you tell her she can't. The problem is, it only works once. Maybe. The women who succeed get their emotional success rush but remain uninterested in the goal and the skill they acquired achieving it. It's as if women can't wait to prove they can do something so they can stop doing it and go back to being girlie girls. Petra has over a hundred feminist and self-help books to empower her but not one book on auto mechanics. Sure, some women are goal-oriented, but most women are predominantly obstacle-oriented.

It begs the question—am I *not* believing in women enough to help them succeed? The answer is no. I believe in the innate abilities of women, but that doesn't seem to help them. In fact, it bores them. There's nothing self-motivating about being your own obstacle. There's no drama in people assuming you will succeed. Offending women and making them angry drives them much better.

It pisses me off to see women in the House and the Senate. I saw another one of those damned T-shirts the other day. Fortunately, there still aren't that many women in Congress. The commanders in the bunkers at Patriarchy Central have maintained our oppression strategy very well. We're keeping women's pay down, so that's good, and we've successfully preventing them from becoming CEOs of most major companies. That was no easy task. We've also been able to prevent women from playing electric guitars. They are only permitted to be vocalists. But there are still a lot of women succeeding, and that has got to stop. If we don't watch out, women will want to think and use logic. They'll become assertive and maybe even buy us dinner. That's just wrong. If they try that, we will stop them. Women are weak physically and always will be. They're uncoordinated and can't even figure out which way to turn a wrench. There. I can see them storming off to sign up for weight training, learn about power tools, and play musical instruments. It won't work, you know, cause you're just a bunch of silly girls! That might keep them going for a couple of months. But it won't be long enough for any of them to become competent musicians. I doubt I'll ever get that dinner either.

Being set up as the favorite opponent of women has its downsides. For one, we never get thanked for being their emotional punching bags. Far worse is that women tainted with anti-male biases really believe that we *are* their opponents, and they fight back for real on all levels. For them it's personal. They want to promote all things girl *and* tear down all things boy. Feminists celebrate male failure as if it were their own personal victory. Not many women want to acknowledge this, maybe just those with young sons. There's some real damage.

Playing a Different Game

It's interesting that feminists describe sports as the ritualized celebration of male violence—unless women are playing. Then it's breaking down barriers. When women gain entry into men's sports teams, they say it will benefit women everywhere. It's time to ask if such things also benefit men. This question is never raised by feminists, because disruption of male success is half their agenda.

I think all girls should be taught how to throw balls and be on teams. They should develop coordination and dexterity. After that, why try to funnel girls into a place where they don't have a future? The answer is that feminists are worried that sports give men a competitive advantage in life. So feminists encourage the herding of girls into sports teams, and if there aren't enough girls interested, they use Title IX to restrict sports opportunities for men.

Title IX perfectly suits the dual feminist agenda of promoting girls while restricting boys. Why should sports that generate enough revenue to pay for themselves be subjected to funding limitations? It's because feminists want to limit the success of men to that achieved by women, a la Susan B. Anthony.

Of course, feminists complain there are not enough opportunities for professional female athletes. Is this my fault too? I'd say women's sports will achieve equal recognition when women become equally interested in sports. Why did the US women's soccer league fail? Did the sponsors drop out for lack of a male audience? No, it's that very few women experience the same level of excitement watching sporting events as men. Still, I hear women's sports being hyped and marketed to men, as if we should rush in and save them. I would ask, why should men support women's sports while female athletes continue to benefit from the destruction of men's collegiate athletics?

I watched Annika Sorenstam play golf with men at the 2003 Colonial PGA event. She seems nice. Give her credit for teeing off from the same place as the men. I found myself hoping she would do well. It's fine with me if those pampered millionaires get their butts spanked by a girl. The television coverage did manage to show the male leaders occasionally when Annika wasn't playing, or holding a club. Or walking. CNBC had Annika's score listed along with their stock quotes all day. Sometime around the third commercial featuring Annika I noticed I was losing interest. Then I remembered I don't really care about golf. I regained my balance and began to *not* care equally about all the players regardless of their gender or national origin.

But there was something unsettling about her playing with the guys. Why all this Annika drama? You can't tell me suddenly women care about golf. Why was this woman transformed into Mother Theresa with a 5-iron? It's the same drill as always. My God, someone has uncovered another holdout of male dominance and oppression. Sound the alarm! A gender hero emerges from her shackles to save the day. It's like a worn-out Broadway show that won't die. Any volunteers to play the dumb male oppressor for the media piranhas to chew on? Vijay Singh dove right in, stating his view that the PGA should be for men only since there already is an LPGA. He must have bought into that free speech thing you hear about. That Vijay had a valid point didn't matter. He didn't understand the game being played was not golf. What is the game that invokes such passion? It's grown from simply "beating the boys" to a broader call to celebrate the defeat of men.

I noticed the bar for generating hype has been lowered for Michelle Wie. Unlike Annika, Michelle doesn't need to *win* a PGA tournament to fulfill that old gender fantasy of beating the boys—she just needs to make the cut. Please, spare us the hysteria and the over-glorification of any female infiltration into male sports. As men, we should not have to compensate women for their physical differences. We are not holding women back. It's not misogyny, it's biology.

Why shouldn't women be allowed to play in men's leagues? Because they will get more credit for doing less. They will receive attention unworthy of their performance. Annika's inclusion was a gender publicity stunt. Can't say I blame her for participating, but let's not act like this is about oppression. Please. Women's sports are more about social activism than sport. Otherwise, very few women would be interested.

So many times I've heard women ridicule men and our fascination for getting a little white ball in a little hole. Comediennes have milked this for years. Funny how suddenly it became of *monumental importance* for this woman to get *her* little white ball into a hole. It was the triumph of feminist social activism. At least it would have been, except that Annika posted a lousy score. She was tied for 73rd place after the first round. Even so, it was reported on TV that she was "hanging tough with the guys." She was just "a few strokes off the lead." She missed the cut the second day, finishing in a tie for 100th place out of 111 golfers. Fact is, it didn't matter how she did. Not to the media anyway. It's sad when it's a victory for a woman not to come in dead last. Women will know when they've achieved parity when they no longer get special recognition for achieving the ordinary.

Every so often we hear about a female athlete who wants to join an all-male team. Those men who object are labeled as pigs that want to turn the clock back. As usual, women never like to turn the comparison around. Let's try. How about if a male student wanted to join a girls' volleyball team that played at his skill level? Would that be acceptable to women? Probably not. If women object are they pigs? How about if a boy wanted to join the girls' gymnastic team? Would people stand for that even if he were capable? No. They might accept him just to mock everyone. I doubt the female gymnasts would appreciate him taking up a space on the team.

A couple of high school guys in Maryland were actually allowed to join the girls' lacrosse team and wore kilts to the games. Sure, it was amusing, but I thought they should have been thrown out. Girls who want to join boys' sports teams should be denied in the same way. Find a different sport or create an all-girls team. Rules are different for girls. We can't be as rough, and if they get hurt it's somehow worse than if boys get hurt. A girl on a male team disrupts our male bonding. Female success is treated as more significant than male success. Please acknowledge this.

In the summer of 2003 I caught part of the boys' little league world series game on ESPN. The Guam team had a girl on the otherwise all-boys roster, and the commentators exuded the mandatory glory. She must be an outstanding player to be on the boys' team, they said. Why can't we ask what the hell she was doing on a boys' team at all? The commentator went on to recite the names of all the girls since 1984 who played in the boys' little league world series. Aren't they special? Just a few days earlier I was watching the girls play *their* little league world series, but there weren't any boys on *their* teams. I guess there weren't any boys special enough to be on the girls' teams.

In real life we try getting the girls to play sports with us. It's a lot harder to get them to participate when we aren't excluding them. Play a sport without making a political statement about equality? That's boring. IBM adopted the now standard corporate rules that allow women to join any men's team, but permit women-only teams to exclude men. They can do this even though there are mixed leagues. Special incentives are offered to get women to participate in mixed league softball. If a guy gets walked, the next female at bat can choose to bat or just walk to first base. They always take the walk. Female batters get a smaller, lighter ball to hit. Even with incentives, it's still difficult to get female team members to actually show up at their games. It's like they sign up out of some ideological obligation, but they dread actually having to play.

On the other hand, you can't keep the corporate feminists off the field if they have a political statement to make. I knew a woman from work who played in the women's soccer league—while pregnant. She continued playing her position as goalie into her *8th month*, which obviously made the opposing teams hesitant to shoot any goals. Someone needed to tell her to get the hell off the field. Oh, but that would be limiting her. And since she was a known feminist manager, a comment like that could get you into sensitivity training, or worse. I wonder if a woman on the opposing team would be reprimanded for kicking a soccer ball right at her womb? I'll answer that. In the current reality it would be more acceptable for a pregnant woman to get hit by a ball and give birth right there inside the goal than for someone to suggest she quit playing because of her pregnancy.

Just how much of this are we expected to ignore? If women are performing poorly in areas because of strength or biological limitations, will we ever hear about it? I doubt it. If men are better at something by nature of our strength or body type, why must we grant women equal opportunities at lower standards? Women use all of their female traits to their own advantage. Men's physical strength is deemed irrelevant in modern society, but women still want to retain physical appearance as a form of power. Breasts have become more powerful than muscles. Shouldn't men be allowed to use our own strength and biology when it is to our advantage? Shouldn't men get credit when we perform better physically than women? Or maybe we should ask to be compensated for not having cleavage. Clearly, our lack of mammaries puts us at a disadvantage in life.

Gender-Normed Equality

During the non-stop coverage of the Iraqi war in 2003 one of the news channels showed a tiny blonde female soldier trying to give orders to some looters with her Minnie Mouse voice. It wasn't working. How much more of this are we *not* seeing? I saw on CNN that women were flying combat missions in the war. Everything was going just fine. Nothing was mentioned about the "gender-normed" standards that have allowed women to become pilots. It's true that military personnel may be reprimanded for criticizing double standards for women, since that's like questioning an order. But why can't CNN report it? The military is rampant with gender-norming, sexual harassment, fraternization, and pregnancy problems. Apparently, our 24-hour news services don't have time to go into it.

To my male mind, there's something bogus about the way we're supposed to turn our heads to all this, but everyone has been conditioned to support all female efforts to appear equal. I don't like how women want to live a dual standard with every advantage in their favor, wanting equality only when it benefits them. I bet the female fighter pilots still like men to move their furniture and buy them dinner. I bet they want to be able to take maternity leave for a couple of years then come back and fly jets again if they choose. Shut up and let it go, says the voice, you might hurt their feelings.

I went over to a girl's house and she put on *GI Jane* with Demi Moore. Fine, I hadn't seen it. It's the perfect gender equality fantasy with plenty of obstacles facing the oppressed female. As we watched, I sat quietly thinking how absurd it was. My friend was totally into it, shouting at the TV and cheering for Demi as she went through the Navy SEAL training. I was rolling my eyes at both of them. Some male SEAL candidates were DORing because it was too rough. Not Demi. No gender-normed standards? There's some fiction. She has no political gender goals? Not bloody likely. Later, the navy SEAL commander rapes her as part of her "psychological training," so she kicks the crap out of him with her hands tied behind her back. And she doesn't file charges? Oh, please! She's set up for *failure* by the government? I don't think so. More likely she would be guaranteed success. A real female candidate would be given special treatment and well protected from harassment. None of this mattered to my female friend, who was so wound up she looked like she needed a tranquilizer. She got her gender fantasy re-enforced. Women really are equal. It's men who are the problem. Yes, the movie spoon-fed us that line too.

The feminist-centric media is desperate for such fantasies. The 2003 Iraq war offered up Jessica Lynch, and the media did its very best to transform the cute blonde into GI Jane. We all heard how the aspiring kindergarten teacher emptied her weapon during the am-

The Overcoming of Obstacles

bush, killing at least four Iraqis before being shot and taken prisoner. We learned how she was tortured in captivity. The Bambi-like private was beaten, stabbed, and the bastards even broke her legs. I confess, I bought into it. Hey, it was carried by all the major news outlets— even the Washington Post. It had to be true. I was ready to admit I may have been wrong on some fundamental levels. Maybe I *was* the one with the problem. I always thought women in dangerous situations would look to men for protection, and men would assume the risk for them. It's just how we work. Here was dramatic proof that a woman suddenly thrown into combat can respond with valor equal to that of men. I don't mind being wrong. It's happened.

A few days later the real story was brought to light. No dramatic last stand, no torture, no gunshot or stab wounds. Jessica's broken bones were from an accident during the ambush. She didn't fire her weapon at all. In fact, she sought shelter between two male soldiers who took on the traditional male protective role, firing their weapons and accepting the risk for her.

Even though it was clear Private Lynch had been the standard helpless damsel in need of rescue by the nearest cavalry, the media still held out hope she could be transformed into the new female superhero. Weeks later I watched live coverage of Jesse delivering her simplistic homecoming speech in a sing-songy, girlish voice. It sounded like a third-grader reading a report about what she did on her summer vacation. No statements of female empowerment. Nothing about equality for women. Not a single heroic sound bite for the media. Feminist organizations must have been devastated that she wasn't actually tortured, or at least a lesbian. They're still holding out hope that maybe she was raped.

For me, the Jessica Lynch story will always be about the need to portray females as having more intrinsic value than men. Especially cute females. I found myself disappointed that I had been right all along. Jessica Lynch and GI Jane are equally fictional heroes. Pfc. Patrick Miller only got recognition because of the publicity surrounding Lynch. Why can't some of this caring be redirected at all the injured men coming out of Iraq? Why is male heroism so insignificant? Why do male casualties amount to little more than numbers? I doubt I'll find the answers to these questions in Lynch's book, but then, I don't think I'll ever read it. I'm just afraid we'll keep hearing about her forever for no reason. And I'm not helping matters. Andy Warhol, please be right.

Why do women need so badly to believe they can do anything?

There's plenty of stuff I know I can't do. There are lots of people stronger and more capable than I. What is so damned traumatic about that? Why is it news when a woman succeeds? Why are we presented with an entire documentary about it? It's always a variation of the same theme. Oh, no one believed in her, and all the stupid men said she couldn't do it. But she believed in herself and achieved some arbitrary success, now everyone respects her. What did she do exactly? Whatever. Are the writers of those annoying little pseudo-epics trying to rub our noses in it, as if female success is repugnant to us? Will they ever understand it's glossed over female failure that we find repugnant?

Once again we arrive back at the basic nature of women. It's more about feelings than goals. Women view success itself differently than men. Women don't succeed by succeeding. They succeed by trying. They succeed by overcoming an obstacle. And who am I to stand in their way? But I keep forgetting, they *need* me standing in their way. Otherwise, they cannot fully triumph.

Will we ever convince women that men are not obstacles to be knocked down? Remove that mythical "oppression," and women will find out life is still not fair, work is hard, and few people of either gender get justly rewarded for their achievements. Someday women will realize their attainment of arbitrary success is just as egocentric and meaningless as that attained by all those men they loath and try to emulate. Someday it will finally not matter.

Chicks Dig a Spiritual Guy

The major religions have fallen out of favor with a lot of women influenced by feminism. Christianity and Islam are part of the sprawling patriarchy they want to defeat. Religion is an institution in which discrimination against women continues. Religion still supports the oppressive female gender roles of wife and mother. Many churches still prevent women from ascending the male church hierarchy. If you want to be pope, you had better have a penis. Somehow the apostles get to be saints, but Mary Magdalene is a whore. Islam oppresses women everywhere, restricting their education and personal freedom. And it was in the name of Christianity that the heathen witches were burned all across Europe during the Middle Ages.

But most women consider some form of spirituality a necessity, even feminists. The "spirituality" women seek often involves infusing some wonderful cosmic meaning into all events in their world. Their muddled lives must have some meaning, even if they can't imagine what. Why not let some mystical entity rescue them from the torment of living?

There is certainly a large selection of theologies offering to soothe us with their own eccentric versions of spiritual numbness. The thing is, it's normal to have some torment in your life. Pain in all its forms is a part of our reality, and if you really want to escape from that you have to shut down part of your brain. Most women I've met seem more than happy to do this.

When women go shopping for inner peace, they have in mind something powerful that can completely sedate them. They want that spiritual lobotomy. They lay themselves down willingly. Afterwards, they may have that glazed-over look of artificial happiness we've all come to recognize in people who think they are spiritually superior to the rest of us.

But there's a difference between genuine and artificial happiness, at least to me. Chicks into prayer and pseudo-spirituality and religious fiction and follow-the-leader ceremonies are all seeking some form of artificial happiness. It's really a denial of the pain and agony that is part of the natural world and our collective lack of power to do anything about it. Me? I'm comfortable with my genuine misery. I prefer my torment over any flavor of lobotomy. That's not what chicks want to hear. Let's face it, chicks dig a spiritual guy.

Just like chicks dig guys in suits and ties, they dig guys with designer religions. These days an Eastern philosophy is like a fashion accessory. Saying you're Christian is like wearing clothes your mom picked out, so you need to go with something exotic. That's why that Stephen Seagal character is into some nebulous Eastern religion, so chicks will dig him. It's a bizarre blend of yoga and incense and acupuncture and martial arts. Sometimes he wears cool oriental stuff. He's so spiritually deep. No one can tell what the hell he believes, and no one cares, especially the chicks. They seem to dig it most when it's something they don't understand.

Most women prefer men who can be persuaded to participate in whatever spiritual tangent they're on. This can be a form of Christianity or anything from the grab bag of new age gunk. Women prefer men into any weird religion to men with no religion at all. In their judgment, basing decisions on astrology is better than not having any "spiritual" guidance. Women committed to any faith consider themselves superior and wiser than agnostics or atheists or other disgusting people who insist on thinking for themselves. Women want men who believe in something, something that has no connection to facts, something with just faith to support it. They often don't care what. It's the believing that counts.

I understand now. I'm spiritually inadequate. Being agnostic is like not even having a personality. It's the type of religion you'd get on sale at Wal-Mart. How embarrassing for your date! What men need is to get some kind of oriental yin yang thing going on. It gives a chick something to talk about when describing you to her friends. Maybe I should chuck my agnostic wardrobe and try something new. I could start doing yoga, find some obscure form of Buddhism, and even learn to use chopsticks. I could sign up for breathing lessons. I'm sure I'd hook up right away with one of the countless Nirvana babes out there. If I want her to leave me the hell alone, I'll just say I need to meditate.

If I don't want to buy her something, I'll say it's against my religion's principles of austerity. I'll make her get her tailbone tattooed with some oriental writing she doesn't understand. If she asks I'll tell her it says "respect," but really it will say something like "Joe was here."

I met a cute girl who was a strict vegetarian. Even though she worked a minimum wage job, she bought the most expensive organic vegetables at high-end food stores. She invited me over for herb tea and broccoli. As the tea seeped, she lit up a cigarette. I called her on it. "Oh, I eat so healthy that a cigarette doesn't matter," she explained. "And I take lots of vitamins. Besides, I think your personal energy is much more vital to your health." "Oh really," I replied skeptically. "Don't you believe in anything?" she asked. "I believe in science and things I can see with my own eyes," I said. Bad answer. It would have been better to say I believed in UFOs or Vishnu or angels. A normal dinner with intelligent conversation won't cut it with a woman now. Maybe invite her to a nice Wicca ritual.

Most single women you meet will probably be into some trendy philosophy or religion. Just check Shirley MacClaine's website (www.shirley-maclaine.com) for a laundry list of all things flaky for women. She says there are millions of women like her who believe in the supernatural. That's one thing she's right about. If that website is too flaky, there's also an *Idiot's Guide to Women's Spirituality* that explains it all. Yes, now women have their own spirituality just like they have their own cigarettes.

Contemporary women are completely over-therapied. I think they have vertigo from too much "balance." I'm choking on their force-fed inspiration. I just hope someday there will be a cure for "wellness." Besides various forms of Christianity, here are some common philosophies and religions that Western women embrace:

- reincarnation
- monastic dietary philosophies such as macrobiotic food, vegetarianism
- homeopathic medicine, herbal remedies, or any non-scientific methods of healing
- Eastern religions and philosophies, especially if you haven't heard of them
- aroma and color therapy, especially when combined with massage
- feng shui, and anything to do with energy and balance
- astrology

Women shopping for an ideology want something packaged and

ready for immediate consumption. Either they grab whatever every-one else has or something trendy their friends haven't discovered yet. That's why you see all those different flavors of yoga and meditation. It's sold like detergent: the new and improved Integral yoga for a deeper spiritual awakening. How about a little Neuro Linguistic Programming? Or maybe some Psychosynthesis? For the latest trends in enlightenment check the continuing education offerings. Here's what I found in my catalog:

- Vipassana Meditation, breathing, walking and sitting therapy
- Mantra Meditation, transcendental sound vibration therapy
- Hatha Yoga, gentle beginning yoga
- Iyengar Yoga, precision and alignment yoga
- Satyananda Yoga, holistic yoga
- Kundalini Yoga, the yoga of awareness
- Ashtanga Yoga, ancient breathing therapy
- Chi-Kung Yoga, Chinese yoga
- Pre-Natal yoga
- Reiki, the universal life energy of Japan
- Ayurveda, the Indian science of life
- Karmic Cleansing, the clearing of "psychic debris"
- Shiatsu Massage, Japanese finger pressure therapy
- Shamanism, restoring spiritual power and health
- Vedic Astrology, the sacred science of India
- Psychic Tarot, reading messages from the angels
- Canine massage, for emotional and physical healing of pets

Is it any wonder there's a new crop of "pet psychics?" The one on the Animal Planet program claims she can communicate "emotionally" with living and dead pets. The dearly departed dogs always express how happy they are now that they're in a wonderful place where everything is fine. So I guess killing your pets is cool. Just once I'd like that pet psychic to tell someone that their dog Fluffy is furious for being put to sleep. Fluffy wants to say, "I'll be waiting for you at the gates of hell so I can bite you in the ass over and over again for the next thousand years."

I used to wonder why astrology was so popular with women. I think it's because their menstrual cycles follow the lunar orbit, and so they project that into a belief that all celestial activities mirror real events in their lives. We just have to extrapolate what the stars are trying to tell us. It must be a way for women to think of menstruation as a really a cool cosmic thing that connects them with the universe.

Chicks Dig a Spiritual Guy

I wish ancient Jainism was offered as a continuing education course. The Jainists considered sex a fitting way of worshipping the gods. The act of sex is the origin of life, so why shouldn't it be divine? I visited some incredible 800-year-old Jainist temples in Khajuraho, India. They are decorated with intricate stone sculptures of people engaging in various acts of sex. How come chicks aren't into that one? Too eccentric? I guess a religion has to be on the approved menu. I need something that's eccentric in a middle class way.

Mia and Her Yard Salad

I've been out with plenty of "New Age" babes. They know everything better than me. I met a girl named Mia who was into oriental religions and macrobiotic food. She was nice, and whatever she ate was not important to me. Predictably, we went to her favorite vegetarian restaurant. As soon as I put cream in my coffee I knew I was going to get the "dairy lecture." Sure enough, she went on and on about how it was going to make my nose run. "It was made for little cows to drink, not you." I wanted to say, "Yes, and little cows were made for me to *eat!*" Or was she offering to suckle me herself? People wonder why I'm so quiet. Of course she was into all things organic. It was like a religion to her. One time she wanted to show off her plant knowledge, so she went into her front yard and plucked some edible weeds for me to sample. I politely nibbled a little, but then she got all excited and made a whole bowl full. She didn't bother to ask me first. She didn't even wash it, she just plucked and served. Sure, her yard salad was organic, and so were the bird droppings and squirrel piss in there. When I declined to eat it, she was offended and considered me ignorant. Hey, what harm can a little organic dog doo do? I've met these people before. They think that as long as water is not "contaminated" with chemicals like chlorine, everything is pure. Never mind about bacteria. It's organic.

Yet Another Girl Into Healing

At one party, a girl was introduced to me as "currently studying the Japanese art of healing," and that was supposed to be really awesome. She probably had signed up for one of those continuing education classes. I'm not sure why she and her female friend thought that would interest me. Maybe she'd just read *The Rules* and was trying to be "a creature unlike any other." She droned on and on about healing and energy flows. Apparently, she had just discovered her inner deepness. She wants deep? Hell, I visited the Deerpark on the outskirts of Varanasi, India, site of the first lectures given by the original Buddha. I wasn't making a spiritual pilgrimage—to me it was an ancient historical relic. I was sitting in the grass near the temple ruins in a lotus-like position when four Indian teens came up and started treating me like I was an incarnation of Buddha himself. They were extremely respectful and started asking me questions about life, so I played along. I remember telling them, "You have to know what you want from life before you can discover it." They went off all inspired. But I never got to tell my story to the girl into Japanese healing because I couldn't get a word in edgewise. She was a creature like so many others. She just grabbed onto something she thought would enhance her spirituality. Like a boob job for the soul.

The Hindu Health Food Babe

Some friends hooked me up with yet another health food babe who was into the religions of India. Sure, I spent three months in India, but that doesn't mean I'm into Hinduism. In fact, I consider it a collection of ancient superstitions. It's beyond me how anyone can consider themselves cleansed by visiting a place so saturated in organic waste. Holy men drink their own urine. Even Gandhi. India is a fascinating place, but I was happy to leave. I took the health food babe to a vegetarian restaurant of course. Over tofu linguini she described her devotion to Hinduism, astrology and her life on a commune in India. I tried to explain I was more into the history and music of India than the religions or astrology. Still, she was excited because I was as close as she had come to anyone comprehending what India was like. She was actually a very nice person, but I could tell it was going nowhere. She invited me into her apartment and showed me the 2x3 foot photo of her Indian guru she had mounted above the fireplace. I was ready to bail. Then she offered to "do my chart," even though I had already made it clear at dinner that I had no interest in astrology. Doing a chart is a lot of work, so I was supposed to be honored. Maybe I could have gotten laid out of it, I don't know. The problem is, I don't want to be judged by the position of the moon. And I know she would actually believe whatever the chart said about me. I felt like saying, "How about we toss all your astrology books into the garbage and see if we can jump-start your brain?" Maybe we could start with Carl Sagan's *The Demon Haunted World*. As always, I never really say things like that, I just think them. I don't try to force change on women, so why do they all want to change me? Once again I pulled the ripcord. I was free.

A Paranormal Encounter

Just last year I was talking with a girl at a bar and I asked her what she did. She told me she was a "paranormal photographer." Here we go again. She said she had hundreds of photographs of the paranormal, such as images of Jesus and Mary in clouds and screen doors, and lots of "orbs" that center around people. For some reason, these orbs are only visible through a camera lens. A friend of mine whipped out a camera and asked her to see if there were any orbs near me. She indeed saw a "large red orb shaped like a sword" hovering in my vicinity. She attempted to photograph it, but it was too elusive. I suggested she might have better luck without the flash. Of course she was off on the whole new age spiritual trip. She told me she could sense that I needed to work on my chakras. Obviously, I'm an idiot and need to be taught all about this.

Good thing I had my *Idiot's Guide to Women's Spirituality* at home so I could review the meaning of "chakra." It turns out they are the body's seven energy centers. I wonder which chakras I should work on? That's odd, the "throat chakra" contains creativity. Shouldn't it be near the brain? It's also odd that the "sacral chakra" containing sexuality is located near the ovaries in women, but at the spleen for men. The *spleen*? I guess testicles are too disgusting to have their own chakra. But who am I to question such ancient Hindu wisdom? I'd better start meditating right away. Got to get that damn orb off my back. Or was it just lens glare?

Most people seem to need a religion. They'll never be comfortable knowing how much they don't know. I'm sure mathematicians like Stephen Hawking have a much better understanding of creation than the pope. In fact, anyone who didn't sleep through Astronomy 101 does. But people don't want theories and complex explanations they can't understand. People want simplistic answers to all questions about life and death. Any answer is fine as long as other people believe it too.

It's like those people you see on TV after their trailers or churches get ripped apart by a tornado. They insist it must be God testing their faith, as if God had nothing better to do than to fuck with the people who believe in Him.

But if God deliberately destroys His own churches and kills His believers, then He was certainly using that same twisted wisdom when He created men and women. Is there some higher purpose to the torment we inflict upon each other? Are we to believe we are created out of love? Why does God rob us of our youth and make us die? Can religion really make sense of all this? Let's all pretend that it can. Better not to think about it. At least we gain that approval from the larger community by repeating its religious dogma. That's the main reason for both men and women to give in to it. They don't want to be shunned. From there, the genders diverge in their reasons for incorporating religion into their identities.

For men, religion is a power thing. Men discover that whatever they say is more compelling when wrapped in religion. I suppose the pope would disagree. But anyone lacking in credibility can make up for it by quoting the Bible. Or the Koran, or whatever. A church itself is a power structure just like the military. Commands must be obeyed without question. No one told you to think. Throughout history religion has helped consolidate the power of nations. That's certainly why there are still so many state religions. Men often identify with their religion as strongly as their identity with their native country. A religious affiliation is like pledging allegiance and joining an army. They will fight and kill for their religion, right or wrong.

For women, religion is yet another relationship opportunity, a spiritual bonding challenge. This time it's the challenge to show everyone they can have a relationship with God or Jesus or whatever spiritual entity they select from the menu. Just pick one and marry it. It's another commitment for its own sake. They want to connect with God and the universe as a way of wearing that spiritual tiara. It's another feeling to achieve. Prayer becomes a therapy session. Even if women are not into a specific religion, they still want to show everyone that they have a spiritual side. They're "spiritual but not religious." If they can broaden their spiritual identity into something really creative and multicultural, that's extra deep.

I get annoyed when people grill me about my religious beliefs. They just want their own beliefs validated; they don't want to hear what I have to say. I had one girl react with absolute shock when she discovered I wasn't a Christian. I explained that I did not see how the torture and murder of an innocent man benefited me in any way. No, please do *not* explain it again. I don't want anyone nailed to a cross for me. "So do you believe in an afterlife at least?" she asked in an irritated tone. "You remember the 13.7 billion years before you were born?" I asked. "It'll be like that. If I'm wrong, I'll know."

Less Holy Than Thou

I actually dated an atheist once. She told me there was no God and she could prove it. I told her I didn't believe in any religions or a religious type of god that needs to be worshipped or prayed to, but I doubted she could prove anything about the existence or non-existence of any god. It depends on how you define "god." Who are we to say? An intelligence of some form could exist. Rather than producing her evidence, she quickly retorted that I was *too religious* for her. That was a first. Why don't I learn to agree with whatever chicks say? What the hell does it matter? I keep forgetting chicks want a guy who's a challenge, they don't want to *be* challenged. Note to self: discuss religion *after* sex.

What is my faith? My faith is that if there is a God, He will not punish me for being what I was created to be. What does "God" mean to me? "God" is the name we give to everything we cannot comprehend. "God" is the sum of all our hopes. "God" is what you scream when you can't remember your lover's name.

Like all cultures of the world, even our advanced Western civilization has one foot in the Middle Ages and will for a long time. The Islamic world is still locked in its own version of Puritanism. I don't see much difference between the burka and a nun's habit. And I don't understand why people so willingly participate in their own repression.

I am just as connected with the universe as anyone. There is wisdom in religion, but wisdom doesn't need religion as a medium. Religion masquerades as wisdom. My beliefs disqualify me in the eyes of most American women who assume all good people are religious. We don't worship Zeus and Neptune anymore. Can't we just abandon religion altogether? John Lennon imagined it. Was anyone listening?

I've met far more women than men into eccentric ideologies. Pseudo-spiritual goddesses abound. These women are likely to make life decisions based on religion and superstition. Or whatever the phone psychic says. Maybe tarot cards are better than letting them make decisions themselves. With Tarot cards at least they have a chance of getting it right. Make rational decisions? How dull. There's a certain drama involved with casting your fate to the crystals, and it also removes a level of personal responsibility from decision-making. Now that sounds like fun. It's a no-brainer.

Caroline and the Plastic Buddha

It had been several years since I saw Caroline. She was living in Washington, D.C. The "horse's head incident" was far in the past. I was in town on business, so I gave her a call. She wasn't seeing anyone, so I picked her up and took her to dinner. Her big news was that she had dropped Judaism and was now into some Indian religion called "The Divine Light." She was probably waiting for me to ask her more about it. I didn't. We had a good time, and on the way home she wanted to stop by "the center" for just a few minutes. It would save her a trip. Against my own instincts, I agreed.

When we arrive at the *Divine Light Center,* she tells me I should come in with her for "a minute." I see it coming, but to avoid confrontation I comply. She introduces me to people I have no interest in meeting. Not good. Now she wants to show me what she does there. Just as I thought: it's a trap, and I'm pissed. She shows me how they lay down, and a "giver" waves her hand over the forehead of the "receiver," delivering that "divine light." She'll just do it to me for a few minutes, she offers. She's in front of her friends, and I don't want to make a scene; so now I'm about to get the "divine light" treatment. Oh well, it can't actually hurt me. Then there's a switch. Caroline isn't going to give me the treatment, it'll be some girl from India. Caroline is going to receive it too. So I'm lying stomach down on the carpet with a strange girl waving her hand over my forehead. I find it *very* annoying. Every few minutes, she touches a "pressure point" on my back or shoulders with her fingers. Once in a while some people from India sit up, chant in a foreign language, and clap at a plastic Buddha. This is hell for me. After 10 minutes Caroline says she wants to get the "full treatment," which lasts 20 minutes. Whatever, I'm a captive now. I'm just going to play it out. Besides, I already know this will be the last time I ever see Caroline. As I am receiving, I look up at a chart on the wall, and notice the "anus" is a pressure point. I think, *She'd better not try that one!*

Twenty minutes pass. Thirty minutes. Finally after 45 minutes it's over and I'm doing my best to conceal my anger. As we prepare to leave, Caroline tells me to bow to the plastic Buddha. I ignore her. Exiting the building, she starts to tell me I just offended her friends by not bowing. I go off on her. How dare she take me in there against my will, make me to do her weird therapy, and then expect me to bow down before her stupid fucking plastic god? Caroline was great at math and computer programming. Why do so many intelligent women go insane on me?

My Mother the Healer

Lots of women are into the concept of healing and want to see themselves as either the source or the cause of someone's healing—as in prayer or more eccentric means—especially if it can't be measured by science. Generally, women like it when healing is emotion-based, and they see themselves as uniquely qualified to perform it. There's that famous song about sexual healing; but ironically, women don't go for that even though they would be really good at it. I guess sex doesn't heal women like it does men. Besides, women have all been taught that sex is dirty, so they choose to be "pure" emotionally and spiritually. They seek out forms of spirituality that will cleanse them and make them feel whole. And make no mistake, women know everything better than men, and that gives them the right to tell us what to eat and drink. And if that works, they're more than happy to tell us what to think.

My mother was one of them. She was a well-intentioned person but consummately self-righteous when it came to God and the universe. I was about 10 years old when she demanded I attend her Christian Science church. After years of study she became a church "practitioner," working evenings as a faith healer. For her, it was a sweet arrangement—God did the healing, but she got the money. Her goal in life was to rid the world of evil by "casting out demons." My mother actually thought she could influence world politics through prayer. She had a list of world leaders onto whom she would project her spiritual guidance. Richard Nixon was one of them. She spent two or three hours every day on her prayer list, which she called "mental work." And if it wasn't working, she became even more determined. She would emerge exhausted from her bedroom after several hours of mental work. Someone had to protect the world from evil.

As I was growing up, my mother repeatedly tried to deny me medical treatment, insisting that it would ruin her own attempts to heal me through prayer. My father stepped in and did battle with her to get me the medicine I needed when I had rheumatic fever. Once after I was badly injured in a bike accident, my mother scared me away from a hospital visit by telling me the nurses would hold me down and scrub my open wounds with brushes no matter how loud I screamed. Again, it was my father who took me in to get stitched up and examined. He promised there would be no brushes. Years later I found out my mother had published an article in the *Christian Science Journal* claiming she had healed me of my injuries from the bike accident. As far as I'm concerned, prayer is a placebo.

Petra and Her Magic Herbs

Holistic healing is one step away from faith healing. I believe their prescribed treatments are also placebos, with the real treatment being hope and kindness. That's the reason it's vastly popular with women. It's more nurturing than being dissected by a stranger. No, I don't trust traditional medicine without question. Doctors misdiagnose and mistreat problems all the time. The commercial drug companies push their medicines with little regard for facts or side effects. But I'll take my chances with traditional medicine. Just my preference in case anyone asks.

It's still hard for me to fathom, but Petra is a qualified medical doctor. She gained admission to med school in Munich after getting her Women's Studies degree in Montreal. She received a full stipend for the five-year program in medicine and earned the official title of "doctor." She then abandoned everything she learned and became a practitioner of holistic healing.

Petra's primary interest lies in herbology, which I consider a form of quackology. Herbalists don't have the backing of scientific research for the herbs they prescribe. They often select multipurpose herbs for the patient to try, or rely on anything used by the indigenous peoples of Peru. They believe anything "natural" is always better than synthetic medicines. Petra also treats people with acupuncture and Aura-Soma color therapy. Aura-Soma uses a collection of small bottles filed with different shades of colored water and oil. Patients are supposed to pick out the "color key" that matches their inner feelings so they can undergo "soul therapy" and healing. If their treatments don't work, holistic healers send you to a "real doctor."

One time in Munich, I got food poisoning from a vegetarian casserole I ate at a rest stop on the autobahn. That night I was staying at Petra's and having a rough time. I'd experienced food poisoning before and knew my system needed to purge itself, and that I would be fine in a couple days. I just had to wait it out. As always, Petra knew better than I. She has a medical degree, after all. Never mind that her training did not involve herbal remedies in any way.

About midnight, I was half asleep when Petra quietly stuffed some dried herbs in my mouth. I couldn't believe it. She didn't bother to consult with me or explain what the herbs were, as if I were a child unable to make my own decisions. Yeah, growing up I had religion shoved down my throat, but always in the figurative sense. How appropriate that Petra literally shoved herbology down my throat. She was surprised when I angrily spit the leaves out onto the floor and told her never to try anything like that again. But she was just trying to help. Excuse me if I don't say, "Thank you."

Chicks Dig a Spiritual Guy

Have Fun on Ararat

Sure, there are lots of men who willingly shut down their logic for faith. They had it drilled into them as children that they must embrace their parents' religion or be rejected by their family. I was different. At age six I was already rebelling against religion, which was taught in public schools. I remember one day they wanted us to draw pictures of "God's Riches," and all the kids were making pictures of trees and birds and houses. I knew full well what they wanted me to draw, but just to mess with them I drew a picture of clouds opening up with dollar bills raining down from the sky. The other kids saw that and immediately started drawing dollar bills into all their pictures too. Suddenly, all the birds had dollar bills in their beaks. It was great fun. But the grown-ups didn't appreciate my display of artistic license. I'm sure they were also upset at being mocked by a six year old. So I got scolded, and everyone with dollar bills in their pictures had to do them over again. I was supervised while drawing my birds and trees. They should have given up on me right then.

As an adult it amazes me how even scientifically-trained minds can embrace impossible beliefs. It's like that ex-astronaut James Erwin who searched compulsively for Noah's Ark on Mt. Ararat. How can someone that scientifically advanced think 15,000 feet of rainwater (falling worldwide at the rate of 15 *feet* per hour for 40 days) could cover the entire earth and then just settle into the oceans? Would we accept an astronaut who gave lectures on how the sun *really does* orbit the earth? Wasn't it the head of James Erwin's religion who threatened to kill Galileo for publishing the correct orbits of the planets around the sun?

It doesn't surprise me that a believer in creationism was re-elected president of the United States. Our 43rd president also thinks God made him president. With the help of declassified CIA satellite photography of the "Ararat Anomaly," Bush's fellow creationists are busy looking for the Ark and conjuring up pseudo-scientific theories of how the great flood happened. It's one thing to be retarded, it's quite another to *choose* to be retarded. Yes, I think it's possible there was a "great flood" when the Black Sea was formed. But I swear, if they find a huge 5,000-year-old ship up on Ararat and it's scientifically verified, I will convert to Christianity. I'm not worried.

How about the same offer from the creationists? Something like, if they don't find the Ark in the next 10 years, they give up and admit the whole story was a work of fiction. They will never agree to that, of course. The Ark must be on another mountain, or they will look next year, and the year after that, and so on. I think at some level of consciousness these people must *know* the damn thing simply does not exist. It's a faith exercise. The true test of faith is to believe the impossible.

But that's the kind of man almost all women want, the man of faith, even if the belief itself is absurd. Chicks don't dig a skeptic. It's the combination of irrationality and spirituality that appeals to women. They'll follow you up Mt. Ararat and help you look for the damned nonexistent thing. And it doesn't matter that you'll never find it, as long as you never stop believing it's there. Believing is so much nobler than thinking.

The world is full of women who are forever searching for some herb or prayer or therapy that will heal them. What is this deep agony for which women seem eternally in the need of healing? Behind it all is the simple fact that we are mortal. We can't change that. Neither can we do much about the suffering in the world except to seek some temporary sanctuary from it. Knowledge is inadequate in that regard. On the contrary, knowledge can be painful, which is why so many women avoid it. They prefer to wait around for miracles, thinking they have such wisdom.

These women with their eccentric spiritualities consider themselves visionaries. I see them as dillusionaries. To me, the trendy new "awareness" is really an unawareness. Just another way to voluntarily shut down your brain. Women leap at it. You'll see some men embrace it. Yes, men can shut down their brains too. Or maybe they're just getting laid. That's too high a price for me. Maybe. Make me an offer. They don't call it Nirvana for nothing.

Incompatible Histories

I recently was talking to a female friend about the 2003 Iraq invasion, and I wanted to raise the question about the justification of waging a preemptive war without solid proof of Iraq's weapons of mass destruction. She responded that the Iraq war was really an expression of repressed masculinity on a national scale. "Men are losing their sense of masculinity and are desperate to recover it, so they see a big war as the best way to do that." Hmm. Repressed masculinity might be why there's hard rock music and a multi-billion dollar porn industry. But repressed masculinity as the cause of the Iraq war? Where did she pick that up? She's never even heard of Susan Faludi. Okay, maybe I *don't* want to discuss war and politics with women.

I suppose I could have let her go off on some academic tangent about how violence itself is a male phenomenon. Sounds like a research project for a women's studies class. What I found more interesting was her compulsion to assign negative qualities to "masculinity" so she could re-enforce her own perception of "femininity" as superior. That I'm still hearing this nonsense is an indication of how widespread the whole oppressor/victim myth has become. It is *not* dying out.

Women like this believe that if they ran things we would all be peaceful vegetarians living in an emotional paradise free of hatred, racism, oppression, and everything else invented by men. If women could just rid the world of men and masculinity, they could live happily ever after in their vaginal utopia. There are indeed feminists who promote the eradication of men from the earth, such as Mary Daly in her 1998 book *Quintessence*.

Women influenced by feminism think we could end all war today, except that men love it so much. Women are dismissive of real knowledge they associate with any of these issues. War knowledge might contaminate them. The problem is, there are a lot of important things happening in the world that merit discussion beyond the simplistic "woman good, man bad" rhetoric they continue to offer up.

A girl I know lectured me for some 20 minutes about violence toward women and how she couldn't understand why men were so gratified by fighting and war. Later that same day, she suggested we watch a movie. I let her pick one out, and she chose *Excalibur*. She loved it. I sat there amazed at her hypocrisy as we watched images of men slaughtering each other for our entertainment. Apparently, this was acceptable to her since no women were harmed. I think I understand now. Women can't be interested in military history because violence is wrong. Unless the conflict is between two handsome knights willing to wage war as a contest to determine who gets the privilege of marrying a beautiful princess. Then a thousand men can lay down their lives to defend her honor. How romantic.

That women distance themselves from any responsibility associated with violence illustrates how much they limit their understanding of the world they live in. It's another glaring example of female "selective knowledge." Or call it "selective *ignorance*." It's been going on for a while now, even though women have been fully integrated into the educational system. Women aren't interested in violence because they don't see it as relevant to their lives. Why discuss things like how the threat of violence protects women from violence? Don't feel like talking about that right now? Sure, I'll walk you to your car.

Petra and the V2

It had been five years since my disastrous visit with Petra in Montreal. She happened to be in the U.S. visiting relatives when she looked me up in Washington, D.C. We went to the Smithsonian Air and Space Museum to see an IMAX film, and while we were waiting, I took her around to see the exhibits. As expected, she had no interest in historical aircraft. It was like walking around with her in a warehouse. Spirit of St. Louis? Didn't ring a bell. Then we came to the V2 rocket. Not only did she not recognize it, she had never even heard of it. She had no idea that Germany had developed these highly advanced ballistic missiles, produced them by the thousands using slave labor, and shot them at civilian targets in London and Antwerp during WWII.

Her level of disinterest actually offended me. Even after hearing how important this rocket was in her own nation's history, she still had zero interest in it. It could have been a beam holding up the ceiling. Can I put it into an emotional context for her? That the Germans had used their creativity and intelligence to deliberately wreak such terrible suffering is emotional, isn't it? What if I describe how the rocket technology has been used in peacetime? I explained that the V2 was designed by Werner von Braun, the same German scientist who led the U.S. effort to land on the moon. None of it mattered to Petra. Her brain was shut down.

At first I thought it was another case of a woman disassociating herself from history. Then I remembered Petra had studied lots of third world history. Why would she have no interest in technology that changed the world? It amazes me how much more I know about 20th century German history than Petra. Apparently, she thinks her ignorance of World War II, combined with her anti-American politics, makes her a better pacifist. She also uses feminism to separate her from her own nation's history. Jet fighters and rockets are male-specific implements of power. War is not something German, it's something male. Americans have fared better in history because the victors get to write it. Not only do Petra and I have incompatible personal philosophies, we have incompatible histories.

We've had this discussion before. Or more accurately, Petra has evaded the issue before. Like most Germans confronted with their recent history, Petra prefers discussing America's own dark past. She sees America as a nation founded on slavery for profit. I see slavery as a problem America inherited as a colony from the British, French, Dutch, and Portuguese slave traders. I disagree that America profited from slavery. How many young men were lost ridding ourselves of the scourge? How many southern cities and towns lay in ruins afterward?

Petra equates the ethnic cleansing of the Jews in Germany to our Indian wars. She can name all the Native American tribes that were killed and driven off their land. She can recite every incursion by the U.S. military into Latin America. She studied American history as the genocide of native people, the expansion of slavery, the rise of capitalism, and the continued exploitation of people in the third world. But she's never heard of a V2.

I would be willing to discuss whether or not the Indian wars were the same as the Jewish holocaust. But there's no need for any such discussion. Petra has never been any more concerned about the American Indians than the Jews. She just needs to distance herself from it all. She's used to maneuvering herself into the victim role, and she's always looking for that big oppressor.

Petra is convinced there must be a selfish and cruel motive behind all American foreign policy. If America defended Germany from the Soviet Union during the cold war, then it was because America wanted to use Germany as a shield against a Soviet nuclear strike. Never mind about the Soviet subs off the U.S. coast. America only helps nations prosper if it is in our own economic and political interest. But Cuba does only good things in the world.

I can hear the anti-American jargon creeping into her conversation. She talks about America as a "capitalist state" as opposed to a "democracy." We are an "imperialist" nation that wages war for profit, robs poor nations of their resources, and oppresses minorities everywhere. She learned a lot in those "Third World Studies" classes she took in Montreal. I imagine the Canadians are a little kinder when presenting their own history.

Petra's concern about the victims of the world strikes me as very limited in scope. In her apartment she has some framed portraits of Hindu women. Who are these people? They are supposedly women who were thrown onto their husbands' funeral pyres while still alive. Some feminists claim it is still common practice in India. I've witnessed a number of cremations being performed in India, and there were no living women getting thrown onto the fires. I do not believe people in India would be any less horrified than the rest of us. In fact, there are domestic violence and "dowry harassment" laws in India that protect women from reprisals if her dowry is not paid. I'm sure my friends from India would roll their eyes at Petra's photos. But the portraits are important to her because they show women as victims of male-dominated society.

In any case, Petra would have more credibility with me if she also displayed some portraits of Jewish holocaust victims. Maybe she could do some research and find photos of people taken from the very street where she lives, which runs directly into Dachauerstrasse. But that's all part of that big black hole in her head. It's deliberate. Maybe it's because her own father was in Hitler's army that she prefers chasing demons that aren't quite so close to home.

The Restaurant Incident

Petra and I were in a restaurant in Munich just after Saddam Hussein invaded Kuwait in late 1990, and I happened to express my opinion that the United States needed to help Kuwait expel the Iraqis. She got angry and began *shouting* at me in the restaurant that Saddam had every right to take Kuwait, and the U.S. had no right to "interfere." The U.S. only cares about dollars and oil, that's what their military is for. Americans will do anything to keep their snouts in the trough. I completely gave up on her at that point. Apparently, there is no need for Iraq to pass UN resolutions before they invade countries. It didn't even matter to Petra that the Iraqi soldiers were murdering and raping women, as long as the arrogant Americans weren't trying to stop them from doing it. I didn't realize she was *that* anti-American. If she's a pacifist, shouldn't she be against *all* war?

There in the restaurant with everyone staring at us, I understood that Petra would never have the capacity to tolerate viewpoints contrary to her own. I believe people have the right to their opinions, but that includes me. She couldn't see the similarity between the Iraqi attack on Kuwait and the seizure of Czechoslovakia by Germany. That's because she knows nothing about it. But she's still smarter than me. She's the perfect pacifist, so everyone should hang on every wise word she speaks. I hope I never get so smart that I consider learning unnecessary. I was furious with her for shouting at me in public and suggested she pay for her own dinner. She would have gladly slapped it down on the table, except she didn't bring any money.

From Petra's point of view, her struggle against "intolerance" is a struggle against those who disagree with her about anything. Sure, I'm aware of America's dark and violent past. I disagree with a lot of our policies. But that's not the issue. No one's intolerance is justified. I've talked to lots of people who hate Germany. I had a Jewish coworker who refused to go on a business trip to Germany because "that's where the holocaust happened." A lot of people still miss the whole point. I maintain that the horrific things done by Germany are not something German. They are something human. Petra just misses the point from a different angle. She is herself full of political, historical, and gender intolerance. But everyone should accept *her*. She clings defensively to her ignorance of German history. If she were capable of listening, I would tell her that avoidance is not enlightenment.

A Conversation With a Panzer Driver

I don't use Germany's history to pass judgment on Germans as individuals. Not even the people involved in the war itself. When I lived in

Germany in the late 1970s, there were still many who had participated in the war. I stayed with a family for a month in a town on the North Sea while learning the language. It turned out the father had been a German Panzer driver and spent that terrible winter of 1941 in Russia. He wore special shoes because his toes had been frozen off. I had a lot of questions for him, which he was happy to answer. I wanted to know what he thought he was doing while he was invading Russia.

"We were stupid and believed all the propaganda. I was there outside Moscow all winter thinking I was fighting for the Fatherland," he said. Having faced the Russians, he was very happy with West Germany being occupied by the American military. No talk about the Indians from him. No references to America being capitalistic and imperialistic. No points like "the victors get to write history." He made no pretense of knowing the answers to everything, but he knew he never wanted another war. He said he no longer followed politics but considered the American presence in Germany an important deterrent to war. I realized my interpretation of history and political views had a lot more in common with this ex-Nazi Panzer driver than with Petra. Years later it struck me, the Panzer driver was the true pacifist.

A Call from Nina on 9/11

Nina is another Munich girl. She was my friend and an occasional lover for 20 years. She never seemed anti-American. I got a different perspective of her worldview when she called me on 9/11 right after the second plane hit the World Trade Center. She was laughing and telling me how this was exactly what we Americans deserved for our "terrorist" acts around the world. "You think nothing bad can ever happen to you! Now you know how the rest of the world feels under your terrorist threats. Ha! Someone finally knocked you off your high horse!" she said. Nina was *delighted* watching those people dying horrible deaths. It sounded like it was the happiest day of her life. Incredibly, she seemed to think I would laugh along with her. I found it obscene. She didn't know who had sponsored the attacks, nor did she care. A few nasty e-mails later and our 20-year relationship came to an end. She tried the female tactic of, "I can get angrier at you than you can get angry at me." It was as if being a woman entitled her to be as insensitive as she wanted without apologizing. It didn't work for me. Then Nina asked me, "What happened to free speech?" Here's some. Fuck you.

The Ninas of the world, who so callously delighted in the 9/11 attacks, still see themselves as "pacifist" when really they've embraced a lot of intolerant and hateful causes. They do not distinguish such acts of terrorism from the U.S. military's ability to deliver bombs anywhere. "It's the only way they can fight back," Nina told me. Who exactly was fighting back, she didn't know. She had morphed into another Chomsky clone. So if "terrorism" is no different than any other means of delivering death and destruction, then I suppose the U.S. may as well use terror tactics instead of a conventional military. And I guess there's no difference between possessing terrible weapons as a deterrent and actually using them. We could blow up airliners and stadiums, and contaminate cities with anthrax unless our demands are met. It would save us a lot of money, and let's face it, that's all that really matters to us, right?

I understand that as Americans we do not live up to our own hype. Our gluttony overshadows our good intentions. We have such enormous responsibility in the world and so little knowledge of it. The opportunity affords itself again and again for us to be the nation that leads the world to a higher standard of human dignity. We could become the most benevolent nation on earth. Again and again we seem satisfied to demonstrate merely that we are the most powerful.

But if the Germans ever find themselves in deep shit, they'll be screaming for the Americans to intervene. Until then, they are content to let someone else soil their hands so they can remain "pacifists." They continue to sit in their beautiful homes and secure apartments in their unified country while cursing the U.S. military planes that occasionally fly overhead. When is the last time that Western Europe had more than 60 years of peace and prosperity? Never. I don't go around soliciting gratitude from Germans, but there's a time to acknowledge the good the U.S. has done in the world. I could have used some kind words on that day.

I never discussed the 9/11 attacks with Petra. There's no need, I already know where she stands politically. America is her evil empire. We got what we deserved. A few days after 9/11, I saw a poll on CNN that said 65 percent of all Germans thought the U.S. had brought the attacks on itself. Germany is a country full of Ninas and Petras. Like true ideologues, their opinions are predetermined. They automatically take the anti-American position on every issue, which I find just as absurd as taking the pro-American position on every issue. They don't differentiate between legitimate intervention like in Bosnia and Kosovo and outright political fraud like the Iraq invasion of 2003. And they certainly won't admit that they benefit greatly from low expenditures on defense. I'm tired of Europeans droning on about how U.S. foreign policy lacks foresight, credibility, and creates more problems than it solves. And I really wish we would stop proving them right.

Ivana Behind the Wall

I knew one German girl who had an appreciation of the U.S. Ironically, she was from East Berlin and had been taught in school that America was her enemy. Her name was Ivana, and I met her at the top of the Berlin TV tower. This was back when there was still a wall and guards and minefields. Ivana was someone who knew what it was like to live in a police state without personal freedoms. She obviously enjoyed meeting Americans and venting about all the restrictions on travel and the expression of ideas. We walked around East Berlin after her shift, had dinner, and exchanged addresses. We actually corresponded for a few years. She sent me brochures of Dresden, describing how it was destroyed by "Anglo-American" bombing during the "War Against Fascism." She was sick of hearing about it and wished she could go to Paris or New York.

I returned to Berlin three years later to visit Ivana. She had a French boyfriend who was trying to get her across the wall. East Germany only granted one-day visas to people from the West. In order to stay in East Berlin overnight with Ivana, her boyfriend had to return to the border crossing before midnight, leave East Berlin, then turn around and get another one-day visa.

I was irritated by the East German ban on "unapproved" books, so I took it as a personal challenge to violate it. Certainly *Armageddon* by Leon Uris (the story of the fall of Berlin to the brutal Russian army) would violate their policy. It was thick, so I opened it up and stuck it under my belt and made it through East German customs. I gave it to Ivana, who was shocked at my audacity. Like women everywhere, she was more appreciative of the act than of the gift itself. She invited me to stay at her flat that night, so we had to go through the same midnight visa drill at the border. We made it back, and I fell asleep in her tiny living room.

In the morning she brought me some tea. When I walked into the kitchen to get some sugar, I found her standing in the plastic dish basin unabashedly taking a sponge bath. Her little flat had no shower. We did the visa drill again the next night, but this time an East German policeman saw Ivana getting back into my car three blocks from the checkpoint. He stopped us and wrote down her name as a possible prostitute. Ivana was in tears as we drove back to her place. She hated the East German Stasi and vowed again to make it to West Berlin.

Ivana plotted for years how to get out. She married the French guy but still didn't get an exit visa, even though he crossed the border almost daily for two years to be with her. A diplomat offered to smuggle her out in his car for money and sex. She declined. It was probably a scam anyway since he wanted the sex up front. She finally got an exit visa when it was determined she could not have children which apparently made her of little value to the socialist state. Ivana made it to West Berlin seven years before the wall came down.

A Kinder, Gentler Fascism

Why does Petra lack any such appreciation for how the U.S. helped reconstruct and protect her country after the war? Doesn't she value her personal freedoms? Not surprisingly, Petra never visited East Berlin. I wish she could have spent a year or two behind that wall. Let her experience a taste of socialist paradise where everyone fails equally. See how she likes her neighbors spying on her and ratting her out. Militaristic police everywhere. Her life would have been more like Ivana's if it weren't for U.S. foreign policy.

Oh, but Petra thinks American foreign policy is not much different from that carried out by the Nazis. We're just not as efficient. It's taking us longer, but we're slowly achieving that dream of world domination with our advanced weaponry and technology. To her, World War II was not a struggle between good and evil, it was the wholesale destruction of Europe, resulting in the triumph of U.S. propaganda. Just like the Nazis, we indulge ourselves in our own version of superiority while glossing over a few atrocities that may have occurred along the way.

A German telling me my country resembles the Nazis strikes me as oddly entertaining. At the time, I wasn't ready to play the "who's more like a Nazi" game. I'm ready now. How about Petra's personal philosophy? Pages from *Mein Kampf* seem to keep showing up in feminist literature. Since this is not an Internet forum, Godwin's Law does not apply. Shall we play?

When I see references in the mainstream press gloating about how my Y male chromosome has "defective" genes (Maureen Dowd, New York Times, July 9, 2003), I notice the similarity of radical feminism to Nazi propaganda and the master race. When I hear about the study of "masculinities" and "whiteness," I am reminded of the Nazi "science" of eugenics. When I read that men have taken all the power for themselves at the expense of others, I recall the banners in 1930s Germany accusing the Jews of exactly the same thing. Feminism has become an academic attempt to create a female "übergender." When I see that *The S.C.U.M. Manifesto* and *Quintessence* (which call for the extermination of all men) are on lists of required reading for women's studies courses at many public universities, I understand that men are feminism's Jews. We are sub-humans worthy of the most extreme contempt. Feminists have also been very successful in preventing many culturally impure "masculinist" works from being published. You can't burn a book if it was never printed. Of all the comparisons made to Nazi Germany, I think the term "feminazi" is the one that will endure. If the jackboots fit, wear them. I know a lot of women with a pair in their closet. Right next to the "fuck me" pumps.

All the fun comparisons aside, feminists haven't reached the level of the Nazis. Let's not give them that much credit. Feminists don't actually want to exterminate men. They just want to emasculate us and take away our rights. And turn us into financial slaves. And put us in prison. Besides, if they exterminated us, who would they have to blame for all their problems? And someone has to build all the roads and bridges and houses and everything else that just drops out of the sky.

The real difference between Nazism and radical feminism is that radical feminism is primarily a *non-violent* political hate movement. It's is a kinder, gentler fascism. They threaten not with violence but with hate itself. As with all haters, they feel fully justified. Their most effective ways of inflicting "solutions" upon men and society are through legal means. That doesn't mean they don't condone violence when it is committed against men. It doesn't mean they don't celebrate it.

Feminism has gone pathological. I have no doubt that if women were awarded absolute control, the most ruthless feminists would be setting the agenda. We would see the rise of female versions of Stalin and Hitler. The man-hate expressed by Mary Daly and Valerie Solanas in *Quintessence* and *The S.C.U.M. Manifesto* would no longer be theoretical in nature. The radical feminists would gladly carry out their gendercide fantasy. After all men were either dead or in prison, the female populous would explain it away. "We didn't know they were serious."

In fact, Dorothy is already wearing those ruby slippers. That's right, women already have the power to legally exterminate men. We've all heard about the horrific problem of selective-sex abortions of female fetuses in India and China, but where are the figures for the United States? Is the opposite happening here? If single mothers and lesbian couples decide to selectively abort male fetuses, they won't need gas chambers. Perhaps that's what Mary Daly already has in mind. If Dorothy learns to click her heels, America could become that idyllic community of incarcerated males and peaceful lesbian couples. And about a zillion cats. The roar from all the wind chimes would be deafening. I think I'd rather be dead.

Sharon's Favorite Show

Wouldn't it be simpler to have a girlfriend who didn't care about any of this? Why burden a relationship with gender warfare and historical conflict? Isn't there enough to disagree about without fighting over which gender contributed more to civilization? Must I debate U.S. foreign policy and the exploitation of developing nations over dinner? A discussion about the use of the atomic bomb on Japan or the fire-bombing of Dresden is never a good prelude to sex.

Maybe it's good that most women would rather know what kind of shoes the Dresden women are wearing than anything about Dresden's history. Maybe that's the kind of girl I need. A girl who doesn't care about any of this. A girl who has never even heard of Andrea Dworkin or Joseph Goebbels.

I met Sharon after I moved to Austin, and we immediately clicked. As with most sudden involvements, there was a price to pay. To keep her happy I had to spend a couple of evenings per week watching cheesy shows on TV with her. We would curl up at her place for hours with Sharon in control of the remote. Sure, the sex was good, but there's only so much a guy can take. I waste my time all the time, but I can't stand other people wasting it for me. I had forgotten how bad the original *Star Trek* series was. It was actually a relief when *Mr. Ed* came on. Sharon never watched boring stuff like news, history, or science.

Sharon's favorite show was *Hogan's Heroes*, which probably provided the majority of her historical knowledge regarding Germany. I guarantee she knew more about Schultz and Klink than any historical figure from WWII. She and Sgt. Schultz shared the same philosophy: "I know nothing, *nothing!*" I think it's fine to watch that show, but you should also be willing to acquire some real knowledge of the era. Tell Sharon about the Panzer driver I had known? I don't think so. Every time *Hogan's Heroes* came on I felt compelled to offer some commentary. In one episode, the black prisoner in Stalag 13 makes a fake radio broadcast pretending to be Hitler. The Germans are easily fooled. I remarked, "I don't think that black guy could fake a Bavarian accent well enough to impersonate Hitler." "Huh?" She didn't get it. "Bavarian?" I just couldn't dumb it down for her. "Can you just be quiet and let me enjoy the program?" she snapped. "You know, it's not exactly Shakespeare," I snapped back. Things went downhill from there.

At that moment it became clear to me that pure stupidity is not the answer. No, complete ignorance is *not* better that selective ignorance. My relationship with Sharon slammed into the ground like a V2. Like a what? Never mind. Chicks want a guy that makes them laugh, not a guy that makes them think.

I have no doubt that if I ever mention the V2 to Petra again, she will have no idea what I'm talking about. But I'm sure she can tell me all about women's history of the last century. She can't place Charles Lindbergh, but she knows all about Amelia Earhart. She can prattle on about Gloria Steinem or any of her feminist superheroes if you let her. How about the Battle of Verdun, or the defense of Stalingrad? It doesn't matter to Petra how many men died or for what reason. To her, war is just another stupid thing men do. Why learn anything about it? The sun still comes up every day in her world.

I would agree with those who say there is too much hero worship of military figures in the traditional versions of history. What was so "Great" about Alexander? He massacred people from Greece to India and back. Shouldn't we rename him "Alexander the Psychopath"? Why are the French so proud of Napoleon? They should pull his oversized casket out of the Hotel des Invalides and dump it into the sea. Maybe his corpse would absorb some oil from that *Prestige* tanker spill, and finally he will have performed a useful service for France. I don't have a problem learning about these murderers as long as I also learn about what circumstances created either the opportunity or need for such men.

I don't agree that the answer for women should be to introduce gender into history to promote anti-male doctrines. But that's exactly what's happening. War, global slavery, and nuclear weapons? Blame it on testosterone. Just be sure to elaborate on it using scholarly sounding terminology. Alexander the Great was a tyrant exhibiting those "hegemonic masculinities," but Catherine the Great was an exceedingly shrewd and cultured woman who consolidated her power and expanded her empire despite an entrenched patriarchal system. Too bad she forgot to free the serfs. Some call her an "enlightened despot." I prefer "Catherine the Spoiled Egomaniac."

Don't actions speak louder than hormones? How about all the European queens who ruled over the centuries? Elizabeth I financed Drake's attacks of Spanish ships and ports. She knighted him for it. Why would a woman encourage such brutality? Was her estrogen level abnormally low? Why didn't she abolish England's slave trade? Why didn't she strive to end war and make peace with Spain? Yes, it was in Elizabethan times that the Spanish Armada was defeated. Women's history reveres Elizabeth I for exerting power greater than most kings. How about the colonization of India and Africa under Victoria I? She knighted the inventor of the machine gun, which decimated African tribes. Powerful women do not hesitate to send men into battle to do their killing. This is not something that has happened only in the past. Margaret Thatcher responded militarily in the Falklands. More recently, Condoleezza Rice and Karen Hughes of the Bush II administration strongly supported the 2003 Iraq invasion. It's clear to me that women are capable of enslaving, torturing, and murdering masses of people if they are just given the same opportunities as men. I suppose the difference is that none of these women were ever required to wield the sword in their own hands.

Women's history is not about history. It's about women's obsession with gender roles. I was right all along that Petra had no interest in history itself. Her only interest was victimology. Do we really need gender-specific histories? Are we supposed to let feminists fuck with history so they can feel empowered? I'm not sure who I'm asking. I doubt I have many female readers. They're off taking a relationship quiz in *Self* magazine.

The Missing Piece of the Female Brain

When I go looking for a girlfriend, I usually end up looking for answers instead. Women do not make sense. Sometimes it seems like a piece of their brain is missing. Men know what I mean. That would be logic, right? Men are rational and women are emotional. I used to think that. But the logic function can't be missing in females, because it works occasionally. Most of the time in fact. Just look at how women can do math and highly complex computer programming.

As irrational as women can be, I cannot believe men are by nature more logical. But women get all emotional and cry, right? Well, men get all emotional and do stupid irrational stuff too. We just get emotional over different things. And we prefer swearing to crying. Sure, women lack emotional discipline, but let's face it, there's no shortage of bad logic coming from either gender.

No, fucking up is not something that needs to be gender-normed. But women seem to think that when they fuck up, it shouldn't matter. This is what men are talking about when we refer to "female logic." But there is a certain logic to female irrationality. Women's many double standards are rational in the sense that they always benefit women. If logic doesn't get them what they want, then what use do they have for it? So it's not that women are irrational by nature, it's that irrationality works in their favor. Regardless, there still seems to be something missing. If it's not logic, then what is it? After years of pondering this question, I am proud to announce that I've discovered the missing piece of the female brain.

Women do not have the ability to see the world from a non-female perspective. Their brains cannot perform gender role reversal. Actually, they can do half of it—where male behavior is shown to be inappropriate. But they can't role reverse their own inappropriate behavior. Women can't do it because it *never* benefits them. It's as if evolution simply recognized this was an unnecessary function for females and removed it from their brains. It's like those fish that have lived so long in dark submerged caverns that they've lost their eyes altogether. Turning on the lights is not going to help.

Men see it. We're trained all our lives to anticipate female needs and to understand their feelings. We're supposed to agree with women even when we don't agree with them. We have to figure out what they want so we can make them happy. It's part of our provider role. Women are far more comfortable communicating their needs than gaining some kind of male perspective on their own actions. What would the value of that be? Why try to understand men if you can control and change them? Women listen to what we say only so they can "correct" us based on their own estrogen-centric perspective. Lots of men just give up, take the blame for everything, and agree with whatever changes women require of them. I believe these men are commonly known as "husbands."

You doubt what I'm saying? It's men who line up to suck up to women and tell them they're beautiful, smart, and right about everything. It's men who must try not to offend females. We're the ones who have to be sensitive all the time. God forbid we should ever hurt a woman emotionally. We are supposed to meet the needs and expectations of women without even being told what they are. That requires a comprehension of the female mindset, and a willingness to confine our behavior to female standards. Forget those "superior" female verbal skills. Women are much better manipulators than communicators. Women don't care if their actions denigrate men. No need to role reverse offensive female behavior. That's just good entertainment.

How about a role reversal exercise? Here's one. I was flipping through channels and came across *Miss Congeniality* with Sandra Bullock. She's cool, so I watched the ending. She was on stage at a beauty pageant dressed in a cute girlie outfit, and began demonstrating various self-defense moves on a fellow FBI colleague. She hits him in the face, stomach, and several other areas to the delight of the crowd. He takes it like a man. She taunts him, "Are you scared?" Then the camera zooms in for a close-up of her punching him right in the groin. The crowd cheers. He must have deserved it somehow. By being publicly assaulted, Sandra's FBI colleague gains so much respect for her that he asks her to dinner.

Now let's switch the genders. The FBI guy hits Sandra Bullock a few times in public to demonstrate his boxing skills. She is in pain but does not resist. He taunts her, "Are you gonna cry?" Delighted male and female onlookers cheer him on. So then he punches her one more time in the ovaries and she doubles over in pain. "Hurray!" This beating attracts her to him so much that she offers him sex. Make any sense? Sorry, Sandra, you're off my "cool" list.

The classic 1986 book by Warren Farrell called *Why Men Are the Way They Are* has a chapter called "The New Sexism" that gives example after example of how women find nothing wrong with derogatory depictions of men but would be infuriated if the gender roles were reversed. The problem is that you can give women a thousand role reversal examples, and they still will not see them as relevant. Seeing things from the male viewpoint could not possibly benefit them, so why bother? It doesn't matter if men get upset as long as women don't get upset.

The suppression of critical thinking is what enables so much of feminism. It is the basis for the expansion of all female rights and privileges without regard for the rights of men. Only women can be victims because male suffering does not matter. Men do not need any rights, because men's rights do not benefit women. Violence against women is bad; but violence against men is unimportant, since it has little impact on women. Unless the man is the provider for a woman, of course.

Feminists have been trained not to support any male viewpoint regardless of its merit. There were few women who supported Glenn Sacks' campaign to get department stores to stop selling "Boys are stupid, throw rocks at them" T-shirts to elementary and high school girls. "Get a life," wrote feminist Jane Ganahl of the San Francisco Chronicle in February 2004. Since there were no "Girls are stupid, hit them with sticks" T-shirts offered for sale to boys, we just have to imagine what the feminist response would be if the roles were reversed. I'm sure they would be complaining that such shirts encouraged violence toward women and trained boys to be future wife-beaters and oppressors of women. I would be in agreement with them that such hypothetical shirts would send the wrong message to boys.

Role Reversal of "no means no"

Can a feminist use gender role reversal on the "no means no" rule when it applies to her own behavior? Of course not. It wasn't very often when I turned down sex with Petra, but of the three times I did, not once did she accept "no" for an answer. Of these three incidents, once I was tired but she got me going. Fine.

The second time it happened, I had fucked another girl without a condom just a week before I visited her, and didn't want to get interrogated. I suggested a condom, but we didn't have any. So I said "no" to sex. Petra wouldn't give up. I politely said "no" several more times. I didn't think it was a good idea. She insisted she couldn't get pregnant. My concern was more about the slight possibility of her contracting an STD, though I had no symptoms. She undressed and got me hard. "I don't think we should do this," I told her. She ignored me and put me inside her. I didn't physically resist, but then, I didn't consider it a sexual assault. I considered it disrespectful. I just wanted to prevent her from taking a risk. Oh well. She violated my right to say "no," so she assumed the risk.

The third time it happened was probably 10 years after my trip to Spain with her and Ursula. Petra and I ended up staying overnight on Ursula's bedroom floor, and apparently Petra wanted to have sex with me in front of Ursula like we did in Spain. But I remembered how Ursula complained after the trip about our lack of discretion, and I wanted to finally show Ursula a little courtesy. But Petra wanted to show off, and ignored me when I said "no." She continued groping and trying to arouse me. I asked her again to stop and even explained I didn't want to disturb Ursula. Still she persisted. We were in sleeping bags on the carpet, so I zipped mine shut. Petra unzipped it and tried to grope me again, covering her aggression with giggling. I zipped up my bag again and pulled the zipper in so she couldn't get to it, going into a completely defensive posture. She kept at it. I asked her again to please stop. She tried a couple more times to pry my hands away and get to the zipper. Finally she stopped, giving me a look of anger and confusion.

I don't know if it ever occurred to Petra that her behavior fit the feminist definition of sexual assault. The hypocrisy of it offended me far more than her actions. Her brain just could not role reverse the situation. She could have apologized, but she didn't. That would have violated the "women are always right" rule.

The Suppression of Male Views

Women want their way all the time, because that's all that makes sense to them. Most women are at least willing to listen to a male viewpoint, even though they end up disregarding it. But feminists are far more fanatical in their rejection of opposing views. Not only do feminists want to eliminate all challenges to their own opinions, they want to prevent male ideas from even being expressed. We have no right to challenge feminism because our views are sexist and degrading to women. Jack Kammer couldn't find a publisher for his book, *If Men Have All the Power, Why Do Women Make All the Rules*. One publisher rejected it because it offended his female office workers.

Ironically, if you want to find books titled *Cunt, Whore, Slut,* and *Bitch*, don't bother searching the X-rated porn sites. You need to look no further than the Women's Studies section of your local bookstore. Sounds like all the really good titles are taken now. I'm sure it's been done, but when the female clerk at Barnes and Noble asks if she can help you find something, it would be fun to say, "Yeah, I'm looking for *Cunt*." I imagine that book makes a great Christmas gift for ex-wives. Certainly the publishers understood the potential for sales in that regard.

In case you're wondering, *Cunt* (2002 by Inga Muscio) claims that the term was originally a very beautiful word for the female genitalia. A "cunt" should bring up images of flowers. *Cunt* calls for women to take back the word by forming groups in public and shouting the word out loud. So if you're on campus, don't be surprised if you stumble upon a university-sponsored "Cunt Fest," as happened at Boston College and Penn State. *Cunt* also calls on women to use sea sponges for tampons to cut the profits of the male-owned feminine hygiene products companies, since it's all another plot by the evil patriarchy to financially exploit women. I resisted the temptation to buy *Cunt* since I don't have an ex-wife. I'll just wait for the movie.

I wonder why there are almost no gender books from the male perspective? I went to Barnes and Noble and found a Women's Studies section with several hundred books. No Men's Studies section at all. They had one Warren Farrell book in the "Self Help" section. I checked Half-Priced Books and the Women's Studies section contained 31 shelves of books. They actually had a Men's Studies section which contained 10 books, three of which were Susan Faludi's *Stiffed*. Similar story at Border's Bookstore, where I found several racks of women's studies and gay/lesbian literature, and four books in the men's Studies section. I *don't* actually wonder why there are so few men's books on gender issues. Publishing is dominated by women. It's the suppression of literature written by men about gender equality issues. They have successfully categorized anti-feminist books as hate literature.

There's another reason. There are hundreds of women's studies courses attended by thousands of female students who are required to purchase the newest feminist blatherings at full retail price. Sales of several thousand books for each new title certainly drives the genre. And it's not just women's studies classes. Feminist writings are mandatory reading in many sociology, psychology, history, and of course, gay and lesbian literature classes.

In Austin there's a feminist bookstore called Book Woman. It used to be at a very prominent location in the 6th Street entertainment district. A few years ago it was moved to a smaller, more remote location. It's not doing well. I hope it's a sign of the times. There's always a drive to save it. I decided to have a look a few years ago. I walked in and the mandatory ultra-butch lesbian clerk politely asked if she could help me. The pressure was on. Quick, what female author might a white guy be looking for in a feminist bookstore?

"Do you have anything by Camille Paglia?" I asked. At the time, I hadn't read anything by her. "We don't carry her because we don't agree with her," snapped the lesbo clerk. I'd never been in a bookstore that evaluated the contents of books for me. From her hostile tone you'd think I'd just asked for a book on how to pick up chicks. For guys, that is. "I can order Paglia for you if you want, we can use the business," she reluctantly offered. "No thanks, I'll just buy it online," I retorted. Since they're so into "diversity," I would have expected a feminist bookstore to at least offer a little diversity of opinion within the women's movement. Yeah, right. I should have asked for *Cunt*.

The De-engineering of My Gender

Feminists want to redefine masculinity in terms they deem less aggressive and violent and are tying to shape boys to become the ideal passive servants. And what female behaviors are feminists trying to redefine? None, of course; girls are perfect just the way they are. Boys are the problem, not girls. Some studies somewhere prove it. Feminists can't see any legitimacy to masculinity. The hole in their head is showing.

How about a taste of your own social engineering? Let's go ahead and redefine femininity according to the wishes of men. How about teaching girls to stop their taunting of boys? Can we teach women to stop being such teases? And how about teaching girls they are ultimately responsible for their own bodies? If girls want respect from boys, shouldn't we teach girls they must also respect boys? How about some manipulation seminars warning boys what to watch out for?

I suspect all the portrayals of masculinity as inherently evil and attempts to change boys to be more feminine have already resulted in a broadening rebellion by young men. You can't fix something by breaking it more. Rebelling against rules and authority figures is typical of youth, but we are now seeing a male rebellion against the whole educational system. And the neo-matriarchy. As a result, adolescent males are becoming everything they're not supposed to be. Can't say I blame them. As long as we have anti-boy matriarchs in schools suppressing "masculinities" and encouraging boys to behave like girls, male rebellion will continue to worsen. Male enrollment in universities will continue to decline.

Although I think most female teachers think they are doing the right thing by suppressing aggressive boy behavior, why do they continue to ignore the results of their anti-boy biases? According to the National Center for Education Statistics, in 2002 women were awarded 58 percent of undergraduate degrees and 59 percent of graduate degrees. The gap is expected to widen, and no remedial action is planned. It's the deliberate dumbing-down of boys to open up scholastic opportunities for girls. They quickly dismiss Christina Hoff Sommers' book, *The War Against Boys* (2000), which clearly documents the assault on masculinity.

Even though there is nothing preventing women from entering engineering fields, girl-only programs are sprouting up to "end discrimination" in this final area of male dominance. Feminists are anxiously waiting the go-ahead to de-engineer engineering the same way they gutted male athletics using Title IX. Oddly enough, there are no plans to "correct" the dominance of psychology by women, who now make up 74 percent of undergraduate majors. And of course, research done by feminist psychologists heavily influences women entering the education profession, which is also dominated by women. Perhaps we need to connect the dots between the fields of Women's Studies, Psychology, and Education. At some level the neo-matriarchs know they've created learning environments highly favorable to girls and destructive to boys.

Growing up, I was taught by the old matriarchs that my male libido was something to be ashamed of. Girls could wear short skirts, but I wasn't supposed to look. But now that kind of suppression has been expanded to include all "masculine" behavior. We've got to clamp down on boys who want to compete instead of sitting quietly by and obeying all the rules. Keep male teachers away. Let's remind boys to feel guilty by giving them lectures on how sexual aggression equals rape. Make them do lots of homework assignments about women's history. Take on as many effeminate qualities as you can, because that makes you a better person. Remember, all men are oppressors so "get out of the way" and let the girls succeed. And don't forget to take your Ritalin.

The '80s gave us a lot of male rock bands experimenting with a self-imposed androgyny, as if maybe people would like them better if they had clothes and hair and make-up like girls. It continued until Kurt Cobain mocked it and kicked it all into the shitter. More recent bands like Korn, Staind, P.O.D., Papa Roach, Disturbed, Limp Bizkit, Deftones, Drowning Pool, Godsmack, and System of a Down all emit exaggerated aggression and repressed anger. This music contains frequent expressions of desperation, hopelessness, and suicide, which draw a following from of the masses of young males emerging from repressive schools. They're like escaped wolves that just found out they'd been fed veggie burgers all their lives. Yes, there's even a group called "Ritalin Kids."

Much of the loud demonic rock out there expresses the pain of being male in a world that no longer values men. If they fail no one cares, but if they succeed it doesn't matter either. They've degenerated into the male wretches they've been conditioned to believe they are. Adolescent males with their mutated masculinity dare us to hate them, since we helped create them. Obviously the neo-matriarchs would disagree. Oh, this must be happening because we still tolerate too many "hegemonic masculinities" in boys' behavior. Better go commission a study to prove it right away.

Compare male rock to the pop music sung by all the sexy young divas. They don't sit around brooding over the meaninglessness of life. They wear sparkles as they sing songs of beauty and empowerment. They're happy with their sexuality and their personal worth as females. They're cute, and everybody loves them. It mirrors the current female view of success, in which girls get all the attention and credit while guys quietly do the grunt work and vie for scraps of recognition.

I don't think it's possible to fundamentally change masculinity, but it *is* possible to downgrade the self-image of males of all ages. That is the current phenomenon in Western culture. Boys are taught that their success as men is directly proportional to their success in meeting female expectations, and that their purpose in life is to prioritize female happiness by sacrificing their independence, their money, their opinions, their own happiness, and even their lives. Girls are taught not to trust boys, and that the ultimate achievement in life life is to succeed without them.

Men have precious few female allies in the effort to halt the destructive social de-engineering of the male gender. Women capable of comprehending the male mind are as rare as fish with eyes in Mammoth Cave. Feminists will fight us without regard to the validity of our message. They have no interest in helping us recover our rights. It must be because they're afraid men will rise up and attack females in the same way feminists have waged their war on males. But that's not it. What men want might be even scarier. What horrific thing could that be? No more double standards. But wouldn't that be an attempt to take away women's rights? How dare we expect standards to be applied equally? Isn't that just another form of male oppression? When will women be completely free from the shackles of responsibility?

It still baffles me. Have women become so self-absorbed in the last 30 years that they can no longer even consider a male point of view? Are they really incapable of applying gender role reversal to their own behavior? Can it be true that females are missing that piece of their brain? Will they be forever blind to their own biases? Or did they just forget to take the cucumbers off their eyes? Maybe I'm being facetious. Maybe not. I'm not even sure myself.

The Most Sacred of Sacred Cows

My introduction to rape awareness came when I was a college sophomore. I was sitting as the lone male with six girls in a dorm room with the lights low when the topic turned to sexual assaults. I was shocked to learn all six girls had been repeatedly assaulted. Two had to bail out of moving cars to escape being kidnapped and raped. "How fast were the cars going?" I asked. The first girl said "About 15 miles per hour." The second girl said "Probably 25 miles per hour." It had turned into a competition. They enjoyed watching me react in horror as they told of attacks by aggressive strangers, drunken derelicts, and dates. One girl said she volunteered to work at a rape crisis center and recognized one of the male counselors as her attacker from a few months before. The next girl claimed three different men had attempted to rape her in the last two years. The next girl said five different guys had tried to rape her. Do I hear six? It was oddly festive, like sitting around telling ghost stories.

I think some of their stories were true. Embellished perhaps. I suspect some were the equivalent of "the call is coming from inside the house." Since then I've come to realize it's hard to tell the difference between the truth and a good ghost story.

Frank and Dana

One summer I rented a house with a couple of waitresses. One night Dana announced that Frank, the guy she went out with over the weekend, had date raped her. He got her drunk, and she couldn't stop him. I was outraged. Should I go and confront him? No. She didn't want me involved. Was she going to report it? No, but she going to tell everyone what a fucking jerk he was. That's it? She was just going to let him get away with it? That was her choice.

A couple of days later I was caught off guard when Dana mentioned she was going out with Frank again. She told me not to worry, she was going to "let him have it." I was even more surprised when she brought him back to the house, and they disappeared into her bedroom. I guess by "let him have it" she meant something different than what I had in mind. The next day I confronted her. "Wasn't that the guy who raped you?" "Oh, that was nothing. Frank loves me. I probably shouldn't have said that, he's really a nice guy," she said.

Huh? Do I understand this correctly? Is sex either love or rape? Is there no middle ground? I'm sure Frank had no idea she had been calling him a rapist behind his back. I found it interesting that the other waitress in the house believed he had indeed raped Dana, and that she was "suppressing" it by accepting him as her boyfriend. My opinion was that Frank hadn't called Dana for a couple days after they had sex, she got mad, and began to envision their encounter in a more sinister context. Calling Frank a rapist was just another way of saying he took advantage of her. It was another way of saying he was a jerk. The other waitress and I agreed on one thing though. Dana was insane.

On what basis did I decide to believe Frank and not Dana? Besides the fact that Dana's story changed, I also watched them together. If rape is about control, consider the issue settled. Frank was the consummate pussy-whipped boyfriend, totally pandering to her every moody whim. One Friday night I saw Dana rip into him verbally for no reason. Actually there *was* a reason. She just got her period and didn't want to tell him, so she decided to sabotage the evening and stay home. When Frank walked in to pick her up, she called him a "fucking asshole." When he asked what he did wrong, she shouted that he *"ought* to fucking know!" Frank begged to be forgiven for whatever it was. He would try harder. She screamed at him to "get the fuck out of the house." Five days later she took him back and "forgave" him. He brought flowers and pleaded with her for an explanation. "Just shut up, it's okay now," she told him. He was clueless. It was absurd to imagine Frank as a rapist. Dana certainly "raised my awareness" about date rape.

Alexandra Offers a Challenge

When I try to put this all together, I can't help thinking back on my experience with Alexandra, the Romanian barmaid. She's the one who took me home and wanted me to act out a rape fantasy with her. I found the whole idea repulsive. The incident was still disturbing me a week later, so I decided to ask her about it. What was the appeal of being raped? Did she actually like getting hit? Was there some enjoyment in that? She gave me a bemused look and shook her head as if to say, "You silly boy."

"It gets me very excited," she explained in German. "Besides, you would never be able to rape me without my permission." "What?" "It's true, you can't possibly fuck me if I don't want," she said. "Come on, I'll show you."

She quickly stripped off all her clothes. She told me to undress and even gave me a "head start." Then she crawled onto the bed. "Good, here I am. Now come and try to fuck me," she said. Don't mind if I do. I never played this game before.

I quickly got her point. Alexandra wasn't even resisting, just squirming a little and crossing her legs. I couldn't even come close to penetrating her. "Come on, hold me down," she said. I took hold of her arms and held them tightly against her waist. Then with her cooperation, I spread her legs. She could barely move as I got into position. *Ha! I got her now.* I slid inside about an inch when she bit my chin. I couldn't just turn away, she was holding my skin with her teeth and wasn't letting go. I pushed in a little more, and she bit me harder. When I pulled back out, she let go. I put my head down and tried again. This time she bit down on my shoulder. It was just a light bite, but it hurt like hell. If this had been for real, she could have taken a chunk out of me. Once again, I was forced to pull out. It was obvious that I would not be able to fuck her if she resisted at all. Another thing was immediately obvious. I would really suck as a rapist.

This made it clear to me that rape is only possible if a woman is threatened or unconscious. That a woman can simply be overpowered seems to me very unlikely. Sorry, but I don't think there is room for any ambiguity in rape. There's a difference between an overly aggressive guy and an attacker. Any woman who resists can get an overly aggressive date off her. Men get mixed signals all the time, so it's up to women to clarify their position. A girl who mumbles "no" but offers no physical resistance to unwanted male aggression needs assertiveness training, not five years of rape counseling. No means no? I'd say "Get the fuck off me!" means no. "I'll fucking bite you!" means no.

I can see why that dyke at the feminist bookstore didn't like

Camille Paglia. Back in 1994 in *Vamps and Tramps* Paglia said:

> "... consent may be non-verbal, expressed by language or be-
> havior—such as going to a stranger's apartment on the first date,
> which I think should be correctly interpreted as consent to sex."

In 1992 in *Sex, Art, and American Culture*, she said:

> "A girl who goes upstairs alone with a brother at a fraternity
> party is an idiot. Feminists call this 'blaming the victim.' I call
> it common sense."

Common sense means accepting some responsibility for your own
behavior. Girls can't just passively lie there and then decide a few
days later it was rape. Women can't expect the courts to figure out
what happened between two drunken, sexually excited people. Besides, running to the courts after you've sobered up strikes me as
being a bit late to change your mind.

Rape Hysteria, Brought to You by...Your Tax Dollars

I think I've just infuriated the keepers of the sacred cow. I've committed the ultimate heresy. I've told stories contrary to the gospel. Rape
victims cannot be doubted. Certainly a person of male gender dare not
question the feminist authorities. To do so means I have become a sup-
porter of rape. I have become part of the whole rape culture. Or
maybe I mean the "rape hysteria culture."

In the summer of 2003 I started seeing primetime TV ads for the
Texas Association Against Sexual Assault (www.taasa.org). I thought
that was strange, so I had a look at the website. At first, I thought it
was a rape crisis center. It isn't. It's a rape promotion center. Not the
promotion of women being raped, it's the promotion of the idea that all
unwanted male aggression qualifies as rape.

How can I be against a group like TAASA? I'm not against the concept of facilities that shelter women (and men), but I am against the
politicization of rape. I am against anti-male indoctrination camps.
Would TAASA please just rename themselves as the "Texas Ministry
of Rape Propaganda?" What is their mission? It's to get the court system to convict *all* men accused of a sexual assault. Frighten the public
into thinking there is a rape epidemic. Convince young men that acting on sexual attraction is sexual assault. And most important, they
want more public funding for their agenda.

Over the next few weeks I saw several TAASA TV ads. Each presented interviews with a victim of a different kind of rape. One girl was raped, shot, and left for dead in a field. Can't argue with that. The purpose of this example is to disarm any critics and establish absolute credibility for the organization.

The next victim gave testimony about "withdrawal of consent" as rape. This "survivor" consented to sex with the guy, then after a while asked him to stop. He "held her down" and finished. It is unclear how emphatic she was, or if she physically resisted. She decided a couple of weeks later that she had been raped—after discussing it with the helpful feminist counselors at TAASA.

This "testimony" reveals the true political agenda of TAASA, which is to expand the definition of rape, get the rape statistics up, and put more men in jail. They want to cast a wide net and ensnare as many males as possible. They want to appear benign, hiding their political agenda behind real rape victims.

I thought TAASA would be a good place to go for definitions of "rape" and "sexual assault." All I could find was a generic feminist definition, equating sexual assault with rape:

> "Sexual assault, or rape, is a violent crime, not a sexual act. The myth that men who rape women are sexually deprived or pathological has begun to be dispelled and replaced with the understanding that rape is an act of power and control, rather than lust."

Why do they insist on that? I think I have it figured out. By denying that rapists are pathological, they are announcing that "normal" male sexual activity can be considered rape. By saying that rapists are not sexually deprived means it's fine to deprive men of sex, because men will be rapists regardless. By stating that rape is about power, they reveal something about their own power agenda. Rape accusations are about power. Broadening the definition of rape is about power. The cultivation of rape hysteria into a culture is about power.

Susan Brownmiller's 1975 book *Against Our Will* probably launched the whole rape hysteria movement. Reading just a few pages gives the impression that all women are raped and all men are rapists. Men just want to fight in wars and rape women. It's universal.

But it's her famous 2 percent figure about false rape accusations that everyone finds interesting. The 2 percent figure appears in all rape propaganda to justify feminism's dismissal of the entire false accusation issue. I think it's obvious there can be no definitive statistic on the percentage of deliberately false accusations. Therefore, we must rely on estimates. Brownmiller debunks the old FBI estimate of 15-20 percent. She claims when policewomen do the investigating the number of cases attributed to false accusations dramatically drops to 2 percent. Where did that magic number come from? The 2 percent figure that rape hysteria advocates use is the estimated overall rate of *all* false police reports. Never mind that there might be more motivations for women to file false rape reports than false car thefts. No need to investigate any further. Wouldn't want to discover that false rape accusation might be a huge problem, would we?

If Brownmiller can make estimates, so can other researchers. It was reported in the well-known 1994 study by Purdue University professor Eugene Kanin that 41 percent of rape accusations in a Midwestern town were false. This result did *not* come about by sexist male police "determining" that no rape had occurred; the number only represents those women who *recanted* after their stories fell apart. So the actual number of false accusations in this survey must be even higher.

How about this more recent statement in 2004 by former prosecutor Craig Silverman in the Denver Post?

> "However, during my time as a prosecutor who made case filing decisions, I was amazed to see all the false rape allegations that were made to the Denver Police Department. It was remarkable and surprising to me. You would have to see it to believe it.

> "Any honest veteran sex assault investigator will tell you that rape is one of the most falsely reported crimes that there is. A command officer in the Denver Police sex assaults unit recently told me he placed the false rape numbers at approximately 45 percent."

Those numbers do not include misidentifications by legitimate rape victims. As of 2004, there have been more than 150 prisoners exonerated using DNA evidence to prove their innocence. Most of them were convicted rapists who had already served more than 10 years in prison. (See www.innocenceproject.org.) Certainly there are many more innocent men in prison who will stay there because there is no DNA in evidence to test.

How does TAASA deal with issues of false rape allegation and misidentification? Actually I don't need to ask. They pretend these problems don't exist. So what if a couple extra men get locked up? Men are all potential rapists anyway, so it can't hurt, right? Besides, victims will feel safer as long as *someone* is behind bars.

If TAASA is really against sexual assault, why don't they give any examples of men being raped in prison cells? Why is that not an issue for TAASA on their website? Is getting raped part of their sentence? Is it ignorable? What assistance do they offer to survivors of false rape accusations? And if rape (or "sexual assault" as they say) is *any* act of sexual violence, why don't they protest all the gleeful portrayals of men getting kicked in their groins on TV? Don't they care about violence against men too? The feminist response to such questions is always some variant of, "Fuck you, start your own movement." Can someone explain to me again why men are supposed to support women's causes?

I noticed that other cities and states have sexual assault organizations equivalent to TAASA. They do not offer rape victims help, just "information." They "educate" and "train" people about sexual assault. The Oregon site (www.ocadsv.com) describes itself on its homepage as a "feminist organization" with the goal of "raising awareness" about sexual assault through education and social evolution. It is *not* concerned with sexual assault against men.

From reading these web pages I found out that I too am a rapist. Yes, as a matter of fact, I've used alcohol to encourage women to have sex with me. I've continued to fuck them for a while after they asked me to stop. I've ignored the verbal "no" when seducing women if I thought their body language said "yes." Not to mention the offending appendage I carry with me at all times, that instrument of rape. I might as well just go down to the police department right now and register myself as a sex offender. So should all men. Except maybe gay men. But then, why discriminate? They have dicks, register them too.

I saw "information" pages on one sexual assault website that described pornography as promoting male violence against women and causing rape. As proof, they quoted Gloria Steinem and Robin Morgan. I don't know where Gloria and Robin get their porn, but it sounds like they hang out in the bondage section. Are they saying there would be less rape if men were *more* sexually suppressed? Or are they saying the world would be a better place if we all just rented lesbian porn?

The big male fantasy is not violence or rape. The big male fantasy is consent. Porn is about girls saying "yes." Porn is sold to the guys who are tired of getting "no" from real girls. Porn is an escape from all the taunting and rejection. The male fantasy is that girls like sex as much as we do. The male fantasy is being able to walk up to any cute girl, say any lame thing to her, have her drop whatever she's doing and immediately fuck your brains out. That is what porn shows over and over again, not rape fantasies. All the magazines show cute naked girls that look happy. Some sex videos now start off with an extended "interview" with each girl to humanize her and find out why she decided to get into porn. But why am I even explaining this? What right do feminists have to police my fantasies? I don't go around telling women what thoughts they should have in their heads when they hit the "on" switch.

Porn is overwhelmingly non-violent, unlike mainstream entertainment. A few years ago I was flipping the channels and watched some of *Friday the 13th Part III*. I tuned in right as a cute teenage girl gets shot in the eye with a speargun by the crazed male lunatic. It was sickening. But then, at least it wasn't a *cum shot* in her eye. That would be over the line. And thank God that lunatic didn't fondle her. I'd hate for teenagers to see *that!*

Nevertheless, feminists are still trying to sell us the idea that porn promotes violence. Lots of women have bought into the whole concept of equating male aggression with sexual assault. They've been conditioned to view all men as potential rapists and murderers. In the 1990s, television and movies were saturated with the theme of men turning out to be rapists, child molesters, and sadistic killers. A few that come to mind are: *The Ted Bundy Story*, *The Silence of the Lambs*, and one of the most revolting movies ever—*Portrait of a Serial Killer*.

Several times on first dates I've been asked, "You're not an ax murderer, are you?" Once I invited a platonic female friend over to visit, and she wanted me to promise her that I wouldn't rape her if she came over. It stuck me as a stupid request. So let's see, she thinks I have such disregard for her as a person that I might rape her, but I have the integrity to keep a promise not to. I was offended and told her to just forget it.

A few years later it happened again with another female friend when I invited her over. She said, "If I come over you're not going to rape me or anything, are you?" This time I was ready. I told her, "Normally it's my policy to rape all women who enter my house, but *just this once* I'll make an exception." She came over. I managed to control myself somehow.

Professional feminists preach that all sex not initiated by women is rape. It's the party line. Well I live in the real world, not academia, and I know that if men wait for women to initiate, there will be very few people having sex. Other than lesbians, of course.

Most men don't know they are considered part of the "rape cul-ture" by women who have taken women's studies courses. If you want to talk about a rape culture, how about those lesbo sharks I saw pa-trolling a dance floor recently? As soon as any cute girls came out to dance, two fat lesbians would try to molest them. They would come up behind the girls, get them in a body hug, and then go for the crotch. The girls were unprepared for such assaults by other females. A man trying that would be smacked, beaten up, or thrown out, and rightful-ly so. But I watched those trailer trash dykes go at it with impunity all night. Why is that? It's because in our current reality only men are con-sidered capable of sexual assault and molestation.

When men pursue underage girls for sex, they are considered crim-inals who should be locked up for several years. Or forever. Which-ever is longer. When women pursue underage girls for sex, it's called art. Among the convoluted collection of interviews known as *The Vagina Monologues* is a glorification of lesbian sex with a minor, which author Eve Ensler describes as "good rape." The skit called "The Little Coochi Snorcher That Could" depicts the lesbian seduc-tion of a 13-year-old girl by an adult woman. The 2001 edition omitted the term "good rape," and changed the girl's age to 16. Why didn't I hear an uproar? Why did female stars like Calista Flockhart line up to participate in the production?

And how about the more recent movie called *Birth*, in which Nicole Kidman kisses and "falls in love" with a 10-year-old boy? If a grown man were depicted in an erotic nude bathtub scene with a 10-year-old girl, it would be called "child pornography." When an attractive fe-male star does it with a boy, it's a "controversial film." Why can't we hold both genders to the same standard?

It's very telling that females who display sexual aggression are not only tolerated, they are celebrated as progressive and empowered. Somehow, it's always about love and feelings. But male aggression is demonized as assault and a prelude to rape. We're not even supposed to *look* at women for more than a couple seconds, or we're "raping them with our eyes." Whatever.

As for exactly how aggressive a man can be without risking crimi-nal charges, don't look to me for an answer. How should I know where to draw the lines? I'm not a lawyer. I'm not a psychologist. Neither am I a mind reader. Besides, I've been too busy raping my right hand to give it much thought.

Is It Love, Or Sexual Assault?

I dated Amanda off and on for a couple of months. I was out with her once and we had a few drinks. She always seemed lukewarm, but this time she accepted an offer to come back to my place. We began with some caressing and light kissing, but she seemed unresponsive. Bored, in fact. I was going slow with her, but then I lost patience. I decided if she was going to reject me, I just wanted to get it over with. So I grabbed her rudely by the cunt. She voiced no objections. In fact, she livened up. Finally I slept with her. The next day Amanda told me how happy she was that I had stopped holding myself back and began expressing my feelings toward her. It's interesting looking back on that in the context of the rape culture. When Amanda spoke of my "feelings," she was referring to my sexual desire for her. "Expressing" meant grabbing her by the cunt. Men are expected to just try stuff, and leave it to women to decide if it's love or sexual assault.

I met a beautiful Argentinean girl, and we met up a couple times. I invited her over for a drink, and she accepted. I thought I was picking up vibes from her, so I kissed her as soon as she got inside. "No, I don't want this to happen," she said. She wasn't backing off though, so I kissed her again, this time a little longer. "No, no, this is wrong," she said. But she still had her arms around me, so I kissed her again for about a minute. Suddenly she dropped to her knees, pulled down my pants and gave me a blowjob.

I understand that no means no. Even though it doesn't. I know "maybe" always means "no," and "yes" usually means "no." "Later" means "never." I think "no" actually means "not now." "No" means she wants to continue to taunt and tease you for a while. "No" usually means "don't give up now." If women really want to say "no," they say "maybe later." That definitely means "no, never."

I may as well continue with my blasphemies, I'm already a heretic. Am I a rapist? I must be. I've dared question the dogma. I have a penis and I'm heterosexual. I've initiated sex. I've lied to women and gotten them drunk. I'm no different than guys who kidnap women at gunpoint. I'm no better than the guys who stalk women and break into their apartments.

How about the time I was in the middle of having sex with a girl and her phone rang? She wanted to get up and answer it and I said, "Jesus, we're having sex, you can talk on the damn phone later!" "Let me up, I want to answer it." "That's just rude, you are *not* getting up,"

I said as I continued to fuck her. That was 10 years ago. Can I still be put in jail?

Women's advocates know that rape is their most powerful and emotional issue. They understand it can generate the most anger against men for the feminist agenda. They have used that anger to help them expand the definition of rape and threaten opponents. Even the word "rapist" has been replaced with the more ambiguous term "sex offender," lumping men who have committed some minor infraction together with child molesters. Anyone challenging the validity of the "new rape" is a collaborator as guilty as the rapists themselves. Rape is the most sacred of sacred cows.

The Rape of Linda

I've experienced for myself that sense of rage that drives women to become man-haters and volunteers at rape crisis centers. A co-worker of mine at IBM named Linda became a close friend. We went to lunch twice a week, and the conversation was often personal. I told her the story about how Alexandra, the Romanian barmaid, picked me up, took me home, requested a rape fantasy, then offered me money in the morning.

In response, Linda told about something that happened when she was 19. She was dating a male model, and he invited her to his apartment for a swim in the pool. She was very attracted to him so she stopped by in her bikini. He came on to her right away. She told him "no." He wouldn't stop. He was so strong Linda couldn't move or fight back. He raped her.

Linda thought it was over, but it turned out this male model was bisexual. His male partner stopped in, and they took turns raping her. Then they both raped her at the same time. She had never reported it or told her family. "It hurt for a week," she said. I was horrified. Livid, in fact, even though it had occurred seven years before. I was not the same for several days. I walked around dazed and angry. I wanted to do something. I started having fantasies about finding the guy and beating him to a pulp. He lived in a different state, but I could find him. I dwelled on the exact details for hours. I would identify him, observe his routines, then go to his door with a stun gun. When he answered, I would stun him into submission, duct tape him, and inform him that this was payback for hurting my friend. I'd stun him a few more times, then I'd break his legs with a ball bat. Maybe his arms too.

It felt good visualizing him trying to scream with tape over his mouth. I told Linda about my imaginary plan, and she thought it was "very sweet." Neither of us had any intention of actually carrying it out. It might have been different had he been local.

Months passed. Linda invited me over to her place and I started looking through some magazines on her coffee table.

"Oh, there's a picture of that guy I told you about in this catalogue" she said.

"Who?"

"You know, the guy that attacked me."

"Why would you have a picture of him on your coffee table?"

"Remember, I told you he's a male model. See, here he is. Isn't he great looking?" she said proudly as she pointed out a guy wearing a dorky sweater in a men's clothing catalogue.

Then it hit me. Linda had embellished her story to one-up my own story of sexual conquest. Here it was seven years after the alleged rape, and she still had the guy's catalogue out on display. He must have given it to her as a memento. Had she really hated the guy she would have scratched his eyes out of the photo or burned the damned thing. The sex must have been consensual. I don't think it ever occurred to her that I would be traumatized by her story.

My guess is that she actually did have sex with both him and his bisexual partner, but she couldn't brag about that, being a nice Baptist girl. Whether or not any of it actually happened, I think I finally get the point of her story. She's so hot even gay guys are driven to gang rape her. She was just trying to keep up with me. After all, the point of my story was that I'm so hot that women invite me to rape them and then offer me money afterwards. I did learn something important from all this. It's best to hear both sides of a story before breaking anyone's legs.

If only our justice system were so wise. Too much to expect I suppose. It's become the norm that women have rights that supersede those of men. They think their rights even supersede those guaranteed by the constitution. What? Oh, that "presumed innocent" thing. That doesn't apply to men accused of rape. According to the sacred theology, women don't lie about rape. It's just not in their nature.

Leslie's Sister

I know a girl named Leslie who always hated her sister. We went out a few times. I learned not to ask things like "How's your family?" because it would cause Leslie to go off on her "lying piece of shit" sister. "If my sister showed up penniless and starving at my house I would slam the door in her face!" she told me. Whoa. Change subject.

As expected, when Leslie got married her sister was not at the wedding. Her ex-boyfriend explained it all to me at the reception. Back when Leslie's sister was 15, she was becoming uncontrollable. Her father grounded her, but she wasn't going to take that. So she called up the police and reported that her father had been raping her. He was immediately arrested and jailed for a month. Eventually she recanted. It took the father three years to untangle the legal mess and get his name off all the lists. He still had to move out of town because everyone had their doubts. Of course, you never hear of false accusers getting charged. They won't recant if they can be prosecuted. Just give them a couple of therapy sessions and call it even.

I see similar stories played out again and again. A high school girl accuses boys from the school of rape. The police rush in and arrest the accused boys, whose names are printed in the local paper even though they are minors. The girl's identity is protected. The community holds emergency meetings to seek answers to the problem of sexual assault in schools. Then the girl's story falls apart because of inconsistencies. She admits the story is false, but remains anonymous. The charges are dropped against the boys, who have become pariahs in the school and the community. The police recommend "help" for the girl, and say they may "consider" filing charges against her. The story is dropped from the press and no charges are filed. Community groups claim the event had the positive effect of raising awareness of school safety. This is exactly what happened in Ellicott City in April 2004, as reported in the *Baltimore Sun*. I saw the same thing happen at a high school in Austin a month earlier. The girl recanted and the story disappeared.

And Vengeance for All

How many times must false accusations ruin the careers of Air Force cadets, athletes, and college professors before men realize they need just as much protection from women as women do from men? I routinely see photos of men accused of molestation and rape on the local news. They are arrested on allegations alone. Their reputations are ruined regardless of the outcome. They can be fired from their jobs. Why are there no identity shield laws to protect accused men?

Women's groups have succeeded in eliminating the presumption of innocence in sexual assault cases. Just as Petra prophesized back in 1974, boyfriends and husbands (and even fathers) can be arrested solely on the word of a woman. And just as she demanded, women automatically believe *all* accused men must be guilty. I just never thought the courts would go along.

Feminists are now lobbying for *lower* prison sentences for convicted rapists, especially for marital rape and date rape. Why lower? Feminists believe this will motivate juries to convict more men of rape based solely on the testimony of the alleged victim. Oh, the sentence will only be two years instead of 20? In that case, go ahead and convict. Angry feminists don't mind punishing a few extra men.

Women's advocates don't care about the falsely accused. They don't want justice, they want vengeance. Anyone refusing to kneel before the sacred cow risks becoming a sacrifice unto it. Legislators and judges are among the devoted worshippers. The sacred cow has an eternal hunger which must be nourished by the sacrifice of men. The beast feasts as gladly upon the innocent as the guilty. Besides, it's heresy to withdraw a sacrifice from the altar. Now, let us all pay homage unto the divine bovine goddess. I prefer the dagger.

Love and Porn

Sure, we've all heard the hype. All you need is love. Love conquers all. All's fair in love and war. Love is a many splendored thing. Let love rule. Love, love, love. Blah, blah, blah. We're assaulted by songs on the radio with singers boldly declaring love for some vague imaginary person. I've really heard enough now. Even with all the help from our pop culture, I'm sure I will never completely understand what love is. But there's one thing I've come to understand about love. Love doesn't make you come.

Married couples seem to know that neither love nor sex can live up to the hype. From what I've heard, married people start thinking of sex as just another bodily chore, like eating corn flakes. And a lot of times they prefer the corn flakes.

As singles we're in denial. We don't want our dreams of true love and incredible sex to vanish. With vibrators, romance novels, and porn, singles can hold out longer for that amazing lover that doesn't exist. Be patient, the right person will come along. Years later, our waiting has turned into a lifestyle. Wait around for love? Another year or five? When you've got no reality, fantasy can be very enticing.

You'd think women would view porn as another great labor saving device, like the invention of the washing machine. It frees them from another mundane task that has been forced upon them forever. Finally, a simplistic little way for men to get their libidos satisfied without burdening women with the slavery of our lecherous demands.

So why don't women have that sense of gratitude for porn? It's because porn makes it clear that the male sex drive has nothing to do with love. Rather than accept such an unsavory reality, women treat the male libido as if it were a disease. We objectify them. We're oppressors and pervs. We're "sex addicts" who need to be cured. I've got that disease. Yes, I suffer from a healthy libido. But I know something is not right. Porn can never provide any intimacy. My needs are not fulfilled, they're just temporarily contained.

Tough as it is for us pervs to admit, we need more than sex. Pervs have feelings too. Women need to understand that men actually want relationships. We just don't want bad ones. And bad relationships have been around a lot longer than porn. Whether a relationship is bad or good seems to be irrelevant to women as long as they have one.

Porn is a male sanctuary from destructive love. Porn is something you can count on. Porn is immediate and expedient. Porn never rejects you. Porn doesn't make you grovel. Porn doesn't get its feelings hurt. Porn never feels neglected. Porn never complains. Porn doesn't get pregnant. You don't need to send flowers to porn. Porn doesn't care if you like other porn. Porn leaves us the hell alone.

I've sought refuge in the male sanctuary. But the porn kings aren't doing us any big favors. I doubt Hugh Hefner ever depended on a stack of magazines to provide his sex life. It's guys like me who pay just to have a look at all the girls we're never going to fuck.

At least porn can replace the need for high school guys to use girls they know in real life as objects of their masturbation fantasies. Not that I've ever done that. That would be wrong. I heard some guys talking about it. Yeah, some guy was telling me how he used to whack off every day after school thinking about whichever girl looked hot that day. Do these girls know that 10 or 20 guys might be whacking off to them that night? Do they want that as validation? I guess they think guys should whack off without thinking of anything at all. And not every day. Ew.

I remember in my early teens thinking how great it would be when I got to be an adult—not so I could have a girlfriend, but because I could have all the porn I wanted. I figured regular girls would rarely take off their clothes for you. There's some weird game you had to play. You can't just ask them. They tease you and make you buy them stuff and say the right things all the time. Then they get mad at you for no reason and ride off on the back of a motorcycle with a stranger. I suppose in my own ignorant way, I was right.

In college I achieved that boyhood dream of unlimited porn. My roommate brought in a couple big boxes of Playboy magazines, and we began compulsively pouring over them trying to compensate for the life-long sexual deficit we had been accumulating. It got to be like a homework assignment. We began flipping through each magazine as if cramming for an exam. Can't skip any naked girls, got to look at them all. Damn, another 50 Playboys to go.

Porn seemed like a rare and precious commodity when I was a kid, but as a college freshman with unlimited porn it was apparent how unfulfilling a magazine really is. What was next? I could look forward to having sex on a semi-regular basis after I finished college, got a stable career, and got married—in eight or ten years.

That must be why people used to get married when they were teens. Girls of my grandparents' generation got married when they were 17 to 19. Men got married by age 18 to 20. My great aunt got secretly married at age 16. Love had little to do with it. It was about doing whatever it took to get sex. If a man had a job that was good enough to have a wife. Sex, that is. My great-great-grandfather was a street sweeper. That would never get him laid now.

This raises a fundamental question for contemporary society. How are young men supposed to handle their incredibly strong daily sexual desires? The problem is that none of the choices are "acceptable."

- Guys can try to suppress their needs. This is the worst option because it causes guys to become obsessed with sex. These are the future sex criminals and Catholic priests.

- Guys can use everyday girls in short tight skirts as material in their daily masturbation fantasies. This is unhealthy because they will only get to know these girls as the objects of their sexual fantasies. Besides, what are guys supposed to do in the winter?

- Guys can use porn to eliminate the use of everyday girls for fantasies. This legitimizes porn and makes guys dependent on it. It also causes guys to withdraw from their pursuit of girls, which further isolates them.

- Guys can get a girlfriend and start having regular sex as teens. Very dangerous. It is also not a reasonable choice for guys under the age of 18.

- Guys can get married as teens. This isn't practical because guys need careers first. They are expected to assume full responsibility for a wife and children when married. Besides, marriage is a disaster for most people.

"Abstinence" is just a prettied-up word for masturbation. For girls it's easy. Give them a vibrator, and they can be dating teases for the next decade. For boys it's a different story. We can't give them porn now, can we? But you can't recommend abstinence without recommending acceptable fantasy material. What is the process, please? If you're a high school guy exclusively dating a teenage girl, are you supposed to exclusively whack off to her? Maybe teenage boys should be programmed to think about love and weddings and girls in pretty dresses running through wildflowers as they jerk off. Or maybe stories from the Bible would be good. Hasn't the abstinence crowd caught on? People seek that which has been denied them.

What do feminists and pseudo-moralists recommend for all those perverted teenage boys? Some self-control? How about no masturbation at all? I remember trying that. I was 15 or 16 when I decided to find out how long I could hold out. I was determined to be the master of my domain for an entire week. After three days I couldn't concentrate on normal life. Any cute girl would disrupt my thought processes. Still I held out. After a week my mind was completely dominated by erotic images. I remember getting aroused from a cute girl's face in a cosmetic ad in a fashion magazine. Using only her face as a visual, I sought relief. I checked my watch to see how long it would take. Fifteen seconds.

I guess there's no stigma attached to female masturbation because female fantasies are emotional and pure. Male masturbation is based on perverse sex and the exploitation of women as objects. Men should only be allowed to masturbate when it is into a little cup in a clinic for the purpose of helping lesbian couples procreate. I wonder if the donors and the clients ever use the same lesbian porn?

But there is no "acceptable" fantasy material for male masturbation, thereby insinuating that the sexual needs of single males are not legitimate. Or we pretend the issue doesn't exist. "Morality" doesn't address this problem. Morality is simply an attempt to inflict psychological punishment on us for being what we are. As a result, lots of teens are rebelling by having sex earlier than ever. But let's ignore that and blame pornography for everything. Yes, the whole problem must be that pornography is driving men to oppress and exploit and objectify women. How many times will people hear that before they realize it's all nonsense? That we value women for their attractiveness doesn't mean we're oppressors, it means we're suckers. Our attraction to women doesn't exploit them, it exploits us. Our fascination with women's bodies doesn't mean we objectify them. And even if we do, women are supposed to look like entertainment centers, not baby production facilities.

Fire with Gasoline

For some perspective on the topic, it's useful to dredge up Dwokin's 1980 book *Pornography*. For anyone unfamiliar with her, Andrea Dworkin together with Catherine MacKinnon wrote radical anti-pornography and sexual harassment laws for the State of Minnesota back in the 1980s. Their proposed legislation was so anti-male that it was vetoed. They are also responsible for the widespread myth that nearly all women who enter the sex industry do so because they were molested as children. Under the Reagan administration, the moralistic Meese Commission used their writings to draw the unscientific conclusion that viewing pornography leads men to commit violent sexual crimes.

Some Dworkin quotes from the chapter called "Men and Boys" in *Pornography:*

> "For men, the right to abuse women is elemental, the first principle, with no beginning unless one is willing to trace origins back to God..."

> "In pornography, every object is a slut, sticking daggers up her vagina and smiling."

> "Every image reveals not the so-called object in it but the man who needs it: to keep his prick big when every bomb dwarfs it; to keep his sense of masculine self intact..."

> "Pornography is the holy corpus of men who would rather die than change. Dachau brought into the bedroom and celebrated..."

> "Pornography reveals that slavery, bondage, murder, and maiming have been acts suffused with pleasure for those who committed them..."

I can understand why Dworkin is mad at God. So can anyone who has seen her photograph. But I'm not sure why she's angry at men. Maybe she didn't get asked to the prom. Her passing garnered no sympathy from me. Yeah, ding dong she'd dead, but the damage is done.

Here's a sample of Catherine MacKinnon's world view in *Professing Feminism: Cautionary Tales from the Strange World of Women's Studies:*

"In a patriarchal society, all heterosexual intercourse is rape because women, as a group, are not strong enough to give meaningful consent."

I find it amusing when pop feminists like Naomi Wolf try to write about the male libido as if they have a clue. But who am I to question her ideas about my sexuality? She must know more about it than I. After all, she's got a Ph.D. All I've got is a penis. In her article *The Porn Myth* from December 2003 she's finally figured out that whacking off to porn makes guys *less* sexually aggressive. What an amazing discovery. And even though porn has not yet transformed the entire male population into women-hating serial rapists like Dworkin predicted, somehow Wolf finds a way to pay the demented androphobe some obligatory homage.

What does the lipstick feminist recommend for us deviant males now? Same as always. Sexual suppression. How about that Muslim head scarf? Wolf likes the idea of a man not even being able to see a woman's hair. But this time the reasoning is that men need to be sexually suppressed until we achieve a level of deprivation sufficient for us to be attracted to our wives and girlfriends, thus building a healthy relationship. Starve us, and we'll beg for that bowl of gruel. Finally men will learn to love and appreciate women. How brilliant. She's progressed into the Middle Ages.

Man haters, pop-feminists and matriarchs everywhere continue to miss the point. They cannot seem to comprehend that porn is not the problem. That is because they really *want* porn to be the problem. They insist that they can get men under control by removing all erotic stimuli. The feminist bucket brigade is fighting fire with gasoline.

If women hate porn so much, they should stop trying to get rid of it and focus on getting rid of the need for porn. Offer men sex without all the strings. Maybe start an "adopt-a-perv" program. If men could get nicely fucked by real women on a regular basis, porn sales would plummet. But women will never admit they share responsibility for driving men to porn. That would be blaming the victims, right?

How about women becoming people we want to marry? Marriage itself has become so challenging that lots of men prefer being in a state of extended sexual deprivation. There's the verbal abuse. There's the loss of control over your own life. There are demands and expectations to meet. At some point the sex stops. There's an entire array of complex legal implications. Do we need a prenup? How much is a divorce attorney? Will our assets be taken from us? If we don't agree to her terms, will there be accusations of sexual assault? A growing number of men are choosing porn as a more stable relationship.

The wedding itself has grown into a huge production. The idea of wedding gifts came from the time when married couples could not afford *anything*, so friends and family would chip in to help them get started. Now a wedding is an expensive narcissistic coronation that confirms that only her happiness counts. Men are disgusted at the idea of big production weddings. Those who step up to the altar have learned the importance of suppressing their opinions.

Women say porn gives us unrealistic expectations. I'd say women's unrealistic expectations are more unrealistic than our unrealistic expectations. We are judged by our cars, our income, our wardrobe, our adherence to politically correct ideologies, and anything else specific to a particular female. Do we dance right? Are we successful enough? Do we work out? Are we emotionally compelling enough? Are we thinking about her all the time? All women have to do is control their weight and not be psycho. And they can fake the not being psycho part.

I had a roommate in school who married his girlfriend and spent all his savings on the big diamond she expected. He was supposed to be her ticket to the upper middle class. Instead, he struggled with his accounting career and lost a couple of jobs. Years later I visited them in their tiny house in a run-down neighborhood, one step above a trailer park. They had a kid, but that didn't fulfill her dream of a big brick house packed with expensive knick-knacks. She watched TV all day while the kid was in school. After dinner, she would retreat to the bedroom and read romance novels for hours. She had stacks of them. Hundreds of them. If she wanted to live on a higher materialistic plane, she could have gone out and gotten a job. Instead she removed herself from her bland reality. Don't romance novels get boring after a while? Or is it life itself people are bored with?

I got bored with porn. In fact, I think the porn industry has gotten bored with itself. Do we really need choking and gagging? Whose fantasy is that? Do we need three guys all plugging the girl at the same time? She must be in there somewhere among all the men's asses I'm looking up. Call me old-fashioned, but I think porn is something that should be between one man and one woman. Occasionally one man and two women.

No, I don't expect all my lovers to be cute 19-year-old Czech girls who enjoy participating in anal gang-bangs and swallowing semen. I do expect a lover to be reasonably skilled at sex. I'm sick of pseudo-prudes who think that if they're too enthusiastic or willing to please, then they're subservient sluts. Or they can't have sex unless it's the most special moment of their entire lives.

I also expect some reciprocation. The last time I was with Petra I suggested it might be in her best interest to get me started orally, when she proclaimed, "I don't do that anymore." Oh, but I was still welcome to lick her all I wanted. How generous of her. She thinks her cunt is a beautiful flower, but a dick in her mouth defiles her. Well, I'll let everyone in on a little secret. I prefer lips that can kiss me back. I don't know why after more than 25 years of excellence Petra would suddenly retire her fellatio skills. It's not like I married her. All I know is there's one girl who won't be getting cunnilingus any time soon. Unless she gives that lesbian thing another shot.

The truth is, porn is just a symptom of a growing problem. As men and women, we have lost patience with each other's needs. Men are tired of all the emotional overhead. Women have been taught that men's sexual needs are vile and demeaning. So women withdraw, and men take whatever they can get. The porn industry was conceived to fill a void created by sexual suppression. But feminism itself has driven men to porn in droves by expanding that void. Why be with a woman who thinks of you as an oppressor but treats you like a servant?

Lots of men have given up trying to please women. Men have never known what women want, and even less so now. We know we are incapable of ever satisfying women or making them happy for more than short periods of time. We know all we will achieve will be new levels of inadequacy. We know women will never be happy, but at least when they marry us they know who's to blame.

Women don't want to hear about what men really want because it might be something like having "crisis free" time. It might be having projects to work on that do not involve the relationship. It might be something like having some different sex partners. We might like to have sex without it meaning anything at all. Must we always sublimate what we are? Would it be possible to get a decent blow job without having to pretend it's all about feelings and flowers and candles?

But no. We have to constantly recite all the mandatory lies or we'll never get laid. Love is unconditional and forever. Men have sex with women because we are in love. Men who love women are in love with their inner beauty, not just their physical appearance. Men in love stop desiring other women because love elevates us above such primitive urges. Women turn us into the liars we are. They don't care if we're lying as long as we're reading from the approved script. Why am I single?

I can't act and I don't lie enough.

When women realize the male libido is not about love, they react like children who just found out there's no Santa Claus. Why do we have to keep pretending that sex has anything to do with love? Are women that psychologically fragile? We get sick of sex having to be something deep and profound. But that's why women hate porn. Porn makes it painfully obvious that love is never a required ingredient for an orgasm. Women keep trying to change that about us, but we just learn to tell our lies more convincingly.

Why do men even like porn? What the hell is wrong with us? Don't our brains understand the images aren't real? But then, is love real? It must be, because the pain it causes is real. Is love just another necessary lie in our lives? Is it love or sex that draws us to women? What would we rather look into, their eyes or vaginas? I have no logic for this. Perhaps love and porn are equally cruel illusions.

I would agree that porn is degrading. Degrading to men. It's degrading to seek out images of women instead of a real person who cares about you. It's degrading that we settle for such a minimal experience. But it's not as degrading as being minimized or teased by 10 different women. It's certainly not as degrading as begging psychotic women with bad attitudes for lousy sex. The problem with porn is that it makes it so easy to give up. We've given up on fulfillment. We'll settle for some relief.

The whole porn issue is not about morality. It's not about the exploitation of women. It certainly has nothing to do with violence or rape. It's not even about the objectification of women. Why are women so threatened by porn? I believe it's because women lose power when they can no longer hold men in a state of sexual deprivation. Porn has become a realistic alternative for men who would rather not become financial and emotional servants to women. All the other criticisms of porn are diversions from this real issue.

I would also ask, if porn is so bad, then where is the feminist outcry against vibrators and dildos? Doesn't a dildo objectify male sexuality? Isn't a vibrator equally degrading to men? Doesn't a vibrator reduce a man's sexuality to the level of an electric toothbrush? How is porn any less healthy than that? What does a vibrator do to a woman's ability to love? Go ahead and give me the double standard response. Why are all forms of artificial stimulus for females so harmless and porn so dangerous? Mothers don't burst into their daughters' rooms, smash their Pocket Rockets, and yell at them. No one looks down at women for using them.

Men don't go around saying, "I found out the bitch is a vibrator addict."

Maybe men should start complaining, since so many available women stay home hibernating with their vibrators. What can we do? I think we need to raise women's awareness of the dangers of these appliances. We need to tell them it's demeaning for men to compete with permanently hard and excessively long pieces of plastic. How do you think that makes us feel? Dammit, we are more than just a warm kielbasa. We are not your backup plan in case the supermarket runs out of your favorite phallic vegetable.

Want to talk about unrealistic expectations? My dick does not come with seven attachments. Nor can my tongue oscillate 4000 times per minute. How can we possibly fulfill a woman's needs anymore? Are we supposed to show up with flowers *and batteries*? And haven't we heard women say that a vibrator and a brownie is better than any man? How are we supposed to compete? Maybe women prefer their vibrators, but you never hear a guy say he'd rather have porn than a girlfriend. Porn is just less of a hassle. And more reliable.

I met a cute blonde who offered herself up. We had sex all night, and it was great. We kept seeing each other. We told our friends we were involved. We even started doing things together that didn't involve sex. Everything was cool. It was going so well that I threw out my porn stash. It was a milestone. What a relief. It was an incredible feeling that I had finally cast off that pathetic scourge. Two weeks later she dumped me. Dammit! How could she? That was two or three hundred dollars worth of perfectly good porn. Next time I won't be so quick to exercise such careless optimism.

Will women ever stop punishing us for being who we are? Can't women rise above their adolescent love fantasies and just fuck us without tormenting us? What am I thinking? Do I really expect them to give up all their fun? Women will always enjoy fucking *with* us more than fucking us.

How long must this nonsense go on? When did love get all confused with sex? There's been sex forever. Love didn't come until much later. Probably about the time alcohol was invented. For men, there can be sex without love, but not love without sex. Get good at giving head, and maybe we'll get good at buying flowers. No, a verbal "I love you" cannot compete with a blow job. Words must be quantified. In our world, love must be consummated. In fact, in our world anything can be consummated. Call me jaded, but at least I know the difference between love and a good endorphin rush.

Political Correctness

I often wondered what was so "correct" about political correctness. What does the term mean exactly? I've come to realize it is a world view through the prism of victim and oppressor. Rather than "woman good, man bad," it's "victim good, everyone else bad." The only "correct" opinions are those expressed by victims. In legalese, official victims are referred to as "identifiable groups," since these groups may not be an actual minority, as is the case with people of the female gender.

Just as there are similarities between Nazism and radical feminism, there are similarities between Marxism and political correctness. Women and minorities are like the oppressed proletariat class, and white males are the privileged bourgeois capitalists. Men hold most positions of power in government and corporations. Men own most of the means of production. But the analogy can only be taken so far. For one, the bourgeois capitalists were never obligated to buy the proletariats dinner, new clothes, and diamonds. Neither were the proletariats exempt from ever having to fight in wars. And the oppressed proletariats never had the power to make life a living hell for the bourgeois capitalists and deny them sex. In fact, the presumption of victimhood and the proliferation of female-specific programs have clearly established women as the true privileged class. Even so, feminists everywhere still insist women are an oppressed class and use ancient Marxism as the model for their revolution against people who won't let them have their way.

Although feminism still thrives as an anger-based anti-male ideology promoting the idea of female supremacy and the "gender cleansing" of masculinities from society, the implementation of the "feminazi" strategy has its limitations. The actual extermination of men might raise some eyebrows. The "social revolution" strategy is less dramatic but far more effective in garnering results. So feminists have grafted Marxism onto Nazism, keeping the female supremacy concept and renaming the oppressive bourgeois aristocracy as the "patriarchy." The female cheerleaders for political correctness I've known had no such awareness of Marxist influence on their personal philosophy. They just want people to stop disagreeing with them and criticizing them. It's really upsetting.

I've noticed European feminists are much more acceptant of the old Marxist lingo. The whole concept of socialism is still very popular there. Not only has Marxism never been discredited in Europe, it is highly respected. There are streets named Karl-Marx-Strasse throughout Germany. Why don't they repudiate the evil socialism and embrace the free market? Perhaps one reason is the existence of socialized health care that covers everyone. Besides, they see the U.S. as a foreign occupier exploiting Germany as a military base. European feminists typically denounce the entire oppressive imperialist system forced upon them by the U.S.

American feminists can't be so anti-American, and the archaic "capitalist" and "imperialist" jargon sounds quaint and amusing over here. Although the hardcore American Marxist feminists are still barricaded in academia where they have free reign to wreak havoc in the universities, most American feminists have set the goal to succeed in the "capitalist" system and place themselves in positions of power over men. Even if they aren't CEOs, as high-ranking managers and VPs they are positioned perfectly to support female-specific corporate causes like affirmative action for women, paid maternity leave, work-at-home programs for mothers, and strict sexual harassment rules that apply only to men.

European feminists are more likely to call for socialist reforms that favor women who do not have careers. Pay women for being pregnant. Pay them professional wages for raising their own children. Pay them for making weird art that nobody wants. Pay them for doing nothing. Why should men have all the money? It's gender socialism. The focus of American feminism is more on gaining legal rights that supersede those of their favorite target group, the patriarchy. The redistribution of wealth is to be accomplished at the corporate level—not by an overthrow, but by displacement. The patriarchy is not to be destroyed, just neutered.

Fucking with Democracy

People in the U.S. are generally unaware how pervasive electoral quotas for women have become in other parts of the world. That's because the word "quota" is politically incorrect in the U.S. Whether or not people realize it, most major democracies in the world now have electoral "set-asides" for women (http://www.quotaproject.org/index.cfm).

Germany, France, Belgium, Switzerland, Austria, United Kingdom, Spain, Italy, Netherlands, Denmark, Sweden, Norway, Greece—nearly all European democracies impose these quotas. So do a growing number of democracies in the rest of the world—Brazil, Canada, Australia, Venezuela, Costa Rica, Israel, Ecuador, India, and Argentina, to name a few. It's all justified by male oppression and the assumption of discrimination. Taking down the patriarchy is more important than maintaining the integrity of democracy.

To avoid any pesky constitutional problems that may arise from the deliberate exclusion of male candidates because of their gender, democracy in Europe is circumvented at the party level. In Germany for example, parties set their own quotas for female candidates. The FPD and Greens both require at least 50% of their candidates to be female. The conservative CDU calls for one-third female candidates, and the SPD's quota now stands at 40%.

Many countries outside of Europe have more strict female quotas, reserving a minimum number seats for women in both elected and appointed government organizations. The new Afghani constitution includes this system of reserved seating. It's the same with Iraq. In fact, every nation that has ratified the "Convention on the Elimination of All Forms of Discrimination against Women" is required to provide quotas for women in government. Although the U.S. itself has not ratified this convention, we are quietly supporting quotas as part of our foreign policy. How long can it be before the U.S. caves to international pressure to apply the same quotas to our own government?

But if it comes to pass that women get reserved seating in government, shouldn't there also be seats reserved for all the various ethnic groups? And how many seats should gays and lesbians get? How many seats for crossdressers? Why not just assign all seats in legislative bodies in accordance with "identifiable groups"? Why go through the motions of elections if the outcome is predetermined?

No, I'm not against women in government, but I am against guaranteeing a specific result. If politicians like Howard Dean and John

Kerry were serious about supporting affirmative action for women, they should have stepped aside and called for the Democratic party to adopt a quota system for presidential candidates to correct this historical injustice. Like all proponents of affirmative action, they support it as long as their own jobs aren't on the line.

Why are we required to make the path easier for women in every facet of life? Doesn't it disturb anyone that these set-asides allow the deliberate exclusion of specific candidates because of their gender? Perhaps we're too busy with election fraud to worry about electoral quotas coming to the U.S. We fix elections the old fashioned way—through gerrymandering, bribing, voter suppression, influence peddling, and the grooming of information according to the will of the wealthiest and most powerful investors. We're not going to let foreigners dictate to us how we should undermine our democracy. We're perfectly capable of fucking up it on our own, thank you.

Don't Fuck with Victims

We find ourselves in a victim revolution with feminists at the helm. Heterosexual white males get a free pass out of the patriarchy as long as they don't express any opinions contrary to the party line. But just in case any of us want to discuss our own civil rights, feminists at N.O.W. and within the government are busy working to clamp the lid on such things as "incorrect" speech.

The benignly named Local Law Enforcement Act (LLEA) provides extra levels of protection to everyone, except for bourgeois capitalists. Uh, I mean the patriarchy, that is, white heterosexual males. The proponents of the LLEA (previously called the Hate Crimes Prevention Act) keep trying to slip it into various appropriations bills, hoping the new name will keep it under the radar. Under the LLEA, the negative portrayal of identifiable groups (that is, anyone except white heterosexual males) could be prosecuted as a means of *preventing* violent hate crimes. The ACLU has warned against this scenario and is recommending a provision to exclude from prosecution any speech not directly related to a specific violent crime. Such a provision is necessary because criticism of official victims could be interpreted as inciting violence against them. It's one step closer to the whole issue of thought crimes. The mere categorization of certain opinions as "hate" has already curtailed our freedom of speech. Lots of people are intimidated into agreeing with anything to keep from being called an oppressor, racist, sexist, or homophobe. The message is clear—don't fuck with victims.

However, the U.S. has fallen behind in the race to dismantle free speech. Hate speech laws are already rampant in Germany, France, and Sweden. The Canadian government has a department called "Status of Women Canada" dedicated to promoting feminism and attacking the "patriarchy." These official government feminists submitted a proposal in November 2003 requesting government funding to monitor men's rights websites and "masculinist" writers in Canada and the U.S. as "hate groups" for taking positions contrary to feminism. Status of Women Canada even developed a blacklist of "masculinists" who made statements contrary to feminism and posted it on their government website until legal action forced them to remove it. Some anti-feminist writers who were left off the list felt snubbed and wanted to know how they could apply to be included.

Here are some excerpts from the "Recommendations" section of Status of Women Canada's *School Success by Gender: A Catalyst for the Masculinist Discourse*. The entire document is available at: http://www.swc-cfc.gc.ca/pubs/0662882857/200303_0662882857_3_e.html

> In light of the growing use of the Internet by masculinist groups to develop misogynist sites inciting violence and the growing number of discussion groups used to promote hatred of women, we suggest that a monitoring organization be established, similar to Hate Watch, but focused solely on gender social relations. It would also be useful to maintain, publish, disseminate and update a list of misogynist groups."

> It is also important to support organizations, such as the Media Awareness Network, that are working to provide information and consciousness-raising for young people, especially since they are likely to encounter misinformation about "school-based discrimination against boys."

> Since such action is limited to protecting an identifiable group within the meaning of section 318 of the *Criminal Code* ("'identifiable group' means any section of the public distinguished by colour, race, religion or ethnic origin"), and this section does not provide for the fact that a group distinguished by gender, such as women, may be subject to hate propaganda, we recommend that section 318 be amended to include women among the segments of the public distinguished by sex in the definition of "identifiable group."

It's no wonder women's groups like N.O.W. support "hate crime" legislation. Their own anti-male hate literature is fine, but they want criticism of feminist ideology to *be a crime.* They are serious. The California penal code already states that it is a "hate crime" to "oppress" anyone—and feminists consider anyone who opposes feminism oppressors. In their minds, such "oppression" equals hate and causes violence. The only way to prevent violence is to outlaw disagreement.

At some point it will become apparent that disagreeing with a person of official victim status is not an act of oppression. It is an act of communication. But since I am a heterosexual white male, my views have no validity. If I disagree with affirmative action I am branded a sexist and racist. I must be reprogrammed. Disputing the validity of feminism qualifies me as a gang member into rape and ultra-violence, like the Malcolm McDowell character in *A Clockwork Orange.* And like that villain, the reprogramming didn't quite take with me. I can see there's something not "correct" about it. What would that be? It's that with political correctness, hate and intolerance are permitted, as long as it is not directed toward any of the predefined oppressed victims. Quick, tie him down!

The media now markets victimology like a consumer product. Hilary Swank won the 1999 best actress Academy Award and a Golden Globe for her portrayal of a lesbian cross-dresser in *Boys Don't Cry.* Of course, the character had to be victimized in the worst way. Swank should have gotten an award for "best victim," not best actress. I saw the movie and Swank didn't look or act anything like a guy. At least the *Crying Game* dude looked like a girl.

Then there's the 2003 film *Monster,* a "based-on-a-true-story" account of a lesbian prostitute who murders her johns. According to the screenplay, it was men who victimized *her,* turning *her* into this "monster." The usual band of women-firsters claim the killings were all in self-defense. It wasn't her fault. But didn't real-life serial killer Aileen Wuornos recant her rape story? But who cares? Charlize Theron won the Academy Award for best actress. A Golden Globe too. No surprise here. Victim of the Year.

Like all those who hold strong beliefs, radical feminists and their allies think they are doing good in the world. So do suicide bombers. Any suffering is warranted by their cause. It's time for both groups to sit down and rethink a few things. Are they really doing us a service? Are they really being proactive? I suppose the comparison is unfair. Suicide bombers only strike once. And I suppose feminists don't really want to kill us. But feminism has had a devastating effect on men, families, relationships, and personal freedoms. I know I'm not supposed to say things like that. I can't help it. It's the oppressor in me.

More Victim Than Thou

There are people throughout the West who eagerly embrace political correctness and want some way to demonstrate they are not racists and sexists and oppressors like the rest of us. They want to experience victim-bonding. Black people living in Germany are highly sought after to this end. Petra has a friend who married a black guy and had a child with him. That's like a trump card. You just can't beat that as proof you aren't a racist. It was also a fantastic opportunity for Petra to have a black friend. She has photos of herself tenderly holding her friend's black baby. She's got six or seven enlargements of these photos displayed prominently in her living room. Her best friend Ursula has two children, but she doesn't have any pictures of them. No photos of her sister's kid either. In fact, Petra has more photos in her apartment of her friend's black baby than of her own daughter. They've been up for years now. They're like ideological trophies to her. It's like those photos we always see of Lady Diana holding a black baby.

Why does a black baby turn a white woman into a saint? Since I've never taken any women's studies classes, it took me a few years to stumble across the answer. It's because feminists have been promoting the idea that women have suffered the same awful history of oppression that Africans did in slavery. Women were property. They were beaten like slaves. They were denied the right to vote. They were kidnapped and separated from their children, taken to the town square in chains and auctioned off into hard labor to the highest bidder. Hmm, strike that last one. Regardless, feminists have convinced themselves that white married ladies in the 19th century were no better off than African slaves. The horror. But I doubt slaveowners were expected to open doors for slaves out of courtesy. And I doubt they ever gave up their seats on lifeboats when the slaveships sank. It's absurd. And all the while, oppressive white males were free to live glorious lives performing hazardous construction, fighting in wars, and working in coal mines. So now white women share that special bond with black people as co-victims.

One time in Buenos Aires, I was introduced to a girl who had never met an American before. She said hello, then informed me that I was a racist merely by virtue of being American. She proudly pronounced she had no racial bias at all. I found those statements highly prejudicial. Who was the one expressing intolerance? Who was doing the hating here? And by the way, *all* politically correct people in other countries think Americans are the worst racists in the world. These are always people who have minimal contact with other races, except maybe that occasional photo op.

So I asked the Argentinean girl if she would marry an Aborigine from the outback. "Absolutely," she declared, "they're no different than anyone else." I could just imagine her husband putting on body paint and going to a job interview in Buenos Aires. Recognizing differences in people is not the same as hating them. It is not even disrespectful. It is necessary. People like that girl in Argentina who think they are more ideologically pure than the rest of us apparently have no concept of cultural differences. They don't want to, thinking it might make them racists. So they pretend everyone is the same. She's part of the victim revolution, identifying me as an oppressor by my race, gender, and culture.

Victim Creep

You're not supposed to challenge anything a victim from an approved identifiable group says. We had two Native Americans visit an English class once. They gave us a lecture about how the Native American culture was superior to our white European culture of violence and greed. They told us how we pollute the air and water and divide up the land into little squares. They preferred the traditional ways of their ancestors, they said. Some guy asked them if they drove cars. The girls in the class all gasped with horror. Oh my God! That's not nice! Of course they drive cars and shop in supermarkets. But they're on the list of approved minorities. We're supposed to agree with whatever they say out of courtesy. The girls effectively shut down any real communication with the visiting victims and clapped excessively as they left the room.

If the Native American culture is worthy of respect then why not mine? I think everyone should learn how this land we live on was acquired, but not as a reason to castigate us. I'm tired of being placed in a position to justify every injustice and inequity in Western civilization because of my appearance. A lot of history has become a means to incite people rather than educate them. I learn history to find out how we got here, not who to blame for it. I refuse to wear the mantle of guilt everyone is trying to hand me. I disagree that I am personally responsible for events in world history because of my ancestry. People who give in to that just want to console themselves a little. Feel the guilt, feel the pain. Whatever.

What is Sacagawea doing on a U.S. coin? Was her vision greater than that of Lewis and Clark? Did she draw up the maps? Would she have approved of how her assistance was eventually utilized? And how can we put a likeness of someone on our money if we don't even know what they looked like? Images of women and Indians dominated U.S. coinage well into the 20th century, so the reason can't be to "correct past injustices." Why do we have this need to make ourselves feel better about what was done to the native people of this continent? How does putting Sacagawea on a coin help Native Americans? I don't see the correctness.

We can't right everyone's historical wrongs. Can't we stop pretending like we're trying? I had this discussion with Petra before we added politics to our list of banned topics. She pronounced that the U.S. should return more land to the Indians. I explained I thought the Indians should assimilate into our culture, and that they could continue to maintain their identity like other ethnic groups. Perhaps instead of land we could offer them better schools. Petra maintained her view that Americans should be willing to rectify what we did so the Indians could live like they did before we stole their land. Fine, I said. So we level all the cities and highways we built, we return the land to its natural state, replant the forests, and then give it back to the Indians. We pay the Africans for all the work they did as slaves, apologize to them, and return them to Africa. We rebuild the Aztec civilization so they can proceed with their human sacrifices, then we all go back to Europe and everyone else returns to wherever they came from. Then we do South America. Oh, and I hope Petra doesn't forget to repopulate Europe with Jews and return all their property and wealth. I'm not sure what happens after that.

Someone came up with a great solution to all this. If we don't like our history, let's just rewrite it as a continuing struggle by women and minorities to overcome oppression by white males. Wouldn't that make us feel better about ourselves? I know I could use a little more self-flagellation.

The separation of history by race and gender is now rampant. I was in Kitty Hawk, North Carolina, at the Wright Brothers Museum shortly before the 100th anniversary of powered flight. Although the Wrights certainly influenced the design of World War I biplanes, they had nothing to do with the design of World War II aircraft. So I thought it strange there was a separate World War II exhibition in an annex. As it turned out, the exhibit presented only the Tuskegee Airmen. Why? There wasn't mention of veteran airmen of other ethnic backgrounds. And unless you already knew the history of World War II you'd get the impression that African American pilots flew all the combat missions over Germany. I thought we got rid of segregation, so why is there a movement to create "separate but equal" histories?

The main exhibit at the Wright Museum included a gallery with portraits of aviation pioneers. Orville and Wilbur were there. Lindbergh was there as the first person to fly across the Atlantic. As expected, there were women and minority portraits too. Amelia Earhart was there as the first woman to fly solo across the Atlantic. There was the first black female to get a pilot's license. That's odd, I didn't see a portrait of the first Hispanic female to get a license. How about the first female Pacific Islander? Shouldn't there also be a portrait of the first lesbian couple to fly across the Atlantic? How about the first transgendered male to get a pilot's license? Is it so offensive that two white guys invented the airplane? If it doesn't matter, why does it matter?

Why was Amelia Earhart such a sensation? Her famous flight in 1928 across the Atlantic was as a *passenger* with two male pilots whose names have been long forgotten. She finally made her *solo* transatlantic flight as a pilot in 1932—five years after Lindbergh. So what was the point? She achieved immortality by *failing* in her attempt to circumnavigate the earth, which also had already been done by some other guys we've never heard of. Why is Earhart's flying career still considered significant? It is because Amelia Earhart was a professional gender hero, not an aviation pioneer.

The injection of victimology into history allows women to cast themselves as morally superior to us violent and oppressive men. But our innocent women/victims don't like to think about how they were there making the sandwiches as we barbarian males built our oppressive civilization. Our "more oppressed than thou" sisters have a difficult time acknowledging they too may be among the beneficiaries of war, genocide, and (God forbid) the progressive thought of some white male slaveholders who founded the nation we live in.

How can feminists reconcile their ideological purity with such historical injustices? Someone ought to feel really bad about this. Certainly not women. None of this is their fault. So who can we hold accountable? I think we all know the perpetrators. It's those damned white male oppressors, and they're still at it. Can't we round them up and make them stop? Isn't there a way to transform them, or at least punish them? Yes, in fact, we can do both at the same time. Let's round them up and get them into a "diversity seminar."

I've been to several diversity seminars. Before I attended them, whenever I heard the word "diversity," I heard "the deliberate exclusion of white males." "We must achieve diversity," meant, "We must exclude more white males." "We need to hire role models," meant, "Let's hire unqualified females to be your supervisors, and prohibit disagreement about it."

The seminars really helped. At IBM we were told that diversity is *always* better for a balanced team. A diverse team will *always* achieve better results. There was a study somewhere that proved it. Before the seminar, I thought the team with the most qualified and highly motivated people would achieve the best results, not the team with the most different races, nationalities, and genders. Silly me. Good thing I had that training to correct my misconceptions. Now I understand that diversity itself achieves results, not productivity. It's now clear to me that my old presumptions that race and gender did not matter were themselves racist and sexist. I feel much more comfortable now that I understand there are really good reasons for discriminating against me.

I'm tired of being required to do all the understanding, accepting, and tolerating of everyone else. Perhaps all the diversity proponents need to look at people from all cultures and not simply point the finger at someone with a selected appearance. Yeah, I've sensed that intolerance. Even from my "more progressive than thou" girlfriend. I've always had three strikes against me with Petra. I'm white, I'm male, and I'm American. The only reason she kept seeing me is because she never understood baseball.

To all the diversity theologians I would say: you can find stupid people throughout the world, and they don't all look like me. I still hear that immigrants are disappointed in the level of acceptance they receive in the U.S. I would ask, how would I be accepted in the countries they come from? Can I walk down the street in Nigeria and not be harassed? Can I go and work in Japan, Saudi Arabia, or Pakistan and be fully embraced by their cultures? Why is it that only Western cultures are held up to this high standard? The assumption of discrimination must come to an end. White males have raised their consciousness on the matter. It's time for everyone else to catch up. Being white and male doesn't mean you have no limitations. It doesn't mean you are bestowed with privilege. It means you don't have any excuses.

Emotional Correctness

There are a lot of strange concepts swirling in the rancid caldron known as "political correctness." Not only are they not really "correct," they are also not always "political." The political part has resulted in official policies such as affirmative action and hate crime laws. A non-political aspect of political correctness has been woven into the fabric of our culture, which calls for the praise of emotional women as virtuous, and the dismissal of analytical men as defective.

We've all gotten very used to women's claims of moral (and even genetic) superiority, but in this case it's emotional superiority. Female emotions have become a protected entity, as if they are "correct" and should be used as the benchmark to evaluate the validity of all actions and ideas across both genders. Male criticism of female behavior has become a form of emotional oppression. Of course, this necessitates corrective action.

You can say women are better or smarter than men, but never that men might be smarter or better at anything than women. It's all about feelings. Women can have a double standard and not be criticized for it. It's emotionally justified. It doesn't matter what men think about anything. Men have no justifiable feelings. Male emotion is egocentric, aggressive, and sexist, and therefore not correct. Male emotion causes war and hate and other things that hurt people's feelings. But female anger is empowering and justified. If a man kills his wife or children, he's a murderer who couldn't keep his anger in check and deserves to be imprisoned or executed. If a woman kills her children, she's a confused individual whose cries for help were ignored. If she kills her husband, it must have been self-defense and she deserves counseling to overcome her trauma.

Men are being called upon to "deconstruct" our own primitive emotional set with the new "correct" set of female emotions. I believe it's called "getting in touch with your feminine side." It's been spreading throughout our culture for years; it just hasn't had a name. So, I think it should be officially dubbed *emotional correctness*. The rule for determining if something is emotionally incorrect is whether a woman might get her feelings hurt by it. It's estrogen logic. Womanthink. The least we can do is to agree with whatever they say.

Chick flicks, like *The Bridges of Madison County* and *The Horse Whisperer*, often celebrate a woman's achievement of a higher emotional state. These comply with the principle of emotional correctness that a woman's feelings override all other factors. It's just like guy flicks in which there's a cute young girl challenging a stable relationship by offering herself up sexually, forcing the guy to choose between his relationship and a higher state of sexual excitement. Except that in the guy flicks, he is always vilified if he goes for the cute girl. Men cheat because they don't care about love. Women cheat because they demand true love. That's why women think their cheating is better than our cheating. The poor wife deserves better than her emotionally boring relationship. What choice did she have? The husband in these chick flicks never matters. He's a clueless doofus who doesn't understand she's emotionally starved. The horse in *The Horse Whisperer* is far more central to the girl's life than her father. Eventually, the wife realizes she can't hang onto that emotional high she's achieved with the horse trainer, so she settles for plain old inadequate clueless boring dad.

But when wives in chick flicks get cheated on, they are portrayed as victims who have been emotionally betrayed by insensitive jerks they thought they could trust. Even the old pseudo guy flick "10" is emotionally correct, because the guy declines the cute girl at the end. I mean, what the fuck? He earned it. I wanted my money back. An emotional conquest is beautiful and pure, but sexual conquest is primitive and animalistic. Only female feelings matter. That's emotional correctness.

One glaring example of emotional correctness in the movie industry is the best actress Academy Award given in 1996 for that female part in the movie *Fargo*. Clearly it was not the performance being rewarded—it was the feminist theme of female superiority. We're supposed to believe that a pregnant woman whose water is about to break can bring in a violent murderer without help from any damn men. Even though this "true" story was never substantiated, the female superiority theme always makes women feel empowered, and that's what's important. All the men in the film are idiots or criminals, so that supports the feminist worldview as well.

Apparently, the message of *Fargo* is that we should accept pregnant women in all vital life situations as *more* capable than all the ignorant and violent men who impose their control on society. So, I suppose we should not bar pregnant women from combat roles either. Why impose any unnecessary limitations on women just because of their reproductive status? That's oppression. Besides, instead of killing people, pregnant women would just end all war so that everyone could live happily ever after in their peaceful queendom. Except for men—they would be exterminated.

For years the media has been flooded with emotionally correct movies and TV programs showing attractive, smart women beating up and killing uncaring, stupid men who deserve it. It's the same themes repeated over and over. Men are obstacles to women. Men only understand force and are emotionally ignorant. Since men have no feelings, they are disposable. When will it stop? Men have been saying this for years. Do we have to cry to communicate with women? Is that all they understand?

The 2004 CBS docudrama *Suburban Madness* was sympathetic to the actions of Clara Harris, who repeatedly ran over her cheating husband with her Mercedes. She avoided a life sentence because the jury found she acted in "sudden passion." The narrator at the end of the show proclaims, "Clara Harris was in a life and death fight for her family. Her survival instinct kicked in. I want you to ask yourself, would you kill to save your family?" So, she had to destroy her family in order to save it? Where have I heard that reasoning before?

It has become acceptable for emotions to supersede logic. We're supposed to believe that emotional pain is just as bad as physical pain. Maybe worse. Women now believe their feelings should be protected as a right. They consider themselves emotionally oppressed if they are criticized. The emotional reprogramming of men is just one goal of the broader feminist-led plan to replace masculinity with "superior" female values.

I agree with those who say we are undergoing a rapid feminization of our culture. I noticed while watching the Olympics that male athletes now get flowers along with their medals. So do the stage winners in the Tour de France. Maybe we should give them all sparkly little crowns to wear too. It's all part of the female quest to turn the world into one big estrogen fest. I really hope that didn't hurt anyone's feelings. I better apologize right away.

The Feminization of Government

Emotional correctness is working its way into the courts. Emotions just outweigh reason or common sense. Middle-age feminists are in positions of power trying to enforce all forms of political correctness as if it were an anal set of table manners from the 19th century. They're so enlightened, overcoming that male oppression. Are they out of their minds? Yes. They're also judges and legislators.

Emotion can be a deciding factor in trials. If you evoke enough sympathy, you get a lighter sentence. Usually this applies to female criminals who cry nicely. In the case of 16-year-old Marcus McTear (who stabbed and killed a girl at school in Austin in 2003), Judge Jeanne Meurer needed to make a ruling as to whether McTear should stand trial as an adult. Rather than basing her decision on the severity of the crime, she watched McTear as he was shown morgue photos of the girl. McTear teared up. As a result, the female judge ruled that since he "showed emotion," he would stand trial as a juvenile. She didn't use the word "remorse." His tears made him eligible for parole in three years. I notice myself losing trust for emotion-centric women in positions of power.

The politically correct requirement that women be portrayed as victims has resulted in the characterization of female child predation as extremely unusual. In fact, they make up about 10% of the known cases according to Julia Hislop in her 2001 book *Female Sexual Predators*. Boys in their early teens are not viewed as victims, but as aggressive adolescents who are "experimenting" with their sexuality. "A lot of victims of females talk about trying to report their abuse and say they were congratulated rather than assisted," writes Hislop. Certainly many boys do not report these encounters as crimes until after they realize they've been used as ego boosters or sperm donors.

Only the most sensational cases get much press, such as the recent saga of Mary Kay Letourneau. She's the 36-year-old teacher and married mother of four who got a light sentence of six months in prison for having sex with and becoming pregnant by a 12-year-old student in her class. Certainly a male child predator would get a far more severe sentence without sympathy as a factor. There is no "I was in love" defense for men. As soon as Letourneau was released from prison she got pregnant by the boy a second time and received a sentence of seven years. And guess what? The press had no qualms about putting the *boy's* name in the paper. Letourneau continued to contact him from prison with highly explicit and manipulative letters in violation of her sentence. Sure, they're adults now and free to do what they want, but Letourneau messed up the boy's life in an irreversible way, not to mention the lives of her six children.

Another sensational case popped up in August 2004, in which 46-year-old Kathy Tuifel pleaded guilty to having intercourse with an 11-year-old blind boy in her 6th grade class. She faced three counts of felony rape, and got *six whole months* in prison. Why such a light sentence? She copped a plea. And according to her attorney, she only pleaded guilty because, "She didn't want to put anyone through this, including the *alleged* victim." How considerate of her. She only has the best interest of the child in mind. And we wouldn't want to separate her from her own children, who are older than the blind boy.

In April 2003, I read that Lisa Zuniga of Houston was sentenced by a female judge to 30 days and a $500 fine for luring a 13-year-old boy into impregnating her. I wonder what penalty the same female judge would impose on an adult male for seducing and impregnating a 13-year-old girl? But why penalize Zuniga further? Hasn't she suffered enough emotional pain already? When the boy turns 18 she can sue him for child support. I wonder what the feminist response would be if male child molesters could sue their female victims for not stopping them?

Men don't matter. In February 2004, the Michigan Court of Appeals ruled that Alexander Shire must pay child support for the child he conceived with Laura Evelyn in 1989 when she got him drunk and seduced him. Evelyn was 21 and already married at the time and Shire was 14. It was only when Evelyn divorced her husband that Shire was identified as the biological father. That the act of sex with a 14 year old was a crime was not considered relevant by the court. The bastard had his fun, now make him pay. Of course, Evelyn will not be charged with paternity fraud or statutory rape. And let the poor female pedophile maintain custody. N.O.W. will not be calling any emergency meetings over *this* one.

Then there's the issue of "presumption of paternity." I met Carnell Smith at the first Men's Rights Congress in 2004. After 12 years of paying child support, he learned from DNA testing that he was not the child's biological father. The woman had lied to him the whole time. When he stopped paying, the woman sued him—and won. The Georgia State Supreme Court ruled that since he had *emotionally bonded* with the child, he was considered by the child to be the father and was therefore still responsible for her financially. The mother had identified the real father, but that was ruled irrelevant. The court said he had "identified" himself as the father when agreeing to pay the first child support payment. So Smith still had to keep paying the woman who had defrauded him. In June 2002, the U.S. Supreme Court refused to hear his appeal. Now executive director of U.S. Citizens Against Paternity Fraud, Smith is promoting new laws against paternity fraud at the state level. (See www.paternityfraud.com or www.nfja.org).

Let's not forget the case of Taron James, a Gulf War veteran who also proved with DNA testing that he is not the father of the child he is forced to pay child support for. He was assigned paternity in absentia while fighting in Iraq. He only discovered a default judgment had been entered when the Los Angeles Disrict Attorney seized his driver's license and docked half his pay for child support. He confirms he was involved with the mother, but he was shipped off to war a full year before the birth of the child. He believes the woman willfully committed paternity fraud to collect military benefits, including a death benefit in case he was killed in action. Apparently, it's okay to commit fraud if you're a mother. So far he has paid $25,000 in support payments, and the Los Angeles County Child Protective Services is now garnishing his unemployment. As of 2004 he's been fighting the courts for 10 years. Even with his DNA test results, he lost his last appeal because there are no laws that recognize paternity fraud as a crime.

There are plenty of elected male suck-ups who unconditionally support the women-first agenda, like ex-Governor Gray Davis, who vetoed California's paternity fraud bill after it was passed by the legislature. Of course, N.O.W. opposes paternity fraud laws because, well, women wouldn't be able to lie and cheat and steal anymore. Women have fought too hard to suddenly have their "rights" taken away.

Only recently (September 2004) did Governor Schwarzenegger sign a new bill to give paternity fraud victims some limited recourse. Assembly Bill 252 now gives men up to two years to challenge paternity rulings, rather than the current one month. Personally, I don't see why there should be any statute of limitation on this. It should be up to the man to decide what his relationship will be with a child he did not father, not the government.

Legislators like lesbian feminist Sheila Kuehl (D-Santa Monica) still oppose any paternity fraud legislation to protect men from the legalized deceit perpetrated against them by women. "It's an ancient practice going back thousands of years for the government or king or chieftain to make a rule about who is the child's parent," says Kuehl. Hey, weren't those the times of barefoot and pregnant women? Wasn't human sacrifice an ancient practice too? It's almost as if she has an agenda other than justice in mind.

Feminists don't like to call involuntary fatherhood or father-swapping "paternity fraud," since that implies a woman may have deliberately done something wrong. That could hurt their feelings if someone found out. Wrong father? Why can't men stop whining about every little thing and take some responsibility?

I would ask, is it really "in the best interest of the child" to lie about who their father is? I wonder if legislators like Kuehl would be more concerned if hospitals routinely mixed up *tens of thousands of women's babies* every year? That's right, over a hundred thousand babies in the U.S. have their fathers misidentified by their mothers each year (www.aabb.org). Those are only the *known* cases. The actual number could be ten times that. Would birth mothers be willing to accept that it's all a "social construct" and the exact identity of a child's biological mother doesn't matter?

Why would feminists want men to continue paying child support for children who are not theirs? Because of their collective blame of all men. All men are guilty and all men deserve punishment. Why aren't feminists the ones wearing white hoods? Is this 1930 again? Apparently, it doesn't matter which guy did it. Just grab any nigger in the general vicinity.

Looks like truth has gone out of style. It's considered rude. Wouldn't want to offend anyone. What ever happened to the tellers of truth? They've been fired, driven from power, and banished from public view. Being right doesn't seem to matter. We award credibility to the most articulate liars. The only honest people left are children and comedians. Everyone else tailors the truth to fit an agenda. As children we seem to understand what is right and what is wrong. As adults we lose our ability to distinguish between the two. We are content that the truth is carelessly misplaced or locked safely away. We prefer caring, passionate nonsense. We use our big brains to refine it into even bigger lies. But why concern ourselves with this ugliness? If it feels good, believe it.

My Favorite Phobia

Women seem to delight in male homophobia. Whatever that is. Why does my dictionary define "homophobia" as "hatred or dislike of homosexuals" when phobia means "fear"? I decided to check another dictionary. Oh, it means the *irrational* fear or dislike" of homosexuals. An online dictionary says it's "prejudice against homosexuals." Another says it's "fear of male intimacy." Gay activists prefer a definition more like, "promotion of hatred and violence toward homosexuals." In fact, "homophobia" is a pop word. It can mean anything you want. It doesn't even appear in dictionaries more than a few years old.

Women seem to use the word in the trendy context that straight guys are afraid of their own attraction to men. Or we're afraid we might get aroused at the thought of a gay encounter. Sorry ladies, taunt me all you want. I'm not afraid of homophobia. And that's what homophobia really is—a taunt. It's a term of ridicule directed toward straight males. Calling someone a "homophobe" is the sexual converse of calling someone "queer."

I personally think it's good to have a healthy revulsion for people of the same sex. That's why I have an entire drab wardrobe. That's why I don't smile in the men's room. When I touch other men, I want to inflict some pain. Even a handshake. I always hated showering at the gym. I don't even like buying men's underwear. Is it necessary to put pictures of the world's gayest men all over the packages?

Don't worry, I also have a healthy revulsion for the religious nuts who claim God created AIDS to punish homosexuals. If that were true, I'd say God is a total homophobe. And that would also mean God is only angry with gay men—but he's cool with lesbian chicks.

I'm all for acceptance, but I keep getting advocacy shoved down my throat. And the concept of homophobia is the enabler for gay and lesbian advocacy. The appearance of "queer studies" at universities is not acceptance, but advocacy. As part of their anti-homophobia campaign, Women's Studies has been expanding to include gay and lesbian literature and "queer theory." The University of Illinois offers *Introduction to Queer Studies* and *Sexuality, Education, and Varieties of Queerness*. The Feminist Women's Health Center of Atlanta even offers a "Lesbian Health Internship."

The fanatical insistence that gay partnerships be called "marriages" instead of "civil unions" is also advocacy. It's the coerced endorsement of gay partnerships as being equivalent to heterosexual marriage. Excuse me for having an opinion, but I happen to think it's optimal for children to have a mother and father, not two fathers or two mothers. I don't think we should teach children that homosexuality is normal; we should teach them that some people are sexually deviant or sexually confused, and to recognize sexual advances by people of the same gender. By expressing such views I get lumped in with religious nuts, Republicans, God, the murderers of Matthew Shepard, and all other homophobes. The only way to distance myself from the homophobic crowd would be to openly embrace the gay agenda. But why does "accepting" someone mean you have to recite their dogma?

I don't see why there's so much sucking up to the whole gay movement. Somehow, they've gotten globbed into the politically correct sanctuary. They've been granted "hypersensitivity status" and are shielded from all criticism. The animal rights people won't even speak out against what they do to all those poor gerbils.

Well, fuck sensitivity. I'm tired of calls to hysteria over things like the California governor using the term "girlie man" while every day it's open season on heterosexual males. No one objects to all the "heterophobia" in the media. I recently saw a program that went on for 10 minutes about why you should never use the term "that's so gay." You could damage the self-esteem of some poor gay person. How horrible. Then I switched channels to CNBC and saw a promotion for John McEnroe's show culminating with a man getting hit in the groin by a tennis ball. How funny. Unless the man happened to be gay, then it would be terrible. I have no patience for such double standards. So, don't expect me to bend over backwards for gay rights. I don't care what people do in private. I just don't think the gay lifestyle needs to be actively promoted.

My Favorite Phobia

Psychologically-Induced Drama

University psychology departments have experienced an influx of gay and lesbian students intent on turning the profession into a tool for activism. They now influence policies, agendas, and distribution of grant money. The American Psychological Association (www.apa.org) has become a political group, promoting causes like affirmative action and diversity in addition to the entire litany of gay and lesbian issues. In 1973 the APA voted to stop treating homosexuality as a "mental disorder." Now, gay psychology activists want homosexuality to be promoted as *preferable* to heterosexuality. They've turned it around, and no one seems to have noticed. Now straight males are the ones in need of counseling to rid themselves of homophobia. We're the pervs with a "mental disorder." We're sexually constipated dweebs from another century. Hurry up and re-educate us, please.

In the mid 1980s my psychologist friend Lindsey told me her psych department was dominated by lesbian feminists. She complained that they stigmatized her for her stubborn preoccupation with men. Apparently, they weren't impressed by her single liaison with another woman. Her heterosexuality may have impacted her career, since the lesbian head of the department wrote her performance evaluation and references. Lindsey described the department lesbians as extremely aloof, as if their sexual "disorientation" distinguished them from everyone else and their blasé personal issues. They had broken through more emotional barriers, overcome more obstacles.

I've seen that attitude in general. Gays and lesbians are so much deeper than we simple hets could ever understand. They're "more tormented and oppressed than thou." Of course, bisexual girls don't get full credit. After all, we kinda like them. I've lost track. Are we supposed to call them "women who have sex with anyone" now?

Sexual Orientation for Children

Hypersensitivity has actually led to the cultivation of homosexuality in children. The punishment of "disruptive and hegemonic" masculine traits is bound to confuse boys who do not understand the larger political agenda. Feminist-indoctrinated educators now nurture effeminate qualities in boys as preferable to the traditional masculine traits of dominance, aggression, and homophobia.

Gay and lesbian advocates want children to be taught that it makes no difference if they date boys or girls. So let's teach kids that the only way to find out if they are gay or bisexual is to consider dating people of both sexes. They want it taught in schools. Or anywhere. I saw a lesbian couple deep kiss for a full minute in front of a big group of kids at Disney World. See? Everybody does it.

Gay activists are doing their best to "educate" everyone. I was on campus one day, and busloads of nine year olds were coming to visit the university. All the student organizations had their information booths ready. At the gay/lesbian alliance booth, fourth graders could get information about their options concerning sexual preference. I found myself wishing I was in the fourth grade again so I could be like the kid on *The Man Show*. "Hey mister, ever taken it up the ass from a nine year old? Ever gag on a really big one?" Kids these days don't need the gay/lesbian booth for information. It's all over TV and the Internet. Even MTV has gay/lesbian episodes of *Room Raiders*.

Looks like it's working, at least as far as young girls are concerned. They're all lesbian-aware now. I was on the S-Bahn in Munich in 2001. There was a group of six American girls who went to an international school there, and they assumed no one on the German S-Bahn could understand their American slang. They were all 12 to 14 years old. I know because they told each other their ages. The 12 year old was talking about how she had been conversing with some high school guy in a local chat room. They had not actually met, but he had offered her some "weed" if she would let him lick her. "Should I take the weed and let him do it?" she asked the others. Their objection was not to the weed, nor to her getting licked, but that he was trying to buy her. The 12 year old asked the other girls if any of them had ever gotten licked. The 14 year old explained that she was bisexual. She hadn't had sex with a guy yet, but she'd been licked by both a girl and a guy. The 12 year old replied that she'd rather be licked by a guy. "Isn't it weird getting licked by another girl?" she asked. "Not really, it's all good," said the older girl.

Isn't it great that even pre-teen girls are becoming aware of their sexual options, and are willing to consider a lesbian experience? The collective advice to the 12 year old was that she should "get to know" the guy better before letting him lick her. "Let us know if you do it, it would be great to have some weed!" said one girl. "Anybody hear what we're talkin' bout?" said the 14 year old in rapid English, looking around the S-Bahn. I had my head down thinking, *Jesus, times have changed.*

My Favorite Phobia

So now teen and even pre-teen girls are casually trying out lesbian sex as if it were a Hula-Hoop. Even the Girl Scouts are being aggressively targeted by feminists for doses of indoctrination. The Girl Scouts organization is frequently listed by Women's Studies departments as a career opportunity for graduates. Some parents have caught on and have organized boycotts of cookie sales after discovering feminist "guest lecturers" had been invited to give talks to the girls on topics including homophobia and the acceptance of homosexuality. Maybe we should also explain to the girls that it's perfectly normal for men to want anal sex with them. It's just another way men express their love for women.

"Confuse them while they're young" seems to be the current approach. More and more girls are engaging in same-sex encounters. But lesbian feminists and women's studies professors can't take full credit. Porn marketed to heterosexual males routinely contains lesbian sex. Sure, cute girls kissing is a turn on. Unless one of the girls is your girlfriend. They don't even think licking each other is cheating. The reality is, girls into girls may fuck you, but they'll never love you. They're ruined for normal relationships. I doubt anyone bothered to explain *that* to the Girl Scouts. Shouldn't we be *warning* children about same-sex sexual predators instead of clearing a path for them?

My Introduction to Homophobia

I wish someone had warned me. Growing up I never realized there were really men who liked men. I heard the kids at school say, "Suck my dick" as an insult. Obviously, no one would ever want to do that, male or female I thought. Naïve perhaps, but they also said, "Eat shit" and nobody does that. I had to learn all this on my own. I was a 17-year-old freshman in a dorm room when a guy came in and offered to suck my dick for real. Jesus, people *do* that? I know what you're asking. "How was it?" Sorry to spoil everyone's fun. When he reached over and started caressing my pecker, I told him to get out of my room. I learned something else that day. The friendliest people are the most evil. It's true. That's why you can't just go up and talk to people on the street. People assume you must a sexual predator or a financial planner. Either way, at some point they'll ask you to bend over.

Another Friendly Guy

I didn't have a car at college, so I occasionally hitchhiked to visit my parents back home. I could usually make the run in four hours. One time on my way back, I got stranded at a remote exit ramp and began walking down the freeway with my thumb out. It would be getting dark soon. After 20 minutes a car pulled over driven by a really friendly guy. What luck. He would be happy to take me to the university. The conversation quickly turned sexual. He liked girls, but he also liked guys! Had I been with a guy yet? *This must be how it happens*, I thought, *this is how people disappear.* I struggled to keep up a sexual conversation, never actually having had sex yet. Trying to dissuade him, I told him I had a girlfriend and that she sucked my dick all the time. "It feels just as good if a guy sucks it," he responded with intense enthusiasm. He explained that when he was 16, a woman offered to take him home and have sex with him. He got to her place and discovered she had a husband. She went ahead and fucked him, and before he even knew it, her husband jumped in and started sucking his dick. Now he wanted to afford me the same opportunity. Without the girl.

Two blocks from the university he reached over and grabbed my crotch. "Hey, I think you're getting hard!" he proclaimed. Yeah, hard like a slug. Finally, he delivered me to the dorm. Whew. I survived that one, but I had a serious case of the creeps. It was the only time I actually feared someone gay. I told my dad later, "I've *got* to get a car!" No more hitchhiking for me. So, perhaps I *do* fear gay men. Yes, fear is good. In fact, I'd say homophobia is my favorite phobia of all.

The Money Changer at Positano

Just a few years ago I was in Positano, Italy, and I went into a little shop to cash a traveler's check. The friendly old man had a bunch of currencies on display under the glass of the countertop. I remarked about them, and he came out to discuss them. He was standing too close, so I moved away; but he was still too close. Then I realized he had his hand on my wiener. I looked at him in disbelief and said *"What?"* In a heavy Italian accent he said, "Is strong?" How was I supposed to answer that? "No! Uh, I mean, Yes?" If I was a girl I could have slapped him at least. He was fat and disgusting and gave me the same creepy feeling as that "friendly" guy who groped me in his car years before. I had my cash so I was outta there. It disrupted a beautiful day in a beautiful place. So no, homosexual men have not generally endeared themselves to me.

Later that day in Positano, I was telling a tourist girl about how I got groped by that decrepit old geezer, and she was ready to fall on the floor laughing. "What, no dinner? Will you be meeting him again tomorrow?" Sure, I was deliberately serving it up for her, but I knew she would savor this kind of story. I think women see male-on-male groping as a kind of payback for all the ugliness of male aggression. "Ha! See how we feel?" But the analogy isn't valid. I would never walk up to a woman and grope her. I always kiss her first. I also know that if some old guy had groped *her*, we wouldn't be sitting around laughing about it. It would be a huge abomination, and I'd be forced to listen to another lengthy diatribe about the evils of men and the rape culture. Call the police. Call a therapist.

The Confessions of Odair

No, I'm not intolerant. In my backpacking days, I met a guy named Odair in São Paulo, Brazil, and ended up staying at his place. For a couple of weeks we became close friends. I learned most of my Portuguese from him since he didn't speak English. He had a captivating girlfriend, and the three of us would go to rock concerts and Brazilian punk clubs together. It was just after Carnival, and we were talking about the transvestites that sprout out of nowhere and parade around for a few days each year. Odair casually volunteered that as a young teen of 15 or 16 he used to go and fuck around with the transvestites during Carnival. I was surprised to hear that because he seemed straight. He was. He shrugged it off. Oh, that's just something he did back then, he didn't do it anymore, he said. His girlfriend was totally unfazed. That's cool, I thought, he just saved himself several years of expensive therapy working through sexual orientation issues. How different from our American culture. I didn't look at him any differently after that. But then, he wasn't pushing any sexual agendas at me either.

The Politics of Flamboyance

I've had gay friends just like I've had religious friends. It's not a problem, as long as they don't try to preach to me. If I've learned anything from my discussions with gay men, it's never to debate them. Gays can go on for days about how normal they are. I find people who sermonize about the virtues of gay/lesbian relationships just as annoying as religious fanatics. In fact, I think homosexuality *is* a religion.

I was at a party where an effeminate gay guy had corralled everyone's attention with his soliloquy on the wonders of gayness. He was going on and on and on about all the successful homosexuals throughout human history. He had the list ready to recite like a speech. Walt Whitman, Herman Melville, Oscar Wilde, Michelangelo, Sir Isaac Newton, all the Romans and all the Greeks. Gay men just make better artists and writers and architects, fortified by all that extra angst. Apparently, every major advancement in civilization has been the result of the creativity and passion of gay men. Wow. No wonder I'm such a miserable failure.

Besides the gay supremacists, I've noticed that I'm also irritated by gay men who have betrayed their masculinity as a means to foster gay visibility. I had a gay office mate at Compaq several years ago. The first time I met him, he immediately hit me with that affected gay accent, but it was so extreme that I just wanted to say "Come on! I got it already!" He was very excited about how he got his picture with his partner printed in the "Wedding Anniversary" section of the local paper. I had to act all happy for him, even though I thought it was another example of excessive advocacy. He had the hyphenated last name and everything. Apparently, he thought flamboyance was the best way to promote acceptance of his sexual preference. He liked to go around and clean everything in the office with spray cleaner. Even the phone cord. He kept saying he was very "anal retentive." Okay, you can stop now. He was really annoying. I wished I could have told him to please turn down the "gay." But I never said anything because I could be the one accused of sexual harassment. That's what I was told by my manager when I asked to change offices. I'm sure my anal-retentive office mate would have jumped at the chance to squash such intolerance. If he really wanted to promote acceptance of the gay lifestyle, he should have tried speaking and behaving normally.

At Compaq, I occasionally worked in a test lab full of straight guys. They talked all day long about ass fucking, "cunt lapping," and prison sex. It was amazing how they could stay on topic for hours. They seemed to be having a competition to conceive of some diabolically profound anal reference that had never before been uttered in the English language. My gay office mate never said anything truly explicit. Still, I found him far more annoying, with his exceedingly flamboyant "accent" and self-righteous banner waving. He used his effeminate persona to inject his sexual preference into every conversation. Whatever words he was speaking, he was constantly communicating that he liked it up the ass. I was expecting him to break out into a show tune about it. At least the lab guys were joking, not trying to drive a real agenda into everyone. And I had the right to complain about the lab guys if I wanted. They did come up with several highly creative anal references that day. Alas, I did not commit them to memory, and thus they are lost unto the world forever. "Alas," they'd be all over that one.

I'm sure I've unknowingly worked with gay guys. I prefer it that way. I do not consider it vital information how a co-worker's dick gets hard. It is not my purpose in life to validate someone's lifestyle. This is why the "Don't ask, don't tell" policy makes perfect sense to me. I wish something like it would be expanded into corporate environments. Maybe, "Don't ask, don't dwell on it." No, I don't think gays should have to misrepresent their sexual preference. If I ask, then tell. Otherwise, spare me the sermon. Please, leave me out of your gay universe. I just want to not care in peace.

A Phobia of One's Own

I see the defense of gay men by feminists as disingenuous. It's not tolerance of gay males so much as it is intolerance of straight males. Sure, women like effeminate gay men. They come pre-emasculated. It saves them a lot of work. And every gay man is a man who will not be sexually harassing women. Feminists want the best and most powerful corporate professions to be reserved for women. They envision gay men as the ones who will design their clothes, style their hair, and wait on them in restaurants.

Radical feminists also want to eliminate fathers from families. Why? Because fathers will encourage their sons to be violent and their daughters to be sexy. Fathers are potential wife beaters and rapists. And of course, heterosexual fathers are homophobic. Why should women expose themselves and their children to such a risk? Better to have a peaceful lesbian family.

They're promoting the lesbian household as the new family model—the antithesis of the traditional family with an abusive father. They've reduced the concept of fatherhood to the practice of animal husbandry. The feminist concept of the perfect man would be a homosexual sperm donor into fine arts. Straight men should be mechanics, bricklayers, and people who fix toilets, not fathers. Their primary role as fathers is to pay child support. This is all part of the rampant phobia within feminism itself. Their phobia has less to do with heterosexuality than it does with masculinity. I believe it's called "androphobia."

The Assault on Gender Identities

The next thing we're supposed to swallow is that there should not be any gender identities at all, and that crossdressing and transgendering are normal personal choices. Not only is sexual orientation a "social construct," now your gender identity is as well. Whatever equipment you have between your legs is irrelevant.

In the interest of "civil rights," gender is being quickly redefined in cities across the United States. The Human Rights Law passed and signed by New York City Mayor Bloomberg in 2002 defines "gender" as:

> "...actual or perceived sex, as well as a person's gender identity, self-image, appearance, behavior or expression, whether or not that gender identity, self-image, appearance, behavior or expression is different from that traditionally associated with the legal sex assigned to that person at birth."

So, now you can represent your gender on an employment application form according to how you perceive your self-image. I can state that I am female if I decide my gender identity is female. If anyone makes fun of me, I can have them charged with civil rights violations. I can also qualify for affirmative action benefits simply by declaring myself female. Think of what would happen to all the equal opportunity statistics if men began doing so *en masse*. Think what that would do to women's sports. And how about the census? I guess I can have a "woman-owned business," too. Obviously, New York City is having problems figuring out how to apply their Human Rights Law.

As an indication of how mainstream the transgender issue has become, even National Geographic produced a show about the acceptance of transgendered people of other cultures. And in 2004, the Olympic committee fell like a domino, announcing it would accept transsexual athletes if they had completed two years of hormone therapy. In this case, women are *not* delighted by the removal of men's manhood. But aren't these poor ex-men just trying to escape the confines of a gender identity imposed upon them by an oppressive culture? How are feminists going to handle it when transsexual females start winning Olympic medals by defeating "natural" females? Will they see it as a victory for women of all genders?

I believe people should be free to fuck up their personal lives all they want. In environments such as work and school, people's right to be fucked up should not be so absolute. People in such environments should be required to truthfully represent their original gender identity. They can be crossdressers when they get home. Tolerance means we treat people civilly and agree not to harass them. It doesn't mean we have to change our minds about them.

I remember a male transgender candidate at IBM in the mid '90s, and how the company didn't know what to do to keep from being sued. They ended up letting him use the women's restroom while he was undergoing his "gender identity therapy." That is, while he still had a dick. I don't know why everyone should be expected to dance around some guy just because he likes to wear dresses. None of the rest of us get such extreme consideration. When I started out at IBM, I got sent home for not wearing a white shirt. "Come back when you're dressed appropriately."

I read an article about yet another transgender candidate at an Atlanta IBM location in 2003. Service representative Margaret Tolbert sued the company because they let him use the women's restroom. Why does IBM allow that? It's because IBM fell in line and added "gender identity" to their diversity policy. Besides, the guy probably had a note from a lesbian psychologist saying it's perfectly normal for men to want to get their winkies whacked off. Another self-improvement program for men, I suppose. If an employee with an eccentric mental disorder is disrupting the work environment, why can't he be dismissed? Obviously, he would qualify for severance pay.

Pardon me for not giving a rat's ass, but there are a lot of people in the world with real problems, like not having a place to live or enough to eat. You were born with a penis? Yeah, life is harsh. Transgendered males will never be women no matter how hard they try. They will always be surgically altered males. They're gender anarchists. We owe them nothing.

Boys Will Be Girls

At least transsexuals and crossdressers are adults fucking up their own lives. They have equal rights with everyone in that regard. But in May of 2000 I read that the parents of a six-year-old boy named Zachary Lipscomb decided he had "gender identified" himself as female, so they renamed him "Aurora" and were dressing and raising him as a girl. No, he's not a hermaphrodite, he's a genuine boy. Someone at his school noticed and called the authorities, who removed him from his parents. Just because you're a parent doesn't mean you have the right to blatantly fuck up your kids. For once, sanity prevailed. Transgender proponents attacked the decision, claiming the parents were absolutely right to crossdress their child. What better way to transform boys into girls than to actually transform them into girls? The National Organization for Women promoted a seminar supporting the parents' position, referring to Zachary as "she." Anything to emasculate another boy. They're so progressive.

In 2002, an effeminate 14-year-old boy named Ben Brownlee from Rockdale, Texas, was watching a discussion of "gender dysphoria" on *The Oprah Winfrey Show*, and decided that's what he had. For some reason, he hated everything male. His mother did what she thought was best, and sought professional help at a counseling center specializing in Gay-Lesbian-Bisexual-Transgender (GLBT) issues. Having a pro-GLBT agenda, they convinced the mother that the best thing to do would be to "gender identify" her son as female. Ben agreed, so they gave him a girl's name and had him attend public school wearing girls' clothes, make-up, and hair. Then all they had to do was re-educate everyone in the whole school. Ben bought female hormones online without a prescription, apparently with the knowledge of the counselors and his mother. He took them and began to develop breasts. Predictably, he was harassed and taunted by the other kids. Perhaps they didn't get the memo. In November of 2003 Ben hanged himself. Time to round up the usual suspects: an intolerant society, the school, the principal, the teachers, the students. For some reason, the counselors were not in the line-up.

My question would be, Is it really best to push *children* down the path to become candidates for sex-change surgery? Wouldn't it be better try some "gender acceptance" therapy first? Would it have been so traumatic for Ben to wear male clothes until he got out of high school? Maybe someday it will be perfectly normal for children to wake up and decide what gender they'll be that day before getting dressed and going to school. Is that what we want?

I see the Ben Brownlee tragedy as the willful exploitation of a teenage boy to impose politically correct GLBT social engineering upon a school. Sure, ideally schools should be free from all harassment regardless of the motivation, but I find it arrogant that the counselors expected the world to revolve around their therapy. Nevertheless, the GLBT activists believe it's all justified in order to eradicate the dreaded "homophobia" from our culture. To defeat it we must "educate" the gullible public that gender identity disorders are normal. Are the rest of us *required* to agree with whatever the transgender lobby dictates? Will no one join me in proclaiming that the emperor has no clothes? Or at least the wrong ones?

It all comes back to the theory that people have no choice about their sexual orientation or gender identity. Gay rights advocates insist that homosexuals are "born gay." Their researchers are still looking for that gay gene. I find that odd, since man-hating lesbian feminists (like Dworkin in *Woman Hating*, 1976) still insist that heterosexuality is a "cultural construct" created by a male-dominated society that subjugates women. So you can be born gay, just not born straight. Got it.

But I don't have a problem calling "bullshit" when I encounter it. I've only seen it once, but that was enough for me to know that *Rocky Horror* misses the point. Sex is far more psychological than it is physical. Sorry sweet transvestite, but it matters to *me* who's sucking my dick, even if it feels the same in the dark. As I recall, a creepy guy in a car already tried that line on me. Go ahead and dress it up all you want. I don't care how many times you see *The Rocky Horror Picture Show*, it doesn't make the premise any truer. It's so gay.

Affirmative Actions

As boys we notice how happy girls are when we let them win. We learn to take a fall for them now and then. Complain and act like it wasn't fair to heighten the drama. Let them taunt us and do a victory dance at our expense. It's therapeutic for females of all ages to reign superior over us for a time. I certainly didn't see it coming. It astounds me that the concept of "letting the girls win" has been institutionalized into a program called affirmative action, and has become the law of the land. How the hell did that happen?

I remember in my early debates with Petra, she would never admit men were physically stronger than women. She suggested we wrestle to prove it. Fine. She sprang on me like a wildcat. Yes, she was pretty damn good, so I let her pin me down and acted like I couldn't move to reward her enthusiasm. I was too busy laughing to actually fight her. Had I really tried, she wouldn't have stood a chance. Petra was convinced she had genuinely earned her victory. I whined and complained that it hadn't been fair. She was absolutely ecstatic, and I was sexually rewarded for my defeat. If I could get laid whenever I let a girl win, I would just let them win all the time. But men know it doesn't happen that way in real life. With affirmative action, we don't get to choose when we take a fall. It's done for us. And we sure don't get laid for it.

Affirmative action is one of those well-intended programs that is impossible to administer. It is simply not feasible to correct a perceived injustice toward a few women by creating a blanket program. Affirmative action pampers women who have only heard about discrimination in corporate seminars. The result is unqualified women being selected for rapid advancement. Don't tell me it's my imagination—it's official policy. To the disciples of political correctness, merit is not a consideration. It is an assumption. Affirmative action is artificial success.

Brushes with Discrimination

I was on a transatlantic flight to Europe a few years back. A few minutes after takeoff, one of the female flight attendants boldly announced that the captain in command, *she* is flying at an altitude of some blah blah thousand feet. *She* estimates our time of arrival at whenever, and so on. I didn't really care that a woman was flying the plane. No, I wasn't scared or surprised. What was the big freaking deal? I assumed she was qualified, or she wouldn't be at the controls. By that time, I'd been on a couple hundred commercial flights, but when *she*, the captain landed the jet, it was *by far* the hardest landing I'd ever experienced. I thought the landing gear was going to collapse. The plane slammed down and then sprang back high in the air before settling onto the runway. I was amazed that none of the tires were blown. Well, since the flight attendant made such a political issue out of the captain's gender, I had to conclude that *she* was the worst pilot I'd ever flown with. Obviously, the goal had been to bestow the knowledge upon us biased male passengers that women can fly planes just as well as men. It had the opposite effect. Now I began wondering if *she* might have been a barely qualified affirmative action female pilot.

I did a web search and found that airlines indeed hire female pilots with minimal qualifications and far less flying experience than men. (Search on Kathleen McFadden or Patrick Smith.) Why am I still surprised at such things? The female pilot was there at the cabin happily bidding passengers goodbye on their way out like everything was just fine. Clearly, they were going with the version of reality that she did a great job. For all I know she got a promotion. You don't think that happens?

Delores was a black woman with a technical job at IBM trying to get a promotion to "staff," a high-ranking position. She began working three or four hours overtime per day. But there were lots of people who stayed at work that long. This went on for a month or two. Why was Delores working late? She didn't have a project due. Word in the hall was that Delores was bucking for a promotion, and had been told "no." Then the word hit the hallways that Delores had called the NAACP. She was promoted the next day.

Years later when inquiring about my own promotion to staff, my female manager explained that "the bar is being raised." I suspected the bar was being raised for me, but lowered for people of "identifiable groups." I asked my second line manager who told me that if a white male was recommended for promotion, he was required to write an explanation of why the promotion should not be given to a female or racial minority. I had been working 50 to 55 hour weeks for two years. I came in on weekends and holidays. None of that seemed to matter. Not only that, but I was the technical lead for a female who ranked *two* levels above me. I wonder what group would be willing to defend the civil rights of a white male? The National Organization for Men? I doubt the NAACP would be willing to intervene. Is there an NAAWP? The closest thing might be the KKK or Aryan Nations. I don't think IBM would have responded well to a call from them on my behalf.

It wasn't just promotions that were reserved for women and minorities at IBM. I had a hard time getting a raise, even though my productivity was high. I found out from a manager, after leaving IBM, that people in "identifiable groups" were *automatically* flagged for an extra 3 percent raise over white male employees. How can this be legal? Obviously, this had cost me thousands of dollars over the years. Consider it my contribution to help end the "wage gap."

IBM had anonymous surveys every year with the intent to show that the company was not sexually or racially biased. The results were broken down by company, division, and department. At a department meeting our female manager put up the figure that 70 percent of the department thought there was sexual or racial discrimination at the company. She was very surprised. There was only one female in the department, one Asian contractor who didn't count, and the rest were all white males. She asked who in the department felt they were discriminated against. No one raised their hand. It was a dumb question. After all, it was supposed to be a *completely confidential* survey! She finally said that it was probably *just* white males expressing disagreement with affirmative action. Complaining would probably have impacted my career. Still, I learned I was not the only one disgusted by it all.

Kim was a sexy young corporate flirt at IBM who often wore high heels and short skirts to work. One time she was standing at a supply cabinet as I walked past, and she deliberately dropped something and slowly bent over to pick it up without bending her knees. Her panties were showing. Nice. Months later, she came into my office to discuss a software problem, scooted up her chair, and positioned my knee in her crotch. She continued to talk about technical issues as she massaged her clit on my kneecap, apparently to see if I could maintain the conversation without being distracted. I stayed on topic without flinching. What a fun game! She flirted with all the guys, married or single, and was curt and bitchy with all females. She added a lot of spice to the work environment.

Then something woke me up. Kim saw me in the hall and said she wanted to tell me something herself rather than let me find out from someone else. She had been chosen to go to the Olympics as the IBM technical support person for our product's networking layer. Hey, I was the owner of that source code! She had nothing to do with the support of this product, that was my job! I should have been the one going to the Olympics, and she knew it. Through her flirting connections she had found out about the trip and gotten herself assigned to it before it was generally known that support people were being selected. She hoped I didn't feel bad, and wanted my home number in case there were any problems with the network protocol stack. This time it was my turn to initiate some body contact. I backed her up against a copier, bent her over backwards, and looked directly into her eyes as I expressed my thoughts to her. "How the *hell* did you get that job? You don't own that code, *I do*. You are *not* qualified to support that code!" She seemed surprised she couldn't flirt her way out of it. Even so, I didn't complain to management. It wouldn't have done any good. Management had already given her the trip. Sure enough, she went to the Olympics with the support team, had an all-events pass, met famous athletes, and had a drunken great time. There were no problems with the network layer during the entire games. And all I got was a lousy Olympic T-shirt.

A year after that, Kim got a division award for an outstanding technical contribution. A division award is the largest award I'm aware of at IBM. You receive it in front of several hundred people. Word in the hall was this was a $10,000 award. Kim had written a software driver for a new network card, and had it up and running reliably within months. Rumors flew in the halls that this was really an award for sexual favors. It died down in a few days, and people forgot all about it. Kim was rapidly promoted for her achievements.

It must have been three years later that I took over support of the network driver that Kim had written and received that huge award for. There was a minor technical problem with one of the system calls in the code. System calls all have their little quirks that you have to understand or they can cause problems in certain conditions. The issue centered around a system call that was known to be problematic, so I decided to call Kim for a consultation. After all, she wrote the code. Not only had she never even heard of that system call, she was not familiar with *any* of them. It was immediately obvious to me she had not written *any* of that code. It is very common for the manufacturer of network cards to supply working drivers with them. Kim probably fixed a few bugs during testing of the supplied driver, but "somehow" got credit for writing the whole thing. How *did* she get that big award? I don't know, but I suspect a clit massage was involved.

So it looks like there are two separate corporate programs for women. One is affirmative action, and the other is "success for sex." My question is, *What's the difference?* The end result is the same: women making more money, getting recognition, moving to higher levels, and the overall stats look better for the company. I'd say "success for sex" is the male implementation of affirmative action. But if one is wrong, then both are wrong. I regard the two sets of women in about the same way—having gotten where they are without any obligation to earn it. In both cases women are given preferential treatment. Kim figured out how to work it from both sides. Several times I've seen female trainees promoted above their technical leads. I know guys who actually wrote entire drivers and protocol stacks but couldn't even get a promotion, let alone a big award.

When I think about it, I'm more disgusted by affirmative action promotions than "success for sex," because I am *required* to agree that affirmative action promotions are warranted and fair. At another technology company I worked for in 2002, there was a section about support of affirmative action on my *performance evaluation form.* That meant I was required to support discrimination against myself as part of my job description. Since this section was the only part of my evaluation that I got a low rating on, I asked for a copy of the affirmative action policy from human resources so that I would know exactly what policy I was required to support. They said they didn't have one, but it was "the standard corporate affirmative action policy." I didn't have much recourse, since my manager was female, as was the entire HR department. I suspect they indeed had an official affirmative action policy that favored women and minorities, but they didn't want me to have the opportunity to challenge it. Who do I talk to about this? How long before this shit is ruled unconstitutional? After the 2003 Supreme Court ruling on affirmative action in college admissions, its supporters were saying we need it "for another 25 years." "At least." Better sign me up for more sensitivity training.

Affirmative Actions

And Who Dragged the Rifle?

My mother was an early voice against sex discrimination. This was in the 1940s, before anything like affirmative action existed. She protested the "male only" policy of the Ohio State Marching Band. As a result, she and two other women became the first female members. I heard her tell the story a hundred times. As with most women, I was never able to have a rational discussion with my mother about affirmative action. When I mentioned I was against it, she became furious and flew into the "marching band" story again, assuming I was opposed to her joining. In fact, I've always thought it was good that she stood up for herself. But I couldn't get a word in.

It's very likely that female students had never expressed interest in joining the marching band before my mother raised the issue. The concept of a marching band originated from the military, so there was no precedent for female participation. And I wonder if it ever occurred to my mother that the same discrimination that kept her out of the marching band also kept her out of World War II? I can't imagine her dragging a rifle across North Africa and Italy for three years like my father did. In any case, my mother was allowed to join the marching band after taking her case to the college dean. And she wasn't let into the band because she was female, it was because she played her instrument well.

My mother was always a one-way communicator. I never got to explain any of my concerns about affirmative action to her. She never understood that I was also speaking up against discrimination. I never got to tell her how my promotions and raises were given to other people because of my race and gender. I never got to tell her I want women to have their rights. I just don't want women's rights to exceed my own. I don't want success arbitrarily taken from men and awarded to women, since that only perpetuates gender inequity. Ironically, it was my mother who told me over and over, "Two wrongs don't make a right."

I like women succeeding, I just don't like women being handed success as if it were a bouquet of flowers. It diminishes those women who actually earn it. Yeah, I know affirmative action is supposed to counteract the scourge of discrimination we of the male gender are forever presumed guilty of. It's supposed to right wrongs. But the supporters of affirmative action are never concerned with those wronged by it.

My female friends all believe in it. They think men are holding them back. They think affirmative action is a right, like free speech. Except that they don't support free speech when *I'm* doing the talking. Disagree with them about affirmative action and suddenly you become the one erecting barriers to keep women from succeeding. They're convinced they've got to fight us day after day or we're going to render them powerless and make them wash our dishes. You get the "barefoot and pregnant" quote, whatever that means. They're like those survivalists in Montana who think the world is out to get them.

That feminist paranoia seems more prevalent in older women. The young women entering the workforce who are the beneficiaries of affirmative action don't consider themselves oppressed. They look at it as another cool girl perk. It's the corporate equivalent of getting your dinner paid for without having to put out. It's one more example that confirms to women that men are totally gullible. They've come to expect that guys will just take their crap and not even complain. Serves us right for being idiots. It's not feminism so much as it is "feminitis." They've contracted the "it's all about me" syndrome. Their success is more important. Men exist to make life easy for them. Finally, the world *really is* rotating around them. Regardless of the motivation, women of all ages are perfectly happy to take our money and jobs and promotions. Let's buy them some drinks to celebrate.

Affirmative action makes a few people feel good, provided they can ignore the injustices it enforces. Every time gender is used to arbitrarily award success to a female, a male is arbitrarily denied it. This is why I believe all affirmative action must end immediately. Injustice in the past does not justify injustice now. It will end someday, but unless men speak up, it will be a long time. Together we will have to stand up to the anger and intolerance thrown at us by the disciples of political correctness. They will always demand that white males take the fall for them. Please get it through your heads. Men are not limiting you. Affirmative action will never remedy the limits people place upon themselves. In any case, white males getting dicked over is never an issue. I'll start listening to their talk about equal rights when it is.

Personal Affirmative Action

A lot of women like the concept of affirmative action so much that they have incorporated it into their personal lives. In the last three decades, women have become conditioned to expect preferential treatment in their work environments. But they also understand that affirmative action was originally intended for minorities. At some level, white women know they hijacked the whole concept—they feel a sense of guilt for taking the place of minorities at the trough. They want to show their commitment to the ideals that have benefited them for so long. Why should universities, corporations, and governments be the only ones favoring minorities and women? Why not implement the policies on a personal level? The more affirmative actions, the better.

In a relationship with a white guy, a politically correct female expects to get her way as compensation for thousands of years of oppression. Besides getting her dinner paid for, she wants men to unconditionally accept her opinions as important and valid. Her ideas should be given credence and his none. It is her right to be right. Points are to be conceded to her regardless of merit or logic. Disagreement is a violation of her civil rights.

It's different with minority boyfriends. Their rights supersede those of white women, who are less oppressed. Women respect the oppression pecking order. The effect is that a minority male in a relationship is once again the dominant figure, since he has suffered greater oppression than the non-minority female. Offending or challenging a minority is not an option.

Women incorporate this "personal affirmative action" into the boyfriend selection process itself. It works the same way as universities awarding bonus points to minority candidates. Being economically disadvantaged is not a disadvantage in this case. Personal affirmative action males don't need to be successful, since they are not "permitted" to succeed. Minority males may still exhibit oppressive "masculinist" traits such as aggression, intimidation, control, and being sexually demanding. Got to cut them some slack. That's their culture, and cultural bias is a form of racism. White women are also less likely to dump minority guys. Even if some of the disadvantaged minority guys behave in sexist ways, are jobless, or are abusive, white women will show tolerance. It's probably not their fault. They don't need any more intolerance in their lives. That's personal affirmative action—holding someone to a lower standard and feeling really good about yourself for it.

My first encounter with personal affirmative action was with Petra's Peruvian boyfriend during my disastrous visit to Montreal in 1977. At the time I didn't understand that Jorge was Petra's political validation of her personal crusade against imperialism and oppression. Years later I asked Petra what ever happened to Jorge. He left Montreal, but not before turning Petra into a mule. Yes, she actually agreed to smuggle cocaine out of Colombia for him. Even a small amount would help him financially. He described in detail how to get it across the border. Once she found a "reputable" dealer and bought the cocaine, she should cut the bottom of her toothpaste tube, squeeze out half the contents, then hide the coke inside and roll it back up. She followed his instructions and actually made it through customs, but when Jorge sampled the coke, he said it was no good and threw it out. Of course, it was Petra's financial loss. Not to mention the risk of a long prison sentence in Colombia or Canada.

Many times since then I've seen how white women will hold minority men to a lower standard of behavior as long as they're getting politically validated. But a relationship isn't about making a political statement to yourself or anyone. At least it shouldn't be.

Over time I've come to realize what an ideological challenge it was for Petra to maintain a relationship with an American "oppressor." One time in Munich we ran into a couple of her lesbian feminist friends at a flea market. They asked where I was from. From the look of shock on their faces you'd think I was a war criminal. "Oh, he's American," mumbled one of them stoically. Petra stood there cowering with embarrassment, realizing she had just lost credibility with her important dyke friends. My God, not only was Petra not a lesbian, she was with a Caucasian American. Word would certainly get out. What a disaster.

Why does Petra tolerate intolerance when it's directed at me? And by the way, I've been called a "kraut lover," but not by anyone I would consider a friend. If someone made a negative comment about a girl I was with because she was German, I'd tell them to go fuck themselves. I would have appreciated the same courtesy from Petra.

Don't worry, I get the message. I'm the white male oppressor. I must be punished, scorned, and scolded. I'm the one keeping everyone down. Several years ago at the annual Folk Music Festival in Kerrville, Texas, a white guy from South Africa got on stage with an acoustic guitar and performed a song he wrote. It was about how bad the white people have been in South Africa, and he wanted to give white people the opportunity to apologize to all the black people for it, even though there were no black people in the audience. Well, I doubt many people in the audience had ever been to South Africa, nor had they done anything to harm black South Africans. Or black anybody. Nevertheless, all were invited to join in and sing the chorus together.

I'm sorry I'm a white person. I'm sorry, I'm sorry
I'm sorry for the things I've done, I'm sorry, I'm sorry

A few "white persons" actually joined in. Please, indulge yourselves. Think of me what you will. Just don't expect me to sing along.

The New Hostile Workplace

In relationships, a woman's self-worth is constantly elevated above a man's, like a habitual courtesy. Got to buy her stuff, tell her she's smarter, more important. Suddenly, that's what women want in the workplace. Forget equality. They want their corporate self-worth unconditionally recognized as a higher priority than we lowly generic males. They want bigger salaries, faster promotions, and more personal time off. They want their relationship perks carried over into corporate life. Their own happiness and prosperity should be assured. Criticism is verbal abuse. They want corporate chivalry. And just like in relationships, they're never satisfied.

I'm not sure why men should be expected to welcome women into their work environments. With the enforcement of affirmative action and the nebulous threat of sexual harassment charges, we find ourselves in an immediately hostile situation. Why should we be expected to embrace impediments to our careers? The growth of female privilege and the suppression of criticism have created new occupational job hazards for men. It's called "leveling the playing field," but really it's an attempt to change the scoring system. Women use affirmative action to help them succeed, then talk about how much adversity they've had to overcome in the male-dominated world.

As men we are taught that we should be willing to make sacrifices for the good of women. We should not hesitate to risk our own safety or even lay down our lives so that women may endure. But the context has always been related to the physical protection of women. Now we are expected to sacrifice our careers so that women may succeed. We have become political cannon fodder for the benefit of the feminist agenda. It's always been our role to be casualties for the benefit of others. It's also been our role to shut up and take it like men.

Adventures in Social Engineering

I recently saw a report about female smokejumpers presented by National Geographic's *Ultimate Explorer*. It was a whole hour of Lisa Ling raving about how well the female firefighters were performing. There was plenty of time, so why couldn't I get my questions answered? Were there any "targets" for the number of females to be hired? Were any performance standards "gender-normed" to allow less capable females to be hired over males? I saw a female recruit slowly drag heavy gear during a fitness test, but she was given unlimited time. Why? Were qualifications tailored to guarantee female inclusion? Does pay reflect actual contribution? Are there special gender privileges reserved for females? Do females get menstruation leave? If not, how do they cope?

Of course, the *Ultimate Explorer* show did not examine any of this. I already know the answers to some of these questions, but I'd like more specifics. I don't think menstruation qualifies as such a taboo subject any more since we get those explicit tampon commercials thrown in our face every 15 minutes. If we can watch endless demonstrations of wings and applicators and leakage, we can know if female smokejumpers get special menstrual rights.

According to the report, all the men on the team were completely supportive of the weaker female firefighters. Could they express concern if they wanted? Could they stand up and say, "We do a lot more work than the women, so why aren't we paid more?" No, they can't. Questioning gender propaganda can get you fired. Are the men at risk for sexual harassment charges if they catch a glimpse a female taking a leak in the woods? Are men allowed to use profanity in the presence of females, or can they be reprimanded for that too?

I've read elsewhere that female firefighters are in fact *not* well accepted by their male co-workers. Why would there be hidden resentment by male firefighters? Maybe it's because men cannot openly express their frustrations. Will this ever get reported by the media? Probably not anytime soon. Certainly not by Lisa Ling. I just wanted to form my opinion about the female smokejumpers, but the *Ultimate Explorer* program was produced to make me reach each spoon-fed conclusion. Women are every bit as capable as men. The female smokejumpers aren't just fighting fires, they're fighting sexism.

They're heroines changing the world. Women triumph again. It's feminism masquerading as journalism.

How about a reality check? According to an AP report on 3/17/2002, only 28 of New York City's 11,400 firefighters are female. The city so far refuses to lower strength standards. I read that in Melbourne, Australia, the handful of women firefighters are demanding that standards not be gender-normed for them. I respect that. But are they as willing as men to accept risk and injury in an extreme crisis situation? And there's still that menstrual issue no one will talk about.

I support social engineering only when it is used to eliminate itself. I say, feed women "equality of results" until they gag on it. If we can't have equal justice, then injustice needs to be applied equally. If we are to give preference to lesser qualified women over more qualified men in the name of equal opportunity, then less capable female soldiers should be doing equal amounts of killing and dying in combat.

There are a number of reasons why this will never happen. One problem is that women can always get out of military service by becoming pregnant and going on maternity leave. Yes, I've read how an unusually high percentage of U.S. servicewomen got pregnant prior to their deployment during the 2003 Iraq war. Another problem is that the public will always insist on extra protection for women.

Nor do I trust the media to report it when women avoid taking risks or fail in combat. The media will always exaggerate female accomplishments and portray women's lives as more valuable than men's. If a cute female soldier is killed in active combat, she gets a five-minute obituary on the national news. It is an obscene double standard that men get so little credit. Society still can't accept that it is *not* worse for a cute girl to take a bullet than it is for some generic guy. Perhaps our reliance on military intervention would be tempered if we knew our attractive young women would be the ones thrown directly into the vortex of war.

But if equality of results is what women want, let them try it. So far, the only women in active combat roles are those who volunteer. And they get handed the sanitized killing, done from far away. Let's require women to engage in street-to-street combat the same as men. I just hope they have *entire female divisions* so that men don't have to die rescuing them. Segregated divisions would also help prevent so many female soldiers from becoming pregnant. Maybe we could spike their diet drinks with progesterone. Obviously, the military would have to lift the ban on lesbian sex. And a segregated military would prevent allegations of sexual harassment or rape from eroding morale. No more gender-normed affirmative action female commanders ordering men to hold their ground. Send entire female divisions into battle and see how they fare.

Whenever things get tough, why do women have all the options and men all the obligations? Let's require women to register for the draft, and draft them in equal numbers to men. Currently, men who do not register can be fined up to $250,000 and imprisoned for up to five years. Men who do not register can also be denied federal student loans and federal jobs. Women face no such penalties. State universities now require male students to provide proof that they have registered for selective service as a prerequisite for admission.

Oh, but women are the ones obligated to have children, so shouldn't they be exempt from a military draft? If that's the case, we should be able to conscript women into childbearing. I wonder how they would like it if they were lined up naked for physical exams and selected at the will of the government to be impregnated? They would become pregnant via government-approved sperm two or three times before being released from service. Even that would be better than getting shot.

There are bills pending in Congress that call for the inclusion of women in selective service and compulsory national service programs. House Bill H.R.163, introduced in 2003, would require both men and women to register with the selective service system, and for both to serve two years of compulsory national service. However, the President may step in and decide that female draftees will serve only in civilian rather than military capacities. This is an obvious escape hatch for women to avoid facing any danger. They get to spare themselves the trauma of war and acquire marketable skills in their safe support positions. Given the huge block of female voters, it is unlikely that any bill calling for female conscription will pass. Oh yeah, that's why the Equal Rights Amendment failed too. It's all coming back to me.

Some of the more radical feminists are perfectly happy to send women (other than themselves) into battle to die. Not for their country, but to become martyrs for the sisterhood. But the women-firsters are happy to sit back quietly and let people like Elaine Donnelly (of the Center for Military Readiness) win political battles to keep women out of the draft and combat roles. They consider it unfair to expose women to such risks. Apparently, it's worse for a woman to get raped than for a man to get an arm or leg shot off. It's more of that selective equality. They prefer that men retain their traditional gender roles when it comes to being designated killers and risk takers. So much for "equality of results."

So if men will forever be the ones designated to fight in wars and die and get our limbs shot off, what does that earn us? It means that we shouldn't use social engineering to force the inclusion of women in any occupations. It means that since it's acceptable that nearly all combat deaths and injuries are inflicted upon men, then it should also be acceptable that nearly all corporate CEOs are also men. It means if innate aggression makes men better soldiers, then innate aggression can also make us better leaders of nations. It means if men are more competitive, then we should expect more men to be in government than women. It means let the numbers fall where they may. It means we do not owe women *anything*. If anything, they owe *us*. Let us be done with all selective social engineering.

The Fairer Sexism

If one gender is better suited for something, why can't we acknowledge it? Why can't teenage boys come over from Europe to work as au pairs? Because they would suck at it. We could provide them with special training to get them up to speed, but what's the point? Who would actually want them? Guess I can say *that*.

So what does the phrase "equal work for equal pay" mean? To men it means if a woman does the same work as a man in the same time, she should get the same pay. To women it means women should be allowed to work at the same jobs as men and receive the same pay, but without the workload itself being quantified. A good example of this would be professional women's tennis, where prominent female athletes are demanding the same prize money as men. Sure, it's the same job description, but they only play the best of 3 sets instead of 5. I realize that men are physically stronger and play better, but are female athletes also conceding that they have less endurance than men? I've always heard they can kick our asses in aerobics. Why is there no discussion of this topic? It's because we've all been conditioned to disregard lower performance levels by females. This conditioning is now prevalent throughout Western culture.

Why do women's groups continue to insist there is a "wage gap"? In June 2004 the latest cause for alarm was sounded by the feminist think-tank, "The Institute for Women's Policy Research," claiming that "women in their prime earning years make 38 cents for every dollar that men earn." Such conclusions are only possible by the constant evasion of certain realities. For example, a study by the General Accounting Office in 2003 found that men work 2,147 hours a year compared to 1,675 hours for women, but this is not taken into account by the "median" income always cited in these studies. Warren Farrell devoted an entire book to the topic. *Why Men Earn More*, now available, explains how women now make *more money* than men for the same work.

As part of equality in the workplace, women want to be exempted from any physical requirements they cannot meet, without it affecting their pay. They want to be able to call in some generic guy to do the heavy lifting, or to prevent women from being in a position of risk. Feminists call it "comparable worth." I call it "men getting dicked over."

I was in a giant hardware store recently and saw two clerks working together, one male and one female. They both were wearing lifting braces, but when the female clerk needed something lifted, she called over the male clerk who immediately did the lifting for her. Most likely they had the same job description and pay, but it's become institutionalized to ignore greater contributions by men. Women are "considered" equal. It's just like in the military, where women are promoted to positions of authority over men without having to take equal risks. Why isn't it a policy violation when men are discriminated against? Can we at least rename "Equal Opportunity Employer" to something like "Preferential Treatment for Women Employer?"

Let me guess what will happen at the hardware store. Since the female employee cannot lift as well, she will be promoted and become the guy's manager and earn a higher salary. If she lacks home maintenance or management skills, it won't matter because the company needs the numbers to avoid discrimination lawsuits. Besides, the company will spring for her management training. They guy will be stuck doing heavy lifting at a low wage.

Encounters with Corporate Feminism

I've worked for lots of managers of both sexes in my computer career. I don't automatically prefer male managers, but I know there are differences to consider. Rather than writing an entire book on the subject, I'll summarize. Male managers treat people like soldiers, female managers treat people like children. Female managers bring pies and cookies to meetings, male managers bring nothing. Male managers offer you beer to work overtime, female managers offer you candy, and to really, really like you. Oh, and one more thing. I cannot have a realistic discussion about the negative impact of anti-male policies on my career with a female manager.

The New Hostile Workplace

I was at IBM in 1990 when a woman was promoted, becoming our new third line manager. That means she probably had 80 to 100 employees in her organization, most of them male. She was obviously very proud of her new position in command of so many men. During her "welcome" talk she announced that as a woman she would do a few things differently. "For one thing," she said sternly, "if I hear of any men cheating on their wives, I personally guarantee you will be outta here!" Huh? What made her think that was any of her damn business? No, it was *not* a light quip. Dead serious. I wasn't even married and I was offended. I wanted to raise my hand and ask if it was still okay to cheat on girlfriends. I think that incident revealed something about what women want out of all this. They want their own biases validated as superior to other people's biases.

Corporate feminists no longer make people call them "Ms" or "correct" men who use the word "girl." They never call men "pigs" or "male chauvinists" anymore. That would blow their cover. Corporate feminists have gone undercover. They're quietly taking over management and human resources departments, and deciding who will be hired and laid off according to the principles of political correctness. They decide when to mandate more "sensitivity training." Corporate feminism has become invisible, like a secret branch of the occult plotting the demise of politically incorrect men. If you are a man supporting a wife and kids, they may cut you some slack. Single males are expendable. So are young flirtatious females who may threaten feminist control over men. I'm sure they will do their best to get rid of any "cheating bastards." They've just learned not to announce it as official policy. Covert feminism is the foundation of the new hostile workplace.

Sexual harassment has evolved into a silent threat against men. It's no longer limited to actual sexual comments or actions. It's also about disagreement with affirmative action and "equal opportunity" policies. It's anything that might possibly even *annoy* a female. I think we need sensitivity training to teach women the difference between being sexually harassed, and sexually annoyed, and sexually frustrated.

One time at IBM, I ended up working in a test lab with a very flirty young co-op student. She had discovered a bug in my code, and I was using her lab machine to do problem determination. Sure, she was sexy and fun. After introducing herself, she stood over the floor fans and let her skirt fly up like Marilyn Monroe. Great stuff. Thirty minutes later I was sitting at the computer working when her female manager burst angrily into the lab and demanded to know what business I had there.

"I'm debugging a problem, why?" Obviously, she assumed I was sexually harassing the young female student. I had to explain exactly what the problem was and why I was using the girl's machine. Upset that I had a valid reason to be in the lab, she stormed off without apologizing.

I had another female manager who sent humor via e-mail to the mostly male department. Every few weeks there would be something along the lines of why women are smarter than men. Of course, she never sent out anything questioning the intelligence of women. The jokes were the same old recycled material from the last 20 years. Women still seem to love it. And it's not that any of the jokes offended me. I can definitely take it. What I can't take is the hypocrisy. Anti-female e-mails can get you reprimanded by HR. Male managers would never send out a list of reasons why men are smarter than women to an all-female staff. And I know her anti-male jokes were not just in fun. They were a red flag indicating her hostility toward men and her willingness to act on it. Yes, as a matter of fact, she's divorced.

I actually got called into a manager's office once and was informed a female employee was considering filing a sexual harassment complaint against me. He asked if I had any idea who it might be. In a moment of brilliance I responded, "I have no idea, it could be anyone." Nothing came of it. No charges were filed, and I never found out who complained. I wonder if I could have filed a complaint against a female co-worker of mine at IBM who wrapped up a tampon and gave it to me as a gift in front of the office gang? No, it was not in fun.

Corporate feminists express their hostility in some bizarre ways. There was one woman at IBM who insisted on knitting during technical meetings. She had big upside down glasses, short formless hair, and multiple chins. Though only in her mid-thirties, she wore grandma-style clothes. I couldn't tell if she was a radical lesbian or just an angry asexual man-hater. During a document review, she continued defiantly knitting while going over each paragraph, never missing a loop. I think she was trying to make some kind of statement, probably having something to do with the patriarchy or men being jerks. Her knitting was angry and aggressive, almost obsessive. She looked cross, as if daring anyone to comment on it. I wonder what would have happened if I brought in some yarn and started knitting just to mock her. I think I would have ended up with a knitting needle in the trachea.

Just like in relationships, women expect to get away with more crap than men at their places of employment. Their own bad behavior is cute and fun whereas men's is sexist and insensitive. I know a girl at

IBM who had a "penis calendar" up in her office for months. It had close-up photographs of penises from various statues in Italy. No one ever complained. Then a guy brought a little "condom tree" into his office and got a complaint the next day from an offended female, and he had to remove it. It's the differing standards for different genders that I find so disturbing. Should I have retaliated and complained about that girl's penis calendar then? No, that would make me a pussy. Besides, I was the one who gave it to her.

Riding with Guys in Trucks

It was another day of listening to the lab guys at Compaq describe in graphic detail what objects might be inserted into one's anus, with an occasional foray into subjects such as "getting your salad tossed" and speculations as to who might be having sex with goats. It was time for lunch, and they invited me along. Not wanting to miss out on any of their creativity, I accepted.

Six of us piled into someone's huge truck and headed out. They gave me "shotgun," the position of high honor. Two minutes out of the parking lot, the guys spotted a cute girl in a car. "Hey, pull up beside her!" called out someone. *Oh jeez, not this,* I thought. But I was in no position to stop it. In fact, as occupier of the shotgun seat, I was obligated to help disturb this attractive girl who was in her car, minding her own damn business. I would be the person to whom she would be displaying her middle finger. Not good.

I've never been one to harass women or be overtly aggressive. I know they don't like moronic comments and gestures. I'm very aware that the male libido is disgusting to women. Unless they're drunk and lonely. Otherwise, leave them the fuck alone. They've had it with us and our primitive need for constant sexual attention.

We pulled up right beside her car and the guys honked and waved and hollered. I was ready to receive the obscene gesture of her choosing. Instead, she looked up delighted and waved back at us as. Huge smile. Amazing. Guess we got lucky with her. But that just encouraged the guys to look for more girls in cars to honk at. Must we press our luck? We must. A couple miles later we came to the next car with the next cute girl. We honked and waved and hollered. Same thing. She was delighted and waved enthusiastically back. It was like we made her day. I thought women hated moronic antics like that. Apparently, they don't get enough. With that I cleansed myself of yet another remnant of feminist indoctrination.

Attempts to Empower Women

Women are capable of achieving all kinds of things they normally relegate to the male realm, if they want to. But how do you want to? I've never figured that one out. Women have been sent the message they must invade the male realm to prove that women are just as good as men. They're not supposed to be satisfied having babies any more. They're off like soldiers with their commands. There are a lot of women who need to stop trying to be feminist flag bearers and become the child bearers they would rather be.

Feminism has become an art form for many women, an expression of desire to do something or be something without actually doing it or being it. Petra has a hundred empowering, feminist, and self-help books on her shelf, assuring her she can do anything; but she doesn't have a single book about automobile maintenance or computers. She didn't learn to drive until she was 33. The most capable women I know are not feminists. They are people who know how to think for themselves.

Talking about the positive changes brought about by the women's movement sounds like propaganda to me now. I've been so hit over the head by it all. They've been too busy raising everyone's consciousness to raise their own. But there has been progress in women's rights. Women were not seen as capable in many fields. The doors were closed to them in many occupations. Changes needed to happen and did—30 or 40 years ago. So, why am I still treated as an oppressor? I continue to believe in women in spite of their assaults on my intelligence.

Feminism has never helped women be anything other than angry. It's become a think tank to generate eccentric complaints. Feminists never consider they might need to improve their own relationship skills. They never want more accountability. They don't look within themselves to see how they can become better people. Feminism is not for the common good. It's a vindictive girls' club that expects men to dance to their every whim.

Petra has always used anger as the justification to do whatever the hell she wants without regard to the impact of her actions on herself or anyone else. Empowerment in this case is another word for selfishness. Petra and millions like her have damaged their ability to have relationships. Angry women are totally convinced men are the problem and it's up to women to take control of men and make "corrections" as they deem necessary.

Apparently, violence and hate are also female empowerment. One of the early anger books was *The S.C.U.M. Manifesto* by lesbian feminist Valerie Solanas, published in 1968, the same year that she shot Andy Warhol. Feminists celebrate the book as classic literature. Solanas was included in Robin Morgan's 1970 feminist anthology *Sisterhood is Powerful*.

What does Valerie Solanas think of male sexuality?

> "Eaten up with guilt, shame, fears and insecurities and obtaining, if he's lucky, a barely perceptible physical feeling, the male is, nonetheless, obsessed with screwing; he'll swim through a river of snot, wade nostril-deep through a mile of vomit, if he thinks there'll be a friendly pussy awaiting him. He'll screw a woman he despises, any snaggle-toothed hag, and furthermore, pay for the opportunity. Why? Relieving physical tension isn't the answer, as masturbation suffices for that. It's not ego satisfaction; that doesn't explain screwing corpses and babies."

Come on, tell us what you really think.

> "Every man, deep down, knows he's a worthless piece of shit. Overwhelmed by a sense of animalism and deeply ashamed of it; wanting, not to express himself, but to hide from others his total physicality, total egocentricity, the hate and contempt he feels for other men, and to hide from himself the hate and contempt he suspects other men feel for him; having a crudely constructed nervous system that is easily upset by the least display of emotion or feeling, the male tries to enforce a `social' code that ensures perfect blandness, unsullied by the

slightest trace or feeling or upsetting opinion. He uses terms like `copulate', `sexual congress', `have relations with' (to men sexual relations is a redundancy), overlaid with stilted manners; the suit on the chimp."

This strikes me as a strange text to study. If there were such a thing as "Men's Studies," I doubt we would be studying the writings of Marc Lepine. If the name doesn't ring a bell, back in 1989 he was the angry lunatic who opened fire on a crowd at the L'Ecole Polytechnique in Montreal, killing 14 female students because he considered them feminists.

But feminist educators consider *The S.C.U.M. Manifesto* just a harmless example of militant feminism. Nothing for us wimps to get upset about. Andy Warhol nearly died of the gunshot wound, but poor Valerie had to serve three whole years for the assault. She checked in and out of several psychiatric centers beginning in 1973 before dying of lung disease in 1988.

There's a more recent 1998 book called *Quintessence*, by Mary Daly, the former Boston College professor who successfully prohibited men from attending her classes for 25 years. It takes place in 2048 after the gender wars have been won by women and the radical feminists like Dworkin, MacKinnon, and Brownmiller (as well as Daly herself) have been proven right about everything. Men have been nearly eliminated because their patriarchal system was waging "gynocide" against women. Daly doesn't describe exactly how the earth is to be "decontaminated" of men, so it must be some benign non-violent form of extermination. The same fate awaits female sympathizers who "refuse to release themselves from the phallocratic dependencies" of the old system. The pure lesbians create their own "gynocracy" and procreate using parthenogenesis. I feel all warm inside.

Anger is the poison of feminism. Anger is not really empowerment, it is just an easy way to emotionalize gender issues so that women can get really excited about them. And anger comes with limitations. Anger can harm, but it cannot heal. Anger can destroy, but it cannot create. Feminism isn't a philosophy, it's an asylum. It's a collection of angry women, each expressing her own individual psychosis.

The Metamorphosis of Molly

Molly was a goofy, cerebral blonde in her early 20s. Her mom was a radical Jehovah's Witness, so of course there had been constant religious fighting in her house growing up. Sounded a lot like my childhood.

Attempts to Empower Women

Just switch Jehovah's Witness for Christian Scientist and you have my mom. Finally there was someone who understood my experiences. Molly and I had both endured years of ideologically bizarre mothering. She was always facing her mother's threats to disown her if she did not become a Jehovah's Witness. My mother claimed the right to indoctrinate me, throwing the occasional tantrum if I did not cooperate.

Molly and I connected immediately. It was unstoppable. Too bad she lived out of state. She came and stayed with me for a couple of weeks that summer, but she was just passing through. She had a great sexual appetite. One time she asked me if I had any fantasies she could fulfill for me. I said, "How about sucking my dick while I read Friedrich Nietzsche?" Hey, I was just kidding; but, to my surprise, she agreed, "as long as it wasn't more than an hour." Suddenly, I was scrambling. Not actually having any Nietzsche around, I grabbed something by Kafka, and we began. Sorry Franz, but it just wasn't the same. I remember reading something about a guy waking up with too many legs before dropping the book on the floor. To be honest, that's probably the only way I'll ever get off on Nietzsche.

So, what ever happened to Molly? I didn't see her again for three years. She had thrown herself into the "womyn's" movement and made the transition to radical lesbian feminist. One day she stopped by with her "grrl" lover. They both had hideous quarter-inch-long butch haircuts. Even more disgusting was how fat and ugly her "grrl" lover was. Well, they can lick each other all they want, fine with me; but Jesus, are you tellin' me I couldn't compete with *that*? They must have done it in the dark. My disgust with their appearance probably validated their purely "emotional" relationship since being unattractive to men was part of the point. "Are you happy to see me?" Molly quipped. "It's interesting to see you," I quipped right back.

The Molly of old was not home. Just like her mom had been a whacked-out Jehovah's Witness, Molly was now off the deep end with her own self-imposed insanity. She and her mom turned out to be very much alike. They both chose philosophies that isolated them from family and friends, and they both committed to them religiously. They both embraced ideological exile. Molly announced that she and her "grrlfriend" were planning a trip to the Greek Isle of Lesbos. I swear I am not making this up. I never heard from Molly again. Congratulations goes out to all the Women's Studies departments across the country. Another success. Feminists measure success one miserable man at a time. Sounds like *I* need therapy, respond all the lesbian psychologists.

But that's what it takes to be a true orthodox feminist of the highest order. Lesbians are so unviolated by us lecherous males. They're ideological virgins. What better way to practice their anti-male theology? So by all means, be a lesbian, and if that's not for you, at least hate the men you love.

While pursuing her dream of becoming an orthodox feminist, Petra tried the lesbian thing, but it just didn't work for her. It strikes me as a strange way to deal with anger. Sure, women have infuriated me on occasion. I've taken plenty of their verbal abuse, their teasing, their vanity, their rejection, their unreliability, their ridicule. "Have fun dating your right hand!" But no one will ever convince me that sucking some guy's dick is the answer. I promise you, I will never be *that* angry at women.

The Anger Strategy

Not all women who get involved with feminism turn into lesbians. But all of them *do* become infused with anger. You don't believe me? Try disagreeing with them about anything. Feminists have an "anger strategy." Get mad at men, and men will cave. If that doesn't work, get really, *really* mad. When it comes to feminism and political correctness, there is no doubt how men are viewed. We are the hated ones.

When opposing these ideologues, be prepared to be called a whiner and oppressor and rapist and sexist and misogynist. Don't take it personally. Get used to it. When they say, "Get out of the way," they mean "Lay down so I can walk on you." When they call you a "woman hater," they mean "How dare you disagree with me?" Don't bother getting upset. Why waste the energy?

Funny what some women consider empowerment. Some women think having control over lots of men in a corporate environment is empowerment. Strippers think they are empowered because they are in control of their clients. The same is true of prostitutes. Empowerment is apparently the achievement of power over men, regardless of how that is accomplished. This reckless empowerment has no specific goal other than to control. The feminist version of empowerment means a woman getting her way, right or wrong, whichever way she wants. Anger justifies the means.

Petra's Big Secret

I'd known Petra probably 10 years when it happened. We were in downtown Munich, when we walked by a peep show. That raised the subject. She asked if I'd ever been in there. I said "No." I asked her if she had ever been a stripper or a prostitute. She told me she had worked as a nude model in Montreal to support herself. That wasn't what I asked her. Besides, I already knew about that. I repeated my question. She laughed and said, "Oh yeah, I go to work in the peep show right after I get out of church." I wasn't laughing. I said, "I asked you a real question, and I expect a real answer." She became stoic and turned away. She was hiding tears.

At that moment I knew. We had to stop and sit sown. I gave her a moment and said, "Tell me." "I don't know what to tell you," she said. "Tell me the truth. Have you ever been a prostitute?" Again, she turned away in silence. An entire minute went by with more tears. She finally summoned up a meager denial and threw her arms around me, crying. That's the last she ever mentioned it.

At first I thought I had it figured out. It must have been prostitution that drove Petra to feminism. Certainly this was the basis of Petra's anger toward men. I felt a sense of relief. Finally I understood her. Then I realized Petra was already into feminism when I met her. Prostitution must have come later.

It took a while, but I now see how the pieces fit together. There's only one time when it could have happened. It must have been when she was a 22-year-old Women's Studies major in Montreal. There's no way her job as a nude model in an art class could have earned her enough money to pay for food, rent, and tuition for three years. She also tried making jewelry, but that paid very little money.

Then there were those nude Polaroids Petra showed me during my visit to Montreal. She was getting ready to take them to some "modeling studios." These "agencies" didn't want headshots. I remember her telling me how she walked into a modeling agency with her nude snapshots and was embarrassed because all the other girls had portfolios. She had accidentally stumbled upon a legitimate agency. Did I mention how naïve I was at age 24? It never occurred to me what was about to go down. I thought she just needed a professional portfolio.

For whatever reason, the Women's Studies program was vitally important to Petra. She used the empowerment excuse to finance it. The "modeling" money would be used to further the cause of feminism. Why not exploit men's carnal desires for the positive good of women? It fit in with the feminism of the time. During the 1970s many feminists were calling for the legalization of prostitution to "give women control of their own bodies." That way prostitutes could organize and demand benefits such as health care. Remember? It was all about choices. That was before writers like Dworkin declared prostitution and pornography forms of slavery forced upon women by male oppressors.

So it turned out to be the opposite of what I originally thought. It was feminism that drove Petra into prostitution. What a great way to fight male oppression. Have sex with men for money. Yeah, that'll teach the bastards to respect women. That'll teach them not to look at women as objects. Of all the reasons for a woman to rent out her body, that had to be *the lamest ever*. That's why Petra can't talk about it. She knows she's an ideological fraud.

I recall that devastating remark she made to me in Montreal after declining to have sex with me. She told me if I wanted sex I should "just go to a prostitute." It all finally made sense. Those personal escorts come from somewhere. I'd lost my ability to love her years before, but I still had my ability to care. Caring apparently means believing her lies. I couldn't hold it against her for lying to me. After all, I had just lied to her that I'd never been in the peep show. And whoring oneself out is not the worst thing a girl can do. Petra's episode with prostitution will traumatize her only if someone finds out. Slavery it was not. I think it's likely she enjoyed it. The Women's Studies program itself would have a far more devastating impact on her life.

Petra's Big Lie

A few years later Petra empowered herself again. I was in Munich so I stopped by to say hello. I knew what to expect of her by that time and knew she wanted a child, so I asked her if she was pregnant. She was. In fact, the tests had just come back, and I was the first person to find out. Not even her boyfriend knew. I got the straight story before she had a chance to construct the fictional version. Her 40-year-old boyfriend was divorced and already had three children from his first marriage and didn't want more. He could barely afford child support and lived alone in a small apartment. None of this mattered to Petra. She had a plan.

She went off the pill without informing him. She thought since she was already 36 it would take a few tries, so she wanted to get started. She figured there was no need to tell the guy she was off the pill because she would take *complete responsibility* for the child if she got pregnant. It was her idea alone, she said. She would not ask for his help at all. It wouldn't be fair, since he didn't want more children. She would raise the kid by herself. After all, a father is only necessary as a means of financial support, and she wouldn't need him for that. Her practice in holistic medicine would cover it. She wouldn't even ask for assistance from the government. Petra got knocked up on the first try. I asked her why she would choose a man to father her child who didn't want children. What right did she have to deliberately go against his wishes? Why had she not even asked me? I may have been willing to contribute more than just the required raw material. She responded in the same way as all women when confronted with their selfish and ir-responsible behavior. She cried. I never felt so free, being able to walk away from the impending dilemma.

In the letters I received from her that year, she described how furi-ous the guy was. I don't know exactly how she spinned it, but it must have been clear to him that her pregnancy was the result of a deliber-ate act. He refused to speak to her again. By this time, Petra had her official story ready. She had completely forgotten about the total re-sponsibility she was going to assume. Now she was angry at him for not wanting to acknowledge he had "fathered" the child. She put his name on the birth certificate and forced him to pay child support. The pregnancy had been "unexpected," and what an awful man he was for not wanting to be a part of his child's life. "How can men do that?" she asked. She was also getting some kind of aid from the German government, which she complained was not enough.

I was disgusted with Petra and considered her persona non grata, and threw out all her letters. But after a few years, curiosity got the bet-ter of me. I was in Munich so I decided to stop by. I met her daughter Gabrielle, who was simply adorable. My anger toward Petra was tem-pered by this playful 4-year-old child. She had never met her father. "Haven't heard from you in a long time. You must be scared of me now that I have a kid," Petra said. "Let's get one thing straight," I told her. "I'm not scared of your kid, I'm scared of you!" Who knows what the hell will happen next time Petra decides to become "empowered."

I recalled Petra's own definition of rape from that summer when she was debating me nonstop on feminist issues. "Rape" was performing any sexual act without the consent of the woman. So how about if a woman performs a sexual act without the consent of the man? What she did to her boyfriend fits that definition. She deliberately impreg-nated herself *against his will*. But sperm stealing is not yet officially a crime. In fact, the guy gets a monthly bill for it. At times Petra is so nice and caring that I forget she committed rape to start her family. Sure, that was a long time ago, but she continues to support herself through financial rape. There is no running away from this.

Am I betraying Petra by revealing her secrets? At some point I had my own Clark Gable moment and frankly, I don't give a damn. All I'm doing is writing about what happened. She's the one who deceived a man and caused him to become a father against his will. She's the one who has denied a child a father. Why should I be concerned about protecting her feelings? I'm tired of remaining politely silent. I *will* speak my mind. What went around has come around. It is time for male empowerment.

The
Culture of
Female Pathology

In case you hadn't noticed, women have become hostile toward men. I'm sure they always have been, but the recent anger shown by women is much more defined. The masses of Western women have all been salted with varying degrees of feminist anger. Women seem unaware of it, but feminism has damaged them far more than it has helped them. Feminist anger has created an environment hostile to relationships and professional life. An obscure word has recently come to the fore. Unfortunately, it's needed in our vocabulary. "Misandry" is the hatred of men by women. It has far exceeded its more famous counterpart, "misogyny."

Since discriminatory laws have been changed in the U.S., Europe, Australia, and Canada to ensure women's rights and independence, women ought to be celebrating their accomplishments. They have far surpassed anything imagined by those first-wave feminists. But there's a problem. Even though those unjust laws are long gone, there's still a huge infrastructure of women's organizations and professional feminists in need of employment. They can't just keep turning over rocks looking for oppression forever. Now what? Besides demanding more and more privileges, feminists on the cutting edge have come up with a creative new agenda to keep all the women's commissions, women's organizations, and Women's Studies departments staffed and plenty busy.

Feminists have gone from targeting laws that they don't like to targeting male characteristics they don't like. The whole focus of feminism has shifted from the accumulation of privilege to an ideological assault on evil "masculinities." These include traits such as aggression, dominance, violence, sexual intimidation, and having a penis.

These "masculinities" are the cause of the universal oppression and rape of women. The radical feminists who control the direction of feminism see the concept of being a man as pathological, which justifies their attempts to re-engineer boys as well as their own contempt of men. They would like to make "masculinity" illegal. Put all men in one big jail. Call it crime prevention.

Although generic feminist anger has been smoldering for over a century, I suspect it really got nasty with the achievement of new depths of hatred in books such as *Woman Hating* by Andrea Dworkin. By the 1980s it had become fashionable for women to truly, madly, and deeply hate all men. In her 1980 book *Pornography*, Dworkin dredges up all the violent images she can and uses them to characterize masculinity and heterosexuality. Her books are detailed and exceedingly well-documented exercises in the unrestrained hatred of men. Dworkin's writings have been endorsed by many leading feminists including Kate Millett, Susan Brownmiller, and Gloria Steinem. These excerpts from *Pornography* illustrate how the book is more about justifying the hatred of men than it is about porn:

> "Marriage is an institution developed from rape as a practice."

> "The penis must embody the violence of the male in order for him to be male. Violence is male; the male is the penis; violence is the penis or the sperm ejaculated from it. What the penis can do it must do forcibly for a man to be a man."

> "the Nazis created a new standard of masculinity..."

It's as if all men would enjoy being Nazis and witch burners and violent rapists if we were just man enough to follow through on it. In her more recent introduction from 1989, Dworkin equates Nazi propaganda with pornography. She describes a Goebbels propaganda film in which victims are strangled with wire, and *can't resist* informing us that this causes erection in the male victims. I would ask, who is being dehumanized in this book?"

The view that violence is innately male is accepted as gospel by feminists. It's their justification for sending men to war. "Men start wars so they should have to fight them." Saying that men have a greater propensity for violence is like saying Asians are better at math. It's like saying black people are criminals by nature because more of them are in prison. It's an indication of how highly feminists regard their own biases. What happened to that "social construction" theory they like so much?

The Culture of Female Pathology

The assertion that masculinity itself is pathological is a huge miscalculation by feminism. Men have always been the ones forced into environments that require violence and destruction to solve problems for the good of society. Whether it be for hunting, protecting the innocent from attackers, or warfare to defend their own civilization, men are the ones called upon to cause harm for the good of others. It follows that men are more frequently the ones to become pathological, enjoying the pain and agony they inflict, because they are valued for it. Women placed in such environments will also engage in pathological behavior, as we have seen in the Abu Ghriab prison photos. And in Beslan, Russia, where children were taken hostage and killed, some of the "gunmen" weren't men at all, they were the "Black Widows of Chechnya." The irony is that feminism itself has become increasingly pathological. It is the infliction of harm upon men for ideological gratification.

There are other more recent "mainstream" feminist books such as Marilyn French's slightly one-sided 1992 book, *The War Against Women*. It's one of those obligatory primers for new feminist recruits. It was French who declared in her previous work, *The Women's Room*, that "All men are rapists and that's all they are." *The War Against Women* is really a personal declaration of war against men. It's more scholarly evidence that women are victims and men are patriarchal oppressors. Women are saints and men are barbarians. It's justification of gender hatred and anger. Apparently, the injustices men experience are trivial, and our own fault.

> "Men's need to dominate women may be based in their own sense of marginality or emptiness."

> "Even a woman who accepts the status of obedient dog or brood cow has capacities for independent thought, action, speech, and creativity that militate against easy consignment of her to inferior status. To suppress these qualities, men must ally solidly against women, creating institutions that foreclose all roles to women except breeder-servanthood, thrust them into and keep them in the position of subhuman inferiors."

> "While men strut and fret their hour upon the stage, shout in bars and sports arenas, thump their chests or show their profiles in the legislatures, and explode incredible weapons in an endless contest for status, an obsessive quest for symbolic 'proof' of their superiority, women quietly keep the world going."

"...it is not necessary to beat up a woman to beat her down. A man can simply refuse to hire women in well-paid jobs, extract as much or more work from women than men but pay them less, or treat women disrespectfully at work or at home. He can fail to support a child he has engendered, demand the woman he lives with wait on him like a servant. He can beat or kill the woman he claims to love; he can rape women, whether mate, acquaintance, or stranger; he can rape or sexually molest his daughters, nieces stepchildren, or the children of a woman he claims to love. *The vast majority of men in the world do one or more of the above.*" (emphasis is author's)

Disregarding calls from within feminism for the elimination of all men, French apparently believes it is men who want to exterminate women.

"Some women today believe that men are well on their way to exterminating women from the world through violent behavior and oppressive policies."

"Now new reproductive technologies can make women obsolete, and the laboratory will become a new locus of violence against women."

That's odd, in 2004 Tomohiro Kono produced a living mouse using a sperm-free technique. Also, Dr. Orly Lacham-Kaplan of Monash University, Melbourne, has demonstrated with mice how it is possible to fertilize eggs without sperm. She explained this means lesbian couples can give birth to a baby girl without the need for a father. It's that "parthenogenesis" they've all been waiting for.

Headlines throughout the world have touted this research in a wonderfully anti-male way. Science writer Leigh Dayton of *The Australian* wrote in her article "Of mice and useless men" that the experiment proves that "males are a biological frill." The gay news rag *The Advocate* said "Look Ma, No Heteros," and the UK tabloid *The Sun* proclaimed "Men Are Useless." Starting to feel better, Marilyn?

Furthermore, Marilyn French offers indisputable proof that women do almost all of the work in the world. I've seen this quote up in several women's offices.

"The statistics presented at the United Nations Conference on Women in Copenhagen in 1980 remain true today: women do between two-thirds and three-quarters of the work in the world."

The Culture of Female Pathology

It makes me wonder though, if women do so much more work, then why are all the daytime television shows produced for female viewers? And did women construct these cities we live in? Who invented everything? Oh well, if statistics are "presented at the United Nations," they must be true, right? I suppose we should just take Marilyn's word on it. After all, she has a degree from Harvard.

I think I know who stole feminism. With writings such as these, feminism became the science of hating men. Perhaps I should use the official term "gender feminism," but I think "pathological feminism" is more accurate. "Gender feminism" is too ambiguous—and too kind. Even "radical feminism" is vague. I would encourage all women who do not hate men to abandon the term "feminism" altogether. It cannot represent equality. Feminism has earned all the extremely negative connotations associated with it. The word itself suggests favoring one gender over another. Even "equity feminism" is an oxymoron.

The "gender feminists" and the "equity feminists" are still struggling over some fundamental issues. In which ways should men be subservient to women? Should men be allowed to serve in the traditional roles of protector, provider, and worshipper? Or should the role of men be limited to the bare essentials such as construction and sperm donation? Should women beat men down and take everything they have, or be nice to them and take everything they have? If men are healthy and fit, they will have more stuff for women to take; but the bastards deserve to be punished. What a quandary.

Women may love us individually, but they hate us collectively. This is why so many women want to both marry us and make our lives hell. Men are bad and must be punished. Frequently. And since women cannot punish men collectively, they punish us individually for the perceived transgressions of the many. The concept of collective male punishment has developed into a culture. Ours is a culture of female pathology.

Even the masses of women who have little specific knowledge of feminism have absorbed its pathology. They're angry, but not for any specific reasons they can think of. Well, other than that men are lying, cheating pigs who won't do what they're told. They've gotten the message that men are sub-human, and that women should be given more stuff for having to suffer our indignities. We are inundated with the promotion of pathological feminism in the media. It is the celebration of all things female in conjunction with ridicule of all things male. It's not that men are above ridicule. On the contrary, I believe all people should be equally ridiculed.

Every positive goal promoted by the "women's movement" has a corresponding negative for men. Otherwise it would be called the "people's movement." Reward women and punish men. Empower women and weaken men. Promote women and denigrate men. Feminists don't just want inclusion of women, they want to displace men in the best careers. The only equality they have in mind for men is that they want all men to fail equally. Many women who support "feminism" are thinking only of the positives, as if the negatives do not exist. They don't understand that men are not against the positives. As men we only experience the negatives of feminism.

Get Out of the Way!

Girls raised according to the "It's all about me" philosophy expect guys to clear a path for them. The princesses are *not* to be encumbered. That holds true in both professional life and crosswalks. I don't go to Austin's entertainment district that much, but when I do, girls in SUVs keep threatening to run me down for having the audacity to legally cross the street in front of them. It's happened twice in the last six months now. At Congress and 4th, I waited until the "walk" indicator lit up, then proceeded. An SUV driven by a cute blonde came around the corner and stopped three feet from me and honked. "Get out of the way!" she shouted. "I have the right of way!" I responded standing defiantly in front of her. More honking. "Come on, run over me," I dared her. She yelled some gender-based obscenities. Traffic was backing up, so I relented as the blonde screeched past. A guy standing there shook his head and said, "That was unbelievable." It happened again the last time I went downtown. A different cute blonde in another SUV came around the corner of Congress and 5th as I was crossing the street with the light. She jerked the car to a stop and honked, so I asked, "What?" "We're in an intersection here!" she replied impatiently. She took off around me before I could ask her if she was familiar with pedestrian traffic rules. The feminist catchphrase "Get out of the way" is no longer just a figure of speech. The new female empowerment is ugliness with a pretty face.

There are very few American women who are uncontaminated by pathological feminism from school or the media. Women have learned they can be total bitches because there are tons of guys with adequately low self-esteem who will line up for their share of female verbal and financial abuse. A girl I know recently got married. At the

altar, she responded to the big question with "I suppose so." Her father stood up and told her he didn't come all this way to hear her say
that. She relented and said, "Okay, I do." The groom just stood there
and took it. Yeah, cute girl. Congratulations.

The "me first" mentality is firmly grounded in American women
and ruthlessly carried out. In how many ways can women express
their displeasure with the male gender? I made a tally. I'm sure I've
missed several. Want to meet someone new? As a man, you may be
dealing with a lot of the following female attitudes, which may not be
immediately apparent.

- Every male achievement is inadequate or unimportant, especially
  after marriage. Men are permanently inadequate. No amount of
  achievement will change this. Men do not have any obstacles to
  overcome like women, so a man's success is not really significant.
- Men are inadequate to fulfill a woman's needs. Male contributions to a relationship are inadequate, obviously, since women are
  never fully satisfied. Men need to listen better to what women are
  telling them, so that they can meet women's needs. It is no longer
  the role of women to satisfy men's needs.
- A man needs a woman to succeed, but hey, a woman don't need
  no man to succeed! You've heard the saying: behind every successful man is a woman. Somehow the opposite is not true. Successful women do it on their own in spite of men. As men we have
  to help women, but not because they need our help.
- Women have to try harder than men to earn success. If men succeed it is not because of hard work and study, but because society automatically hands men success. Women have to fight all the
  discrimination of the world and succeed in spite of everyone.
- We are inadequate in bed. According to women, we don't know
  what we are doing sexually. As with everything, men assume the
  blame. If a man doesn't climax, there's something wrong with him.
  If she doesn't climax, he's not doing it right. There wasn't enough
  foreplay, they tell us days later. We can't even lick them right.
- Men cannot be trusted. Men need female supervision to perform
  any task, to remain faithful, to make correct decisions. Women
  need to track a man's every activity. Men who do this to women
  are called obsessive control freaks.
- Women can do no wrong; they are always justified in whatever
  they've done. That's because women let their emotions guide

them. Men must get female approval for everything. If men cheat, it's because men are hormone-driven morons that do not appreciate good women. If women cheat, it's because men are hormone-driven morons that do not appreciate good women.

- Women do not need to apologize for anything, since nothing is their fault. Whatever they did, they had no choice. Men should apologize for questioning them. On the rare occasions when women apologize, it will be an apology of the female flavor. I'm sorry you feel that way. I'm sorry you don't understand.
- Emotional pain women feel is of paramount importance; emotional pain women cause men is of no consequence.
- Men think with their dicks, women use their brains. The male sex organs are unattractive, the male libido laughable. Except when she's ready for sex.
- Men should be excluded from women's activities or groups, but women cannot be excluded from any men's groups or activities.
- Women can be smarter and better than men at most things, but men are never smarter or better than women at anything. Except maybe war and opening jars.
- Vanity in females is an indication of self-esteem; male vanity is egocentric and, well, vain.
- Single men who succeed are selfish because they aren't supporting a family. Single females who succeed are heroines that have achieved independence.
- A man who insists on his own way is selfish; a woman who insists on her own way is empowered.
- Men are coarse, and need to be molded and changed by women. Women are more mature and refined than men, and need to grow not change. Women can change if they want, but not in ways dictated by men.
- Whatever a woman is paid, she has earned it and deserves more. Men are overpaid and don't have to earn their pay. Women work harder for less pay.
- All men are pervs (except for gay men). Only men are pervs, women have sensitive needs.
- Any criticism of women by men is oppression; criticism of men is fighting back.
- Men need to be restrained; women need to be set free of restraints.
- A man's primary obligation in life is to serve a woman's needs, expecting nothing in return. Women often confirm this by giving

nothing in return.

- Men's sexual needs are selfish. Men are selfish when they don't fulfill women's needs.
- All men are failures in some way. Women are never failures, they are oppressed. Failure is not their fault.
- Men should have to pay for all the oppression of women in the last 20,000 years.
- Men suppress their feelings and should cry more. Women are more expressive. Men should get in touch with their feminine side. No need for women to get in touch with their masculine side.
- A female ego needs nurturing; a male ego is evil and must be suppressed. A man with a big ego is a controlling jerk; a woman with a big ego is a highly motivated and successful, confident woman.
- Men's jokes are not funny, unless self-deprecating. Humor making fun of male sexuality is hilarious; humor about women's sexuality is degrading and offensive.
- Women "settle" for men. Every female is disappointed by a date, lover, or husband. There's always something missing. Women are saints for taking men in spite of all their flaws and shortcomings.
- Teasing men is better than sex, and you can do it more often. Give men nothing because that's what they deserve.
- Violence committed by women against men is always in self-defense. Women are always victims of violence, even when they are the ones who commit the violence. Men who commit violent acts need punishment. Women need therapy and understanding.

For women, "going ballistic" is an illustration of their destructive power. It's a female threat equivalent to men threatening women with superior force. He's stronger, but she can be more psycho. Men fear psychotic women, so it usually works. Men back down, and women get their way. That's what I think when I hear Helen Reddy sing, "I am woman hear me roar." I don't know what the roar is, unless it's her getting ready to go ballistic on you. She's going to break all your favorite things, fuck your best friends, and tell everyone how you deserved it.

Then there's that angry song Alanis Morissette wrote about how she got dumped by some guy after she "went down" on him in a theater. He promised to love her the rest of his life, but he's "still alive." I get it, "love me or die." I don't know why that guy dumped her, although I doubt it was related to either of her superb oral abilities. Could it have been because she's angry and psychotic? And was that blow job really an act of *love* on her part? Does a blow job make a guy love you forever? That makes her a keeper as far as I'm concerned, but come on. *She* oughta know. Yeah, it's not fair. Wah wah wah. How dare anyone dump *her*? Success seems to have subdued her so-called anger, but how about the millions of women who bought that record and internalized the lyrics?

Lorraine's Favorite Story

I heard Lorraine tell the story twice at work. It was obviously one of her favorites. Lorraine was in her late 50s and worked for years on ranches in Texas before getting an administrative job at Compaq. She used to like it when new ranch hands got hired. These would be young guys 17 or 18 years old. Lorraine would show them the different types of farm chores to be done. She had one chore that she saved for special occasions. According to her, she would demonstrate to the guys how to castrate a caged bull, and then take the bloody testicles and throw them to some dogs that would fight viciously for the privilege of devouring them. She loved watching the reactions of these new ranch hands when they saw that. "One guy even passed out," she laughed. It's one thing to be required to castrate a bull, it's another to really enjoy it. There are some demented women around. I never noticed any examples like her in our Compaq sensitivity training films.

Well, Lorraine is just one woman, right? How can I project that onto all American women? It has to do with that whole John Wayne Bobbitt incident. A woman slices off a man's penis, and women everywhere are delighted. I guess it's their idea of instant equality. The women at work all had big demented grins whenever they brought up the topic. It seemed really odd to me. I remember them sitting around and laughing. They *all* loved it. I was standing there wondering, "What's *wrong* with them?"

Men don't go around high-fiving each other whenever a woman is tortured. We don't celebrate stories of rape we hear on the news. But all the women I talked to thought Lorena Bobbitt was some kind of heroine for castrating her husband. She took his severed penis and threw it in the street somewhere—even better. The office girls just assumed her actions must have been justified. Obviously, he was a real jerk, or she wouldn't have been driven to do that. What courage she had. It was a moment of pure joy to them. They also delighted in our male discomfort with the topic. By expressing their delight they collectively castrate us all. It's emasculation by proxy.

The Culture of Female Pathology

There's more. I was visiting a girl named Elizabeth a few days after the whole Bobbitt incident. Elizabeth was one of the nicest, most affectionate, positive girls I'd been out with in a long time. She was intelligent, into history, not weird on any religions, not feminist. Just nice. Elizabeth and I were curled up together on the couch with the TV on, and there was a news update about the Bobbitt incident. Suddenly this wonderful, positive girl sits up as says "Oh God, I'm sooo glad she did that. He really deserved it." As a matter of fact, he did *not* deserve it. It did not even occur to my nice affectionate Elizabeth that her comment might offend me or that I might disagree that castration was such a wonderful tool for dealing with marital problems. Any woman who thinks Lorena Bobbitt was justified in her actions is basically stating that she herself reserves the right to castrate a man if she so chooses. It must be an even better rush than castrating a bull.

Using the part of my brain that is missing from females, I switched gender roles to imagine what would happen if they showed some guy on TV who had cut off his wife's nose or breast and flung it in the street. What if I had expressed delight over it with Elizabeth in my arms? What if I had said, "Ha! I bet the bitch had it coming!" She would be horrified. I would be thrown out, and rightfully so. But I stayed calm and let the moment pass. The alternative would have been to have a huge fight and never talk to her again. And she was the nicest girl I'd met in years.

There was no reason to lash out at Elizabeth specifically. She didn't say anything I hadn't already heard from the office girls. But at that moment I understood how bad things had gotten for men. It was depressing, realizing that *all* women hate us. It's just that some women hate us more than others. And it's not that Elizabeth hates *me*, but she has contracted the same collective resentment of men that has infected almost all American women. The castration of John Bobbitt was just an outlet for her to vent her contempt. As a man, I share in this collective hate that is directed toward us all. I'm man enough to be hated, just not man enough to be loved. A few women I've known have kept me from giving up altogether

Media Feminism As Assault Weapon

Man-hate is now actively promoted in our culture. Regardless of what Naomi Wolf says, "power feminism" is not an improvement over "victim feminism." I noticed the transition from victim feminism to power feminism sometime in the mid 1990s. During the reign of victim feminism, we were inundated with images of men committing acts of brutal violence against innocent, adorable females. All men were potential rapists and killers, a la Susan Brownmiller. With the rise of power feminism, the violence has shifted to female-on-male violence, a la *Buffy the Vampire Slayer*. Men are beaten up, defeated, outsmarted, kicked in the balls, and killed by attractive, empowered females. It's generic "media feminism" which celebrates female-on-male violence and the ridicule of masculinity. Media feminism is dumbed-down misandry for the masses. The basic anti-male theme is repeated again and again as entertainment. It's indoctrination for all via slow hypnosis.

So, unless you're majoring in Women's Studies, forget about victim feminism or power feminism or difference feminism or dissident feminism or militant feminism or gender feminism or equity feminism or whatever feminism. However you qualify it, feminism will always be identified with the mistrust, emasculation, and minimalization of men.

Television commercials are one of the biggest proponents. I saw Mary Chapin Carpenter in concert on *Austin City Limits* a couple years ago. I like her music, and yes, I think she should have a rock and roll band. Even if it *is* all male. But there's one song she plays about how she's upset by a coffee commercial from the 1960s, and how the husband is so impressed with the cup of coffee his wife made that he thinks he'll "keep her." How *dare* he judge his wife by a cup of coffee? I wonder if Mary Chapin Carpenter has seen any commercials in the last 20 years? If so, she should be happy, because men portrayed in commercials now are all incapable idiots, and thank God for the women who keep them from screwing up. One ad in 2003 has the wife taking digital photos of food as a shopping list because her husband is apparently too dumb to read a written list. He's a white guy, of course.

We've been so conditioned to be über-sensitive to anything that might offend women that it's become unimportant how white males are portrayed. For years we have been barraged with offensive anti-male content on TV. We're dorks and cavemen. Homer Simpsons. We're routinely ridiculed as morons, and very few people think it matters.

The inadequacy of men and fathers has become part of our culture. In the movie *Armageddon*, an asteroid is on a collision course with earth. NASA decides to send a bunch of loser men from an oil drilling team into space with a nuclear bomb to destroy it. One of the men has been shunned by his family as an unreliable husband and father. How can he gain their acceptance? He has to go save the whole fucking planet.

The Culture of Female Pathology

In a Verizon commercial from September 2004, a dorky-looking dad comes in and tells his two cute teenage daughters that he just enrolled them in an unlimited cell phone plan, so now they can talk to him all they want. The daughters look mortified. They don't want to talk to dad. Mom step in and tells them they can talk to their friends all they want, too. The girls are relieved. "Group hug," says the dad. His teen daughters and wife hug each other, deliberately excluding him. "Call me," he laments as they walk away with the phones he has just paid for.

I just saw *Terminator II* again. I noticed the scene in which the Linda Hamilton character is watching the interaction of her young son with the protective terminator robot. She thinks about how *this* father will never get drunk and hit him, will never leave, and won't say he didn't have time for him. "Of all the would-be fathers, this machine was the only one that measured up. In an insane world, it was the only sane choice." That's right, robots are the only good fathers. Thanks for reminding us.

Women are always kicking men's butts on TV and in movies, and girls love it, especially young girls. It's empowerment. That's strange, didn't I just read that violence is an expression of masculinity by us male oppressors? Some friends of mine have a 9-year-old girl, and she was ecstatic when telling me about how Xena beat up a bunch of men. Why is that so healthy? Would it be good for young boys' confidence to see girls getting beat up by men half the time? There goes my role reversal kicking in again.

It gets much worse. Sexual violence against men in advertising is now commonplace. Apparently, we deserve it. In 2002 I saw a commercial for Progressive Insurance in which a woman was using a voodoo website to torture some guy who was out on a date with another girl. The ad is supposed to show the power of their insurance sales website. The woman in the commercial superimposes a digital photo of the cheating bastard onto the computer-generated voodoo doll, then uses her mouse to drag and drop torture implements onto him. The guy on the date screams. Finally, after using the typical voodoo tools like needles and fire, she does a drag and drop of some snippers to *castrate* the voodoo image of the guy. The guy on the date grimaces with pain. This is presented as hilarious, and the woman doing the castrating is portrayed as delighted and ingenious. It shows that nothing has changed since Bobbitt. A man getting his dick cut off by a woman is still amusing and empowering. They changed the commercial in 2003 so that the girl gleefully tortures the guy in non-sexual ways. That's nice.

How does that coffee commercial compare with the voodoo castration of a man on a date? I doubt Mary Chapin Carpenter will be writing a song about that. I'm sure she's still out there complaining about the old coffee commercial. In early 2003 there was an uproar over a beer commercial showing two women fighting and ripping each other's clothes to the delight of two male onlookers. Entire TV shows were dedicated to the controversy. Yes, women are still shown in sexual roles in commercials, but at least they aren't tortured and sexually mutilated to sell products.

In 2003 I saw a Trident gum commercial in which a squirrel runs up a man's pants and bites his genitals. This makes him the idiot that doesn't recommend Trident gum. There was a Washington Mutual ad that showed a man getting his gonads crushed by an errant bowling ball, but he doesn't care because he got a great loan. I was at a Superbowl party in 2004 when a Bud Light commercial came on showing a dog jumping up and biting a man in the crotch. The girls in the room erupted in laughter and cheers. I saw later that it got voted best Superbowl commercial of 2004. I saw a Dairy Queen commercial in May 2004 that showed a 2 year old kicking his dad in the groin when he doesn't get ice cream. I did some searching on the web and discovered that the director of client services for the ad agency, as well as the Dairy Queen exec who approved the ad were both female.

TV and movies always portray men getting struck in the groin as hilarious. Gratuitous crotch violence has become mandatory in all action and comedy films. Ever since the spectacular crotch kick in *Butch Cassidy and the Sundance Kid*, Hollywood can't give us enough. It's everywhere. I recently saw an online listing of more than 1500 films and TV shows that depict attacks on the male genitalia.

Even "family" shows like *America's Funniest Home Videos* shows men and boys getting hit by various objects in their groins—and they're always served up with a laugh track. They've desensitized an entire segment of the public to men in pain. Unlike images in the movies, these groin hits are real. A recent episode showed a man falling backwards into a campfire and the host asked, "Who doesn't like roasted marshmallows?" The winner of the best video of the year was for a five-year-old kid who got his nuts smashed riding a mini-motorbike. For the 300th episode, *America's Funniest Home Videos* had a feature called "Greatest Groin Hits," and offered a cash prize for the greatest groin hit of all time.

Why is it acceptable to show men in pain from various assaults on their sex organs? It's because this type of pain does not offend women.

The Culture of Female Pathology

These same women are supposedly against violence. Violence against *women*, that is. Why do women enjoy images of men getting their testicles bitten and beaten? Because men deserve it. All men, damn them. Because every man has hurt a woman emotionally, and since men are devoid of feelings the only way to make them really feel pain is physically. And what more appropriate place than right in the groin? Quick, everyone think happy thoughts. Oh yeah, to women those *are* happy thoughts.

While expressions of violence by women against men are presented in the media as something positive, violence against women is portrayed as the ultimate evil. Cute girls who are murdered or disappear get huge media coverage. As a clear indication of just who is valued within our society, these are almost always white females. Some I recall are: Chandra Levy, Elizabeth Smart, JonBenet Ramsey, Polly Klaas, Dru Sjodin, Lori Hacking, and Natalee Holloway. Fox News dedicated more than 100 entire shows to Laci Peterson. No such concern is displayed for men and boys who meet violent deaths. Violence committed against women is sensationalized. Violence committed against men is minimalized. I can't recall ever seeing a news bulletin about a missing black man.

I just saw an infomercial fundraiser for animal shelters. The female moderator explained that one reason to donate was because apparently when women run away from abusive men, the men beat up on the women's poor little pets instead. That in turn encourages the women to come back and take the beating themselves. Oh sure, we've *all* done that. So now we need battered pet shelters too. Just not *battered men* shelters. Oh, but women aren't violent like men. Just ask the husband of Clara Harris from Houston or the boyfriend of Dana Pierce from Austin. Oh, that's right, they're dead. Brutally murdered, in fact. Maybe that's why we don't need shelters for men.

I don't think commercials and movies actively encourage women to go out and slice off our penises or murder us. At least not generally. More likely is that women get the message again and again that men are opponents. That men deserve punishment. That pain inflicted by women upon men is good fun. That violence toward men is justified. That violence is a form of female empowerment. The result is not so much an increase in female violence as a decline in respect for men. Our value as human beings is diminished. We must be demeaned. It's done more with images than with actual violence. It's media feminism as an assault weapon. It's a daily bucket of gasoline on the fire.

Besides the assaults on male sex organs for fun, the casual killing of men, and the portrayal of all men as idiots, there are more subtle denigrations going on. It's common for TV to show capable and skilled men reporting to young and sexy women who are their superiors. These divas are the decision makers barking orders at docile men, who scramble to carry out every command. It's retaliatory sexism in screenwriting. It's the result of writers exercising "power feminism," looking for every possible way to belittle and ridicule men. It's pathology lite.

Women absorb these attitudes, then try to enter into relationships with us. The old feminists have slowly gotten their way. They are successfully harming men. Feminists have never caught on that damaging men will eventually damage women. "Eventually" has come to pass.

Men don't have the deep sense of vindictive anger women have been harboring. We don't look at incidents of women being mutilated as opportunities to taunt the women we know. We don't look at murdered wives and think, *The poor husband deserves all our support.* Our anger is more about entrapment in dysfunctional relationships, being publicly ridiculed by women, sexual teasing, loss of our independence, becoming financial servants, being disqualified for promotions because of our gender, being exploited by ex-wives, loss of parental rights, false accusations of rape and domestic violence, you know—normal stuff.

Women continue to see their own potential for violence toward men as empowering. I was on a date two years ago, and the girl was bragging about some "self-defense" course she took. She informed me that she could kill me within seconds in two different ways. I asked her which way she would choose. She responded that she would snap my neck. Shoving a pen up my nose would be too messy. "How was your date?" a friend asked me later. "I survived," I told him.

Can women cleanse themselves of this pathology? I don't know. I doubt they want to. In fact, they continue to celebrate it. After all, anger is a powerful emotion, and women thrive on emotion. They need to be able to express themselves. Denying women this anger would be like oppressing them. If women are trying to scare us, it's working. I'm afraid, all right. I'm afraid I'll never be able to relate to women.

The Culture of Female Pathology

Welcome to Dating Hell

I'm tired of buying dinners and not getting laid. Maybe that's why I don't date much anymore. I ended up paying for about 100 dinners before I figured it out, though. Once men are over the "hundred dinner limit," don't expect us to buy dinners or flowers, wear nice clothes, be polite, or stay sober on dates. We've had it.

As usual, women are just the opposite. As women continue to date into their 30s and 40s, their expectations for the dating experience increase. They like "fine dining." Read that as very expensive dining they never have to pay for. They want the guy to have a great car and new clothes and shoes. A suit and tie would be nice. Does he own a tux? "Flowers for me? You shouldn't have!" She wants every date to be the best ever. She expects to be the most fascinating person the guy has ever met. Infuse me with more of your metaphysical wisdom, please! She considers it a privilege for a guy to be in her company— just like her mom told her. Personally, I have little sympathy for women who have used sexuality to manipulate and extort favors from men, then suddenly after 20 years decide they no longer want to be judged by their appearance.

Is it just me, or does it seem strange for people in their 30s and 40s to call each other "boyfriend" and "girlfriend"? Dating is for adolescents. It's a waste of time for adults. Dating is some contrived surrogate activity you agree to perform instead of having sex. That's what dating is. A guy asking a girl out on a date is his official declaration that he wants to fuck her. Her acceptance of the date is an acknowledgement of that. She has *not* agreed to fuck him, though. All she's agreed to is to get free stuff from a guy she knows wants to fuck her. That's what makes dating awkward. Why should I declare my interest in fucking a girl if she will not unambiguously declare her own interest in fucking me? Why do I have to buy her shit just to find out?

Generally, I find myself in some wonderland version of reality when meeting new women. It's like I'm trying to figure out who they want me to pretend to be. I think we all need therapy. Alcohol therapy. Sex happens when I'm at a bar or a party and a girl with the right attitude shows up. No more dinner dates for me, now it's drink dates. We flirt, touch, and kiss, then go to her place and hook up. If everything goes well, dinner will happen another time. I give flowers when a girl earns them or to surprise her, not whenever she thinks I fucked up. That would be too often.

I've spent most of my time in the minor leagues, moving furniture, repairing cars, and playing personal escort for girls for who will never fuck me. But they really like me now, right? Once in a while I try the major leagues, which is all about power and humiliation. The action is too fast for me there. I had a date turn and talk to a black guy standing beside her at the bar, then practically have sex with him on the dance floor. When guys are on dates, we're not supposed to even glance at other women, let alone dance with them. But I know she likes aggression in men, and she expected me to confront her. At least have an intense verbal exchange, something. Me? When women misbehave I get upset all right, but I don't make a scene. I just stop calling. I'm no fun. I'm just like those girls who show up at a game and can't even swing the bat. I'm out of my league, just hoping to get walked. Once in a while I make it to first base.

As part of a date, women have to prove they aren't easy and men have to pretend they aren't desperate. Obviously, nothing happens. I wonder if there ever was a time when a dinner invitation meant dinner and sex. Maybe it's always been a myth. Now "dinner" means dinner and no sex. Women aren't going to put out for a damn dinner. Some guys have figured it out faster than I have, but it's around that 100-dinner limit when most of us realize it's futile.

Everyone who dates says they don't like dating. I can understand why men don't like it. We have to get rejected asking women out, then when one says "yes" we have to plan it, pick her up, listen to her go on and on, then pay for everything and watch her act like she's just done us a favor. Sex is out of the question. Often women critique the date and express their displeasure at the level of excitement they are getting from our company. A friend of mine got an e-mail from a date the next day detailing his dating etiquette mistakes. He's rapidly approaching that 100-dinner limit.

I'm not sure why women say they don't like dating. They get to torture us and complain about everything. They get to act like princesses. Can you imagine a guy refusing to go out unless he is picked up at his house? Yeah, I'd be into "fine dining" too—if it were free. Let's make women be the ones who have to try for a change. See if you can make me laugh. Try to slip me some tongue. When do I want to see you again? I'll have to check my calendar. That other girl had a better car. Oh, I forgot to call you back. What was your number again?

Take back dating? Return to the days of old that never were? Revive romance? Why create that pretend world again? Romance itself doesn't excite women. Romance gets you in the door, dominance gets you in bed. How about equity dating? Try it. Ask out some guys. Maybe get looked at like you're a slimeball. Get treated like you're joking. Get rejected 10 times in a row. Get stood up half the time. Plan an evening and then get cancelled on short notice. Gracefully accept some lame excuse, then eat the tickets or go alone. Make sure the guy enjoys himself even if you don't. Pay for it even if the guy insults you and talks about himself the whole time. Be judged on how successful you are as a woman by how happy he is. Welcome to our world. Welcome to dating hell.

We Have Different Interests

I met an attractive Nordic-looking blonde named Paula through the personals. She was nice, but I could tell before long her body weight would exceed my own. That's a condition my libido will not overlook. I cannot live with a woman who will balloon up bigger and bigger with each passing year. I've seen it happen to other guys. They show me old photos of how their wives used to look. The emotionally correct thing to do would be to rearrange my brain so that I can be attracted to huge women. Focus on her inner beauty. But they haven't come up with a pill or drink *that* strong. I knew I had to get out, but you can't tell a girl the reason you're dumping her is because she will be fat in the future. You *will* get your house burned down for that. The jury *will* take her side at the trial. So I made up some crap about having different interests. Sweet relief. She bought it and wanted to stay friends. That's fine, I don't mind being called "friend" by girls I'm done fucking. Six weeks later Paula called and wanted me to come over and visit. Fine, I went over. She had obviously gone off her diet and had already gained 20 pounds. I've gotten pretty good at it—preemptive dumping.

An Academic Affair

A lot of women in their 30s aren't looking for a lover, they're looking for a baby enabler. They don't even like us, but they want to marry us. I've had them meet me, find out I had a job, and they'd be willing to get married and have kids on the spot. Who am I exactly? Doesn't matter. I'm not in prison. I could tell them I just got out and they'd consider me a "catch." Are we really compatible? Not important. I'm agnostic and she's a devout Catholic? No problem, I can just go to church and pretend. Do we have any common interests? Does she like to travel? Does she like sex? Sure, whatever. I can get her pregnant and pay the bills. Now that's exciting.

Martina turned out to be exactly that. For some reason I knew she would be easy. She was yet another German girl, and I spoke her language. I had a good job, so I paid for her dinner. She invited me into her apartment where I began to sneeze. "Are you allergic to cats?" "Yeah, but it's no big deal," I answered. She got up, yelling "Get out!" I was shocked, then realized she was talking to the cats, not me. She shooed them rudely out the door. *Whoa, this is getting serious*, I thought.

Martina said she actually bought a book on American dating so she'd know what to do. It was a textbook romance. She always offered to pay for "her half" and exuded praise for me when I refused it. We went out the mandatory three times before fucking. I noticed her interest level in sex perked up after I said I was open to the idea of having kids someday. I came to realize that sex was not an erotic experience to Martina, it was a medical one. Protected sex was like a trial run for her, something to get me psychologically prepared to impregnate her for real. This wasn't love. It wasn't even lust. I may as well have whacked off into a cup in a clinic. I think she would have preferred that approach. I'm sure that as soon as I fulfilled my duty as her sperm bank, I would have become her financial bank. I didn't have to lie this time. I told her I didn't think there was any feeling between us. She couldn't disagree. Sometimes it's better not to go by the book.

A Half-Pint to Go

Not long after I broke it off with Martina, I met a girl in a bar with a

German accent named Vera. She was tall, Xena-like, and had just broken up with someone. Opportunity knocks. I switched over to German with her and noticed she stumbled and made grammatical errors. "You're not German, are you?" "No, but I used to live in Germany," she replied. "What's with the accent?" "What accent?" she responded without an accent.

Now she sounded American. I'd met people like this before. They spend a few months in a foreign country and take on a phony accent to be more exotic, acting like they don't notice. Technically, she wasn't lying. But everyone assumed Vera was actually German. Busted! We nicknamed her "pseudo-German girl." Even so, none of this precluded her from being one-night-stand material. As far as female neuroses go, that one was pretty minor. I bought her a pint as I continued to out-German her. Deprived of her fake accent, Vera was out of her element. I could tell she was uncomfortable and ready to bolt, but she was only half-way through her pint of beer. "I hate to waste good beer," she said. I expected her to chug the beer and leave. Instead, she took the half-filled pint glass and carefully placed it into her purse. "Oh, I always do that," she said as she walked off. "Auf wiedersehen!"

An Engaging Arab Girl

I met an Arab girl through the personals. We got along great at dinner, and right there on our first date she told me that she would like to get involved with me. All I had to do was buy her a diamond ring and pretend, for the benefit of her family, that we were engaged. Huh? So I buy her a $1,000 diamond and tell everyone we're engaged? That's a lot of acting. If we break up, do I get the ring back? What happens when I find out her family is planning a "pretend" wedding? Run Toto, *run!*

The Art Class Babe

I'm a sucker for talented artistic women. Art class is a great place to meet them. One day the model didn't show up, so the instructor asked if anyone would like to volunteer to pose for portraits. A girl in the class I'd been admiring stepped up to the platform. I figured if I did a good rendering of her, she'd be impressed and I'd ask her out. I concentrated and got her eyes and nose just right. I put in the lips and they looked good. Next was the jawline. She had a mole, and I was careful to place it in exactly the right position on her cheek. I finished up with the hair. Of course, she came around to see everyone's drawings. As she approached I noticed her mole was actually a zit. She took one look and never came near me again. She could have said, "Hey, you got my zit perfect." Talented or not, she had no sense of humor.

No Breakfast for Corrine

Corrine from France was 23 and still a virgin. She'd never even been touched by a man. She had me over to her room, and I was testing her limits. We's been kissing for a few minutes when I opened a button on her blouse. "Stop that!" she said. We continued kissing, but she didn't fix the button. A few minutes later I undid the next button. "No, don't do that!" she warned. Again, she left her blouse unbuttoned and we continued kissing. I went for the third button and she raised no objections. She had large, wonderful breasts, and I had to go for them. So I put my hands inside her blouse and began caressing them. She sat up and said, "Stop that or I'll scream!" "Oh really?" I still had my hands on the goods. Glaring at me, she took a long deep breath and held it. Then she exhaled a sigh. The blouse and bra came off. I had full reign of that young body. She must have liked the experience because the next time she came over to my place. She said "No" a lot.

"Does it feel good when I touch you here?"
"No!"
"Want me to take my hand away?"
"No."
"Want to get undressed?"
"No."
"Would you mind if I undressed you?"
"No."
Okay, I think I understand this game.

Corrine wasn't physically or emotionally ready for full sex. A finger was all the intensity she could handle. When she got off, it was like a revelation to her, clearly a major event in her life. She was really happy afterward and sang songs to me in French. Very charming. I was falling for her. She stayed over but couldn't sleep from the excitement. About 3:00 a.m. she was wide awake so I tried to calm her, holding her and kissing her.

Suddenly she turned sad. There was something she had to tell me. That's never good. Then she said she couldn't tell me, not yet. Of course that means I'm supposed to dredge it out of her. "Please tell me, Corrine, what's wrong?" She said it had been such a beautiful night with me, and it wasn't fair of her to be so selfish. She paused for dramatic effect. There was something wrong with her. She didn't have long to live. She wasn't going to tell me, but just wanted me to know that she enjoyed this time with me. "That's terrible," I said, holding her. "Want to talk about it?" "No." I held her quietly.

Ten minutes later she said, "Actually, there's nothing wrong with me." "Huh? So why did you tell me that?" "I don't know," she said. A minute went by. "What did you think it was, cancer?" she said giggling like a schoolgirl. So much for "charming." No breakfast for you, Corrine.

She called me back a week later, wanting me to deflower her. For some reason women still think men enjoy that. I've slept with several virgins who were "saving it" for the right guy. It must be another left-over from the Middle Ages. "Thou art a pure unsoiled virgin? Come hither and remove thy chastity belt, young maiden." I suppose I should have felt honored, but I have no desire to watch a girl grimace in pain as I force myself into her. No, it is *not* special. If men liked it, porn would be filled with it. I would have been willing to do it, but I considered Corrine's little "cancer stunt" pathetic. I had no interest in seeing her again, so I chose to break her heart instead of her hymen. It was time for someone else to take over and perform the honors.

Cancer Girl

Speaking of cancer, I met a cute girl at a brewpub who worked as a nurse in a cancer ward. She said she needed to unwind after having seen so many awful things at her job. Very flirty. We had a great conversation about something forgettable; she even gave me her number without me asking. I like that. Then she lit up a cigarette. She works in the cancer ward and smokes? Excuse me, but you're insane. I suppose I could have fucked her because smokers are total hedonists. They think nothing can hurt them. And even if it does, they don't care as long as they're getting a rush. Sure, I've even been involved with smokers before and put up with their stinky kisses, but there was something very disturbing about the lunacy of a nurse lighting up after working all day with cancer patients. Her capacity for denial must have been immense. I couldn't bring myself to call her. Not even for sex.

Stephie's Choices

Stephie was a striking blonde with eyes so benign they could have made her famous. If she wanted an easy life, she could have walked into any yuppie bar and met a guy with a Porsche. She told me that wasn't what she wanted. She chose a tougher path as a drywall installer. Besides being very fit, she was intelligent and articulate. We connected right away. Even if the words coming out of Stephie's mouth made sense, her actions did not.

A couple of dates into this I find out she's already "seeing someone," but she's not happy with him. He lost his job doing whatever and had been sitting around getting drunk and high every day for months. When he got motivated he would deal some drugs. She was just waiting for the right time to break up with him. In the meantime, she started covering his rent. I thought this guy must have been a controlling alpha male who intimidated her into inaction. Then one time at her place, I ran into him. He was a nonthreatening, pleasant guy; he was also overweight and out of shape. A slob. He clearly had no idea I was dating his girlfriend.

When I was a loser, all the chicks wanted successful guys with good jobs. Now that I finally had one of those good jobs, this girl was clinging on to this dysfunctional bum. I put up with it because otherwise she was an amazing person. That and she let me get to third base a lot. She strung me out for weeks. "It's a difficult decision for me," she said. I thought to myself, *Why the fuck would this be difficult?* Finally, I had to bail.

Two months later she still hadn't broken it off with the drug dealer. Then she met another guy. For their first date he picked her up in a limo and had champagne and flowers. She had sex with him that night and got pregnant. It turned out he was a construction contractor who worked most of the year in Uganda, so Stephie packed up and moved to Africa with him. It's such a violent place that they kept two armed guards with machine guns at their house 24 hours a day. So I guess it wasn't a Porsche that Stephie was waiting for, it was a limo. If that guy had showed up in a sedan and said, "How about I get you pregnant tonight, and then we move to Uganda?" I doubt he would have gotten very far with her. Like so many women, she had a much firmer grip on fantasy than reality.

While talking to her roommate, I found out it was Stephie's fifth pregnancy in seven years, all by different men. She had terminated all but this last. For years women have had the ability to completely control their pregnancies, so why don't they? I wonder what was wrong with the other four guys? I wonder if they even knew? Not that it was up to them. She's the one with all the choices.

Welcome to Dating Hell

Can't Buy Me Love

I remember sitting alone in my apartment on a Saturday night and watching a news report about how Ted Bundy was getting married to his new girlfriend in prison. Even a convicted serial killer had a better social life than I did. Something had to be done. I was ready to try anything. Yeah, I know money can't buy me love, but I thought it could at least get me a date. Wrong again. My officemate joined one of those video dating services and was talking it up. He had met a girl he liked, and urged me to try it out. Well, this didn't sound like something I'd ever consider, and it was expensive. It was $800 to join, but at age 37 I didn't have time to waste on endless teasing and rejection. A dating service couldn't be any worse. Forcing myself to try something new, I went in and talked to the young fluffy sales rep. They had "thousands of members nationwide," she said. Well, since I lived in Austin I didn't care about meeting women in Seattle, so I asked how many members they had locally. She said they had "about 1,000 active members." I asked what was the male/female ratio. "It's about even, I don't know exactly," she said. She would have to review all the records by hand to find out. Sounds close enough. I was making decent money and my officemate joined, so what the hell. I signed up. I forced myself to do the dorky video and filled out the profile. It was pure torture, but soon I would be meeting lots of single, childless, intelligent women. Cool.

It should have been easy. I had no ex-wives, no kids, I was fit, employed, decent looking. I looked through the books for childless women aged 30 to 38 and found several. I figured I didn't pay $800 to meet single mothers with two or three kids. The club allowed a maximum of three contacts per week. I turned in my three and waited a week. No replies. I turned in three more and waited a week. Nothing. Three more. Nothing. They're supposed to officially reject me at least! I widened my net to include women from 27 to 40, and they let me turn in five. Still nothing. These *are* single women who want to meet guys, right? At some point I got a date, but I think she was a girl hired by the company to date dateless guys. She told me she dated different guys almost every night, ate her dinner, and mostly ignored whatever I said. Yes, she had dessert too.

After a few weeks, I ran out of childless women under 40 to select. I was getting suspicious too. It didn't seem like there were 500 women in the books. So I did an audit of both male and female members. Rather than the 1,000 members the sales rep claimed, there were 218 women and 432 men. Most of the 218 women had stopped responding to dating requests long ago, but had been left on the books. I presented the numbers to the sales rep and asked for a refund. As I was aware, their policy was no refunds; but, I explained, I had joined because of false representations made to me. I threatened to sue. They suggested I remake my video and have better photos taken, then maybe someone might want to meet me. This was going to get ugly.

I filed a suit in the Small Claims Court under the Deceptive Trade Practices Act, requesting triple damages as specified by Texas law. I also filed a complaint with the Attorney General's office, as recommended by the Small Claims Court. Suddenly, the club called and had two girls who wanted to date me. Nice try! They also concealed their real corporate name, which delayed my lawsuit for a couple of months while I filed papers against a bogus corporation.

However, the club was required to respond to the Attorney General's complaint I had filed. They claimed the 1,000-member number also included people who attend their open house events. Unwittingly, they had confirmed their own 1,000-member lie in writing. I talked on the phone to their "registered agent" (a person required by law to accept legal papers) to make sure I delivered my lawsuit to the correct corporation this time. Their registered agent (probably an investor) attempted to explain that my membership audit was wrong, because there were additional "secret members" in the club who paid extra to protect their identities. These members didn't appear in the books (and got first crack at any new girls). So these secret members would help bring the total number closer to 1000. Also, they held "drawings" where they gave away memberships to any girl that "entered." So the numbers of women can rise suddenly at any time. I imagine lots of these girls tried it out for free and dropped out after a week, but remained "active" in the books for the next year. So really, it was mostly men who paid the $800. My guess is the club had 400 men and 50 women. The other female members were bogus.

I requested the names of all members, including any "secret members" as part of the discovery process. All names would be public record. I needed an attorney for that, and it got expensive fast. Obviously, the club would rather settle than reveal its true membership. Besides, they had confirmed the 1,000-member lie. They finally offered to refund my money. Too late. By that time I wanted triple damages *and* attorney's fees. As part of any settlement I also insisted the club agree to accurately represent their member count to prospective clients. They agreed, and we finally settled on double the $800 plus attorney's fees. It's pretty bad when you can't even get a date from a dating service. Why is this so hard?

Radio Girl

I met another girl through the personals who was in her late 30s and very attractive. She had a cool job as a DJ for a few hours a day at a local radio station. I laid out for her who I was. World traveler, musician, computer professional, homeowner. She wasn't interested in whatever music I played, nor that I'd traveled to 50 countries. She just wanted to know if my house was out at the lake. No. Did I own a boat at least? There were things in life she didn't want to compromise on. I mean, what the fuck? Buy your own goddamn boat. She could have asked me that on the phone and saved me the trip out. But now I was stuck listening to her ego trip and paying for her dinner. She thought she was totally hot because she played songs on the radio and read the news once an hour. Success doesn't make women more desirable, it just makes them more unattainable.

Jamie and Her Collectibles

I met a girl named Jamie at a club that featured live Latin music. She sucked down a couple drinks, and then turned to me and initiated an intensive oral activity that resembled kissing. I'd never had my tongue stretched like that before. It was intimate and exciting without actually being enjoyable. Kind of like how sex must be for women. I was probably 20 years older than Jamie, but it didn't seem to matter. I'm sure I could have fucked her that night, but for some reason I decided to get her number and call her back. I'd lost track of the proper etiquette.

We talked on the phone since we hardly spoke that first night. My tongue had made a full recovery from her aggressive sucking. Jamie mentioned she liked travel, so I told her I had spent some time in Germany and could speak German. "That's where most of my family was exterminated," she said matter-of-factly. Pause. "Can you believe all the rain we've had?" I responded. Nothing seemed to faze her. She was fully cooperative. No "hard to get" in her playbook. She agreed to meet me again with a refreshing enthusiasm.

I brought her flowers, and she was delighted. "How did you know I liked flowers?" she asked. Duh. She invited me into her filthy apartment. We went into the kitchen to put the flowers into a jar and I noticed there was dried dog poop on the floor. The fragrance from the flowers couldn't compete with the scent of pet pee in the air. "I'd show you my room but it's a mess," she said. "It can't be that bad," I said, trying to downplay the disgusting spectacle. "No, it's really a mess," she warned. A few minutes later she went into her bedroom to get something. In that brief span of seconds the door was open I could see at least a dozen wadded up feminine pads on dressers and boxes. What's up with that? Does she collect them as mementos of special evenings? Is she testing their biodegradability? Does she use them for satanic rituals? That *Room Raiders* show would have a field day in there. I once woke up in a gutter that was cleaner than her living quarters. Even so, she didn't seem unclean herself.

We went out for some drinks, and then it was time to call her bluff. She didn't want to come back to my place, so we drove back to her apartment. I knew she wasn't going to invite me back into her rat-hole room. So I made my move on her in the car. I ended up finger fucking her in the front seat with her feet up over the steering wheel. I thought sure she would want to show off her formidable sucking skills, given her demonstration from the week before. But as soon as she got off (or pretended to) she secured her orifices and said good night. With that I decided to declare victory and let the microbes in her apartment keep the party going. I did see her once again, but the intensity was gone. I think we mutually bailed on the whole thing before it had a chance to degenerate into a relationship.

Mary Ellen Leaves Her Mark

I met Mary Ellen at a retro club in Austin. I just went up and started dancing with her. We must have danced for half an hour before saying a single word to each other. Being a true gentleman, I didn't want to immediately proposition her, so I got her number. I picked her up and took her to a salsa club a week later. We had a few drinks, then I took her back to her apartment. After kissing for 10 minutes in my car, I asked her if she would like sex. I told her I was not looking for a girlfriend, and that this would be casual sex, nothing more. I said if that was okay, she was welcome to come home with me. She agreed and spent the night at my place. It's always clearer in the morning whether someone has the potential for becoming a long-term interest. If I'm comfortable with a woman, I'll want her to stay for breakfast. When the sun came, up I knew I wanted Mary Ellen out of my house. The alcohol had worn off. She was older and somewhat larger than she had appeared through my beer goggles.

Even so, since Mary Ellen fucked me, I figured I owed her dinner. Nice guy that I am. Besides, she seemed really sweet. Maybe I was being harsh. A week later I took her out, and it was again clear that our involvement was meaningless. Sometimes that's good, but not in this case. She was a 40-year-old perpetual student and had been in grad school for 14 years. At least it wasn't women's studies. She had been working on her Ph.D. for the last 10 years trying to produce a study on the social habits of Peruvian Indians. She had never actually been to Peru. She didn't want to graduate since she lived from grant to grant. And even worse, she made me uncomfortable by telling me I was the first man in years she felt she could trust. I don't like expectations being laid out for me to fulfill. Obviously, she was looking for a fireman to rush in and rescue her from her flaming life.

I suppose none of this would have been important if Mary Ellen was a babe, but unfortunately looks matter. I think we're all willing to put up with dysfunctional behavior from people we find attractive, but certainly not from marginally attractive people. I doubt any amount of therapy or guilt can change that. So after dinner, I dropped off Mary Ellen without an offer for more sex, thinking that she would get the clue that she had just been dumped. But she called me back and left a message about wanting to get together. Maybe I should have called her and formally dumped her, but I just couldn't force myself to pick up the phone. Maybe I could have used the old standby excuse that I had commitment phobia. But our encounter had been too brief for that. I just couldn't come up with some bogus version of "It's not you it's me." A month later I still hadn't called back. But then, it's my *right* not to call back. I came out one morning to find that my trees had been toilet-papered and my front yard deeply gouged with tire tracks. Okay, maybe she wasn't all that sweet. Forget grad school, go back to high school, bee-atch. It's strange how women think acts of vandalism and violence are justified against men who scorn them. From what I hear, I got off easy.

The Last Resort

Some say I'm trying too hard. I've tried trying, and I've tried not trying. I've run out of things to not try. Women tell me to just let things happen. Sure, they can sit in a bar and that will probably work for them. Someone will come up and buy them a drink. A guy will be sitting there a long, long time. Somehow alcohol doesn't make *us* look better.

Was there anything left to try? Yes, as a matter of fact, I *did* go to Moscow. It wasn't through an agency. In the spring of 2000, a Russian girl I knew set me up with her friend over there. I usually go to Europe every year and a side trip to Moscow wouldn't cost that much. I'd never been there, and it might be fun to go around Moscow with a cute Russian girl with a typical Russian name: Svetlana. My Russian friend gave me some pictures of her, and she was stunning. She was also 25 years younger than me. She spoke a little English, so that would help. Sign me up. We exchanged a couple letters. Hers were in Russian and had to be translated by my friend. Life was hard for her. She was divorced and had a 4-year-old son, which was difficult since she also worked in a clothing shop. I don't have anything against kids, but would my role be that of a passive provider? That was getting ahead of things. Got to keep an open mind.

I began working on the logistics. A flight from Munich to Moscow would cost $320 round trip, quite reasonable. Svetlana could put me up with friends, so I wouldn't have to stay in one of the expensive Moscow hotels. I just needed to send in my passport for a visa. I needed to go through a service, and found out a damn visa costs $200. I took another look at Svetlana's photo and shelled it out. Next I found out that Svetlana didn't know of a "safe" place for me to stay, so I needed to find a hotel after all. I got on the Internet and booked a room at the *Hotel Moskva* right beside the Kremlin for $54 per night. Not bad. Four nights, another $216.

When everyone realized I was really going to do this, I was informed that Svetlana might not speak any English at all, and that I should consider hiring a translator to accompany us. Another $140 at $35 per day. And that might make things awkward. But I remembered how the best times I had with Petra were when we couldn't speak to each other. Maybe it could work. Still, this was becoming an expensive and complicated adventure. Before I left I bought some cologne, bath oils, and dinosaur toys as presents. Another $100.

I blew off visiting Petra in Munich so that I'd be emotionally available for Svetlana. I arrived at the Moscow airport, and Svetlana was there with an older woman (more my own age) who was the translator. Svetlana was terribly excited, as if I were really riding up on a white horse to rescue her. She was even more stunning in person. We took a taxi to the *Hotel Moskva,* a perfect cold war relic, and I checked into my musty room full of original 1957 furnishings. No guests allowed. We had a spectacular afternoon walking around the Kremlin and St. Basil's. I looked around Red Square and there was not a more beautiful woman than Svetlana anywhere. Unfortunately, the translator spoke only broken English. She and Svetlana would talk furiously and I would get a 10-word summary. Better than nothing.

When I got back to the hotel, I noticed there was a woman sitting in the hall on my floor logging when people came and went. Not many people came and went. That's all she did. Five minutes after arriving in my room I got a call from a prostitute offering me sex in my room. It happened each time I entered my room. So I realized it must be the responsibility of the woman in the hall to notify the official hotel whores whenever men arrived back at their rooms. I found it strange that in Moscow, the *only* women allowed in my room were whores. They continued to call and would not stop even when asked.

The visit quickly degenerated into a guided tour. Like most Western men, I was not controlling enough for Svetlana. She did not understand the concept of discussions and joint decisions. She expected me to have an agenda for her and the translator to fulfill. Go here, do this, do that. When I did not seize control of Svetlana, she saw that as a sign of disinterest. She became passive and quiet.

The highlight of the visit was holding Svetlana's hand while riding the Moscow subway. We came to a stop that still had the old bronze hammer and sickle emblems everywhere. It was like I had been transformed into a completely different person with a new life. I imagined living in Moscow, starting life anew. The moment quickly passed. She picked up her four-year-old son, and he immediately dominated her time and attention. I was relegated to the role of a tag-along guy who pays for everything. This was not going to be a replay of the Petra fantasy of a beautiful foreign woman who can't speak English and likes sex. The whole thing was basically an attempted "father upgrade." To Svetlana, a "father" was nothing more than a "provider." More money—better father.

So what happened to the boy's real father? I was told he was a drunk, just like all Russian men. I wonder why she would choose to have a child with such a man? Wouldn't the boy want to know his real father? And what would the father think about never seeing his son again? Can a woman do that? Just marry a new man and run off with the child without informing the father? I probably should have asked these questions prior to my arrival in Moscow. I found it all quite disturbing. Not to worry, my plane was waiting. I think that's the point when I gave up. Sitting on the plane I thought, *Okay, I've tried everything now.*

Gender War Refugees

Women continue to ask me if I'll ever get married. Married? I can't even date any more. When I meet a woman, I find myself wondering if she's the undiscovered gem she appears to be, or if she's concealing some sordid past. Is she bipolar? Has she been on anti-depressants for five years? Was there a bitter divorce? Did she bleed the last guy dry? Is she still out to get him back? Does she have $10,000 in credit card debt? Does she need an emergency "loan?" Did she just break up with her lesbian lover? Did she major in Women's Studies? Does she look at all men as potential rapists? Does she think Lorena Bobbitt was just standing up for her rights? Was she a hooker in Heidelberg or an escort in Montreal? Does she think she's a pagan goddess or a reincarnation of an Egyptian princess? Does she have seven cats she thinks are her children? Does she make life decisions based on her horoscope? Does she think her life will change if she gets implants? Is she really as nice as she seems, or is she looking for a man to be miserable with? Misery doesn't want that much company.

I suppose I'm part of the "marriage strike," but not in any deliberate way. Even now, I like the idea of a supportive partnership, but mostly what I see around me are partnerships rife with animosity. The male/female relationship dynamic is in ruins. War itself is the deliberate inducement of disaster for the temporary benefit of a few. For most, it brings only suffering. Feminism is one of these deliberate disasters. Consider me a refugee of gender warfare. I'm beaten down, and I don't have the energy to care what happens anymore. I just want some solace from it all.

It's not just me. The new reality is that fewer and fewer men want relationships. Men are becoming woman-wary much quicker than I ever did. Even if a woman seems perfectly wonderful, we suspect that within a few years she'll turn into yet another passive-aggressive ice queen. That once-upon-a-time wonderful, supportive woman will be dragging us into court for one reason or another. One by one they degenerate into self-centered psychopaths. There is very little trust between men and women. It's part of the big wedge feminism has driven between us all.

I've met a lot of highly educated young women who are the presumed beneficiaries of feminism. The glorification of career has pushed them into making professional success their top priority, leaving them with minimal personal lives. Although they in no way consider themselves "feminists," they've had it drilled into them that in order to avoid dependency on men, they must be completely self-sufficient. They still want men in their lives, but they're not sure why. They retain their natural attraction to men, even though they've been conditioned by pop culture to think of them as idiots.

Some have achieved high levels of success and wonder why men are so non-committal. They behave irresponsibly but expect men to love and trust them unconditionally. They seem oblivious that their "me first" attitude drives men away. Others are shell-shocked, having spent years in school with little to show for it. They work at jobs they don't like, wandering aimlessly in the no-man's-land created by the gender wars. The "mommy track" is a derogatory term that drives women like these toward long-term academic and professional goals that will likely keep them childless. They've been conditioned to say they want careers, not children. "Have kids? God no." But ask them about a "family" and they are more flexible with that language. Maybe "family track" would be a better term. These women aren't victims of oppression, they're victims of feminism. And they don't even know it.

All the Things I Like about You

B y now, it's possible you've gotten the impression I have some issues with women. Let me assure you, I adore women. When they aren't trying to enforce their opinions on me. When they aren't telling me how to run my life. When they aren't force-feeding me their insanity du jour. Sometimes I wonder if I like women, or if I'm just attracted to them. Yeah, they drive me up the wall. Is that any different than how women feel about men? I think it's normal to be extremely frustrated by the opposite sex. The fact that I could go on ranting forever is an indication of my infatuation with women more than anything truly negative.

Don't believe me? Think about it. It's happened to you. You're fighting with your lover and dredging up all the inconceivably crass things they've done, and suddenly they ask if there's anything you actually like about them. So you both go into that mode of coming up with the positive qualities of each other, but you're so angry that it takes a minute or so to come up with anything at all. Especially if you disqualify sex and physical attraction.

I remember those conversations, trying to point out the positive qualities of someone who has just infuriated you. I might come up with something like, "You're very perceptive about things." She'll say, "Like what?" Then I can't think of anything. She'll say, "You don't always succeed, but you try really hard, sometimes." Is that positive? Fine, count it. I'll say, "You have beautiful eyes, oh wait, appearance doesn't count." She'll say, "You're really strong, almost as strong as me." My turn. I'm thinking. Let's see, she has a clear vision of her goals in life? Not really. She's reliable? No. She's dedicated and faithful to me? Yeah, except for those three or four times. She's waiting. "Uh, you're smart and you don't let anyone stand in your way, certainly not me." This is not going well.

Why is it so much easier to verbalize the bad than the good? I don't know how long this book will be, but I could continue for a thousand pages about the incomprehensible things women do to men. I suppose it's the same for anyone you deeply care about. Maybe it's true after all that my affinity for women really is unconditional, just like they want. Otherwise, how could I take their collective abuse for so long and still so totally want them?

The Last Word

There's a question women ask me all the time—"Have you ever been in love?" I'll answer that. Yes, but I didn't know it at the time. Angela was only 19 when I met her at a party. I was 28. She was thin and gorgeous with long dark hair. Very Italian looking. I asked her to a rock concert, and she accepted. She hardly spoke the whole night, but not out of belligerence. She was just quiet. There was a hidden charm and depth about her. I met her again, and we quickly got involved. Her enthusiasm for sex was shocking. We continued to meet off and on for months. She resisted becoming too attached emotionally. She tried to be someone different each time I saw her—a Barbie Doll, a mousy student, a punk girl, a sex vixen. We never tried to control or change each other. If she wanted to go out, she wouldn't wait, she would call. If she wanted sex, she would call. She was different in a very good way. Once I got to know her, I noticed she wasn't quiet at all. She had opinions. She had a sense of humor. But we were all about sex. It was phenomenal. We hear the message all the time not to prioritize our sexual encounters too highly in our lives. It had been a nice fling. We needed careers. We had our lives to live.

I took a year off to backpack through South America. When I returned, I couldn't wait to see Angela again. It was better than before. She was no longer the flaky teenager I remembered. By now I understood this was more than sex, we were right for each other. I'd always heard you never get everything you want. Either they're an incredible lover or someone you totally connect with. Never both. Someone's always above the other. Someone's more controlling. Someone always tries harder. There she was, disproving all that conventional wisdom.

One time after several drinks, I told Angela something that visibly stunned her. I told her that our relationship wasn't just about sex; I actually liked her as a person. I told her how well we communicate. I told her she was someone I could actually live with. "You're just saying that cause you're drunk," she said, concealing her delight. "No, I can *tell* you because I'm drunk," I responded. "Ask me again tomorrow, you'll see."

She knew it was true. I didn't need some mushy line to get great sex from her. We stayed at the bar until closing, then went to her car. We were in no condition to drive, but we couldn't wait. We didn't even make it to the back seat. At some point during that two hours of drunken bucket-seat sex, she tore the silver chain from my neck, the one Alexandra had given me two years before. Angela knew it was from another girl. She had been lying there breaking it into pieces during sex, as if it were a violation of her domain. She earned it. I became her territory. I removed the offending debris from her seat on my way out.

Our life plans quickly separated us. I had my priorities, and I needed to get a career together. I went back to school in Ohio since I couldn't afford out-of-state tuition. I thought maybe I'd hook up with Angela again at some point when we were both ready. She'd been taught the same thing, that success and career are the highest priorities in life. Besides, a few drunken sexual liaisons were certainly no reason to alter anyone's life plans.

We occasionally kept in touch as we worked on our degrees. Two years later, Angela was accepted into grad school in California. She suggested that maybe when I graduated I could move out there with her and get a high-tech job. Cool, she's holding out for me too. But that was another year away, and I didn't want to wait that long to see her. I was working as a student intern at IBM Austin so invited her to visit me before she moved out west. I'd take care of the tickets. She accepted but was planning on driving out, so she said she would swing south on her way so we could visit for a few days.

She was staying at her parents' place in New York when I called to firm up her plans. Angela wasn't there, but her parents said she decided not to make the trip to Texas. She was going to drive directly to the west coast. Disappointed, I asked them to have Angela call me. Instead, all I got was a postcard from New York saying hello and giving me her new phone number in California.

That's it? She owed me a call at least. Did her parents talk her out of it? She could have visited me a few days and still arrived on the west coast in time. Had too much time gone by? Where did I stand with her? If I meant anything to her, she would call. I decided to wait her out.

All the Things I Like About You

Several weeks went by, and still no call. I found myself losing faith in her. I've never believed in one person carrying a whole relationship. Maybe she was just like all the others. Maybe my expectations for her were too high. Maybe it had just been about the sex after all. Her birthday was coming around, so it would be a good time to find out what was going on with her. She would be expecting the call. I was prepared for her to give me the "new guy" speech. I just wanted some closure.

Her birthday arrived. I tried to suppress my sense of disappointment in her as I called the number on the postcard. Some guy answered but said there was no one named Angela there. I confirmed the phone number. Then he realized who I was asking about. She had never moved in. There had been an accident. My eight weeks of waiting had been for naught. Angela would not be calling. Ever.

Only then did I realize how much I considered her part of my future. I was awake in a daze all night. I began to hope against hope there had been some mistake, but her parents confirmed it for me the next day. They had been dreading my call, but were relieved I already knew. They promised me she didn't suffer. For weeks I went through the motions of living, paying only scant attention. I realized the priorities I had set in my life were all wrong. I realized I would be happier starting over with nothing if I could just know that she was alive and well, somewhere, anywhere.

Many people are touched by loss. My suffering is nothing unusual. We see casual images of death every day. It's romantic in the movies to mourn a dead lover. There are beautiful sad songs. Girls cry in theaters. But real life is different. Just as it has taken me a long time to realize most things, it took me years to realize that the other women I became involved with did not care about my grief nor my sense of loss for Angela. They didn't even want to hear about it. I wrote a letter to Petra just after it happened, desperate for some compassion from her. Petra finally wrote back more than a month later: "Sorry to hear that Angela is dead." Then she talked about the snow in Munich. Other women reacted in a similar disinterested way after asking why I was single, or if I'd been in love. I learned never to speak of her.

You would think since women are so into compassion and vulnerability that they would be interested in this tragedy and its emotional impact on me. Not so. In fact, one woman remained jealous of Angela for a long time after her death. How can anyone be jealous of a dead girl? I didn't obsessively talk about her. I explained what had happened, but only once. She wanted to know me, right? Five or six years later in the middle sex with this woman, she suddenly asked me, "Are you thinking of Angela right now?" I didn't deserve that. I had not brought her name up in years. It upsets me even now.

It took several more years before I figured it out. These women were not jealous of Angela, but of the unconditional love I have for her. They don't understand, they don't need to compete with this kind of tormented love. Is it such a violation to talk about something that has affected you? Is it wrong to reach out for help? Maybe one of them could lead me from my deep void. Where's all that healing I keep hearing women are so good at?

Years later in 2002, I came across that last postcard Angela sent. It is the saddest object I possess. I thought of throwing it out, but it's all that remains of her. That, some letters, and a broken silver chain. Then I noticed it was a postcard of the World Trade Center. That one simple card could encompass so much tragedy was unimaginable. I resisted the impulse to expel it from my house, my mind, my life. I had kept this card for a reason. Then I noticed the last word Angela ever wrote to me was "love." She knew. Yes, I know what it's like to love someone forever. That's not something you can just rip from around my neck. Any women who become part of my life will have to permit a small part of her to reside within me. I kept the card. It was as much closure as I would ever get.

Angela was funny and smart. She always knew when I was joking and when I was serious. I never had to lie to her. She accepted the male part of me without trying to change it in any way. We had no control issues. No, she was not perfect. I have no illusions about that. She was human. Besides, perfection is always subjective. She was extraordinary in ordinary ways. There was an uncanny sanity about her. She was complicated even by female standards, but not deliberately so. She was still defining herself at age 24. I wish I could have met her again. She was growing her intellect while retaining her quietly wild side. I understood her and knew her like no one else. I could go on, but it's too painful. Why is it so easy now to think of all the things I like about you?

I recognize Angela's qualities scattered among the women I meet. Intelligence combined with playfulness and intimacy. Tender affection and intense passion. A sense of caring and gentleness. A combination of trust and fascination for men. It reminds me that at the core of a woman is warmth. They can enrich our lives like nothing else. They attract us in ways that are not sexual. They have a strength that is not physical. They bear burdens that cannot be measured in weight. Their value is not determined by success. We sometimes forget how much they believe in us. We sometimes forget how much we are an integral part of each other.

Angela was angerless. She never placed expectations on me. She gave me the good without the bad. There must be people who have all that without it being casually obliterated. Her hand has slipped away, but her touch remains. Sometimes I still catch myself staring at a blank wall, remembering how once in my life there appeared a woman who I connected with on all levels. Once I experienced what it was like to find all the right qualities in a single person. Once I had a taste of that happiness I've heard other people describe. Once is so much more than never.

What Needs to Happen

Feminism has never reached out to men. Feminism has never cared about us. It has opponetized us. Antagonized us. Dehumanized us. Sorry is not good enough. Very few men have actually read any feminist classics. Men can't tell you anything specific about Kate Millett, Naomi Wolf, Betty Friedan, or Susan Faludi. Certainly, most men haven't even heard of pathological feminists like Marylin French, Robin Morgan, and Andrea Dworkin. There aren't any Men's Studies majors to keep up with the various movements within the chaos that is feminism. Men have no interest in feminist philosophy, even though it has impacted our lives in enormously *negative* ways. We can't be bothered with all that. We think that if we wait long enough it will all go away.

Think again. Although most women don't read those feminist books either, they get the message. It's all homogenized for everyone into simplistic "media feminism." It's incorporated into movies, sitcoms, and the national news. Women are smart and men are idiots. Women beating up on men is good. Women never get enough credit. Men are handed everything but women have to fight for it. Woman good, man bad. Anger anger anger. It's like osmosis. If you hear a lie a thousand times it becomes true. Then it becomes law.

Even if students don't enroll in women's studies courses, feminist dogma is still being drilled into them as part of many sociology, psychology, English and foreign language classes. Girls continue to absorb media feminism from television, but then they turn to things like fashion magazines and gender-biased self-help books for guidance in dealing with men. Their resulting relationship skills are a combination of generic male-bashing and Oprah fluff. As always, men are the ones left scrambling to clean up the emotional disasters they create. Men are just used to accepting blame, because we'd rather have sex than be right. Jimmy Buffett has it figured out by the end of *Margaritaville*. Whatever happened, it's his own damn fault.

Women do not want to hear about a "men's rights movement." No need for that. After all, women still need more of everything! The new height of arrogance is that pathological feminists want to define the men's movement so that it basically has the same goals as feminism. The real reason women don't want a men's movement is that they know they would need to change. They would have to start giving us our rights back. On some level all feminists know their joy ride has to end. They've stolen our credit cards, and they're charging them up as fast as they can before we catch on.

It's payback time. Four decades of gender hostility from women has earned us something. Men now have the right to help redefine the role of women in relationships. We have earned the right to be listened to. There is a vast underawareness of men's issues by both men and women.

It's equality, stupid. As part of the restoration of equality we need to eliminate Women's Studies as a curriculum from publicly-funded universities, or offer equivalent male courses. There actually are some bogus "men's studies" courses offered by Women's Studies departments. As usual, the intention is to reprogram us according to their own self-righteous biases. What's my problem? I need to abandon my masculinist discourse by raising my awareness of my own violent oppressive nature and by deconstructing my anti-feminist, misogynistic, homophobic, privileged identity which is grounded in the patriarchy. Oh, that. Femspeak for "Go to hell."

Enrollment in women's studies courses should be limited to the attendance by men in actual men's studies courses in accordance with Title IX. We need men in the media, government, and courts who are equipped to challenge the feminist dogma that is drilled into thousands of women each year. Women's studies faculty would have no say in course content. The creation of men's studies is necessary for the preservation of men's civil rights. How about these equivalent men's studies courses?

Men's Studies 101—Survey of Anti-male Bias in Education
Men's Studies 102—Feminist Sexist Agendas and Double Standards
Men's Studies 103—The Growth of Female Privilege
Men's Studies 121—Introduction to Female Manipulation

Men's Studies 131—Statistical Deceptions of Feminism
Men's Studies 203—Misandry in Western Media
Men's Studies 211—The Feminist Assault on Male Sexuality
Men's Studies 234—DV, Rape, and the Presumption of Innocence
Men's Studies 251—Feminist Revisionism of History I
Men's Studies 252—Feminist Revisionism of History II
Men's Studies 350—Maternity Sex Crimes and Child Support Fraud
Men's Studies 381—Corporate Feminist Power Strategies
Men's Studies 386—Feminism in the Courts and Government
Men's Studies 473—Straight Male Art and Literature I
Men's Studies 474—Straight Male Art and Literature II

How's that for an exercise in role reversal? Women need more of that. How about role-reversal exercises in schools? How about role-reversal workshops for corporate women to teach them to identify offensive male-bashing tendencies in their own behavior? These workshops would be the equivalent of the current "sensitivity training" courses required by most corporations to reprogram us biased males. But until such courses are offered, how about a moratorium on the ridicule of the male gender in the media? No ridiculing men for 10 years in commercials or sit-coms. No Groin kicks for 10 years. No women beating up on men in movies for 10 years.

Maybe we should make it 90 years, since that's how long it's been since the beginning of the long-running male-bashing cartoon strip, "Bringing Up Father." In case you didn't grow up with it like I did, most episodes ended with the father, Jiggs, being beaten to a pulp by the wife, Maggie, using various objects such as rolling pins and vases. No one ever had a problem with domestic violence committed by a female. In fact, that was always the punch line. So to speak.

How about ending abuse of the "battered woman" defense for women who commit murder? Women's advocates have invented a new concept for female murderers: "innocent even after proven guilty." They want all female murderers who claim abuse to be granted clemency and released from prison. Lots of governors have been bowing to the pressure. How about sending a message to women that murder is not an acceptable relationship tool?

How about restoration of the presumption of innocence in domestic violence cases? The "domestic violence industry" has gotten to be like the old East German Stasi secret police, encouraging family members and neighbors to make accusations against the opponents of the state dogma. We now have our own DV Stasi whose mission is to arrest the

What Needs to Happen

opponents of the feminist state. Mere allegations are fine. Even "emotional abuse" is a form of domestic violence now. And as I saw on a recent TV promo, that includes telling a woman she's fat. Such victims are encouraged to use shelters to escape this terrible abuse. Can you imagine shelters for men fleeing women who tease them for having thin hair?

How about rewriting the Violence Against Women Act (VAWA) to acknowledge that violence is also committed by women against men? How about a Violence Against *Anyone* Act? How about equal funding for men's shelters? And they don't have to be based on the needs of women. A men's shelter could offer legal advice and counseling to men wih violent female partners. Men would be able to file reports whenever their wives threaten to commit suicide for not getting their way. And men could seek emergency shelter when they find themselves thrown out of their own homes because of restraining orders. And no, prisons do not count as shelters for men.

Men don't seem to notice that feminism has become an enormous political lobby group which is now embedded within government. Feminism is the equivalent of a publicly-financed political party without any opposition. There are at least 270 taxpayer-funded "women's commissions" in the U.S., all seeking female-exclusive programs and benefits (www.nacw.org). Are there no legitimate male-specific needs? There have been hundreds of government-funded studies performed by university-trained feminists. As a result, feminists can cite 10 or 20 official government studies to back every demand and view they have. There are no male equivalent studies to challenge these politically motivated feminist statistics.

How about government watchdog departments for *men* equivalent to the Canadian "Status of Women Canada?" The "Status of Men" department would raise issues concerning bias toward men in the legal system and fund studies to challenge the validity of statistics used to create public policy about the "wage gap," domestic violence, and sexual assault. The first such department in a state government was recently created in New Hampshire to the stern disapproval of women's groups (www.ncfcnh.org). However, it does not yet have public funding like all other women's commissions.

How about a Men's Caucus group in Congress, which would exclude women and promote men's rights, just like the *existing* Women's Caucus in Congress that is permitted to exclude men? (www.womens-policy.org). No really, why not?

I see there's a tiny new League of Men Voters (www.leagueofmen-voters.org). Why? Because, according to U.S. Census figures, there are 8 million fewer male voters than female. The disparity occurs in every age demographic. Obviously, the League of Women Voters will not be addressing the issue.

How about an organization that funds candidates based on their support of men's rights, like Emily's List (www.emilyslist.org) does for feminist candidates? Except that we wouldn't exclude candidates based on their gender. In 2002, Emily's List spent $23 million to fund *female-only* registration drives and *female-only* candidates.

How about an Office of Men's Health equivalent to the growing Office of Women's Health? (http://www.4woman.gov/owh/index.htm) The 2003 budget for the federal Office of Women's Health was $29.1 million, an increase of $12 million since 2001 (www.hhs.gov). The non-existent Office of Men's Health still gets zero dollars. Women-only health offices originated in 1990 when Senator Barbara Mikulski indignantly cited data showing that female-specific health research spending comprised only 14% of the National Institutes of Health (NIH) budget. Mikulski declared that such discrimination demanded the creation of an Office of Women's Health, which was quickly approved. No one mentioned that only 6.5% of the NIH budget was male-specific.

There are now Departments of Women's Health in the Centers for Disease Control and Prevention (CDC), the Food and Drug Administration (FDA), Health Resources and Services Administration (HRSA), in addition to the NIH. As expected, there are no corresponding men's health departments. If women's health is so neglected as claimed by feminist groups, then why is the average life expectancy of American women now almost *seven years* longer than that of American men? It's their way of telling men to drop dead. Clearly, lots of men are complying.

Minority women now get their own programs within the Office of Women's Health, (http://www.4woman.gov/owh/minority.htm) which include funding for the tracking of female genital cutting in the United States. It can come of no surprise that there is no funding to discourage the very common practice of male circumcision. While ignoring the chronic lack of foreskin in Western society, feminists decry female genital mutilation in the third world as another example of bizarre sexual demands forced upon women by oppressive male cultures. So, who's forcing all the American teenager girls to get their navels, nipples and clits pierced? Is that male oppression too?

What Needs to Happen

How about parity in funding for men's health research? I noticed that in 2000 breast cancer research expenditures outpaced prostate cancer research by $438 million to $203 million, even though prostate cancer diagnoses exceed those of breast cancer. According to the National Cancer Institute (NCI), breast cancer expenditures in 2003 still exceeded those for prostate cancer by $548 million to $306 million (http://prg.cancer.gov).

The latest estimates by The American Cancer Society predicts 230,110 new cases of prostate cancer in men and 215,990 new cases of breast cancer (http://www.cancer.org/downloads/MED/Page4.pdf). Perhaps better diagnosis of prostate cancer would reveal much higher frequencies in men than estimated. How about free prostate cancer screenings for men, since breast cancer screenings are free for women? In Austin, there's even a program to pick up elderly women at their homes and take them in for screenings at no charge. Why is there no such service to pick up elderly men for free cancer screenings? And can't we come up with a better prostate cancer test than a dude with a rubber glove?

Two years ago I saw an Internet fund-raiser for breast cancer. For every unique Web user that clicked on the pink ribbon, one dollar would be donated for breast cancer research. I clicked on it. Then I wondered, where is the ribbon for prostate cancer? Why do we care more about women than men? There are telethons for breast cancer, 10K runs for breast cancer, collections on airline flights for breast cancer, a postage stamp for breast cancer. I get telemarketing calls for breast cancer. Why should I give my money to a cause that deliberately excludes men? The Lance Armstrong Foundation (www.livestrong.org) isn't exclusively for men with testicular cancer, it's for all people with any type of cancer. That's a cause I can support.

How about eliminating hidden gender advantages for women in corporations? How about a "gender bias" complaint be made available for men to file against women who deny us promotions and raises because of our gender or marital status? How about ending official gender entitlements in government hiring and contracting? My own state of Texas has a department of "Historically Underutilized Businesses" (formerly "Minority- and Women-owned Businesses"), which has quota goals based on race and gender. Did I say "quota goals"? Sorry, I meant, "diversity goals" or "guidelines for the attainment of a critical mass." Like all states, Texas has a government-funded Women's Commission to coordinate and promote women-only programs. Women even get their own "Women's Chamber of Commerce."

How about real penalties and criminal records for women who misidentify the fathers of their children? How about free paternity tests on demand? How about verifying the paternity of all newborns? I wonder how many mothers would be discovered committing paternity identity fraud if all newborns were tested? According to the American Association of Blood Banks (www.aabb.org), in 2003 there were 353,387 paternity tests performed, and 99,174, or 28 percent of them, determined that the man designated by the mother was *not* the biological father. This figure is consistent with the results from 2001 and 2002, when 29% of paternity tests resulted in "exclusions." Even though these figures do not represent the population as a whole, they are astounding. I think after it becomes standard practice to verify the paternity of every newborn, we will look back in disbelief that we simply trusted women to tell us the truth.

Why do "reproductive rights" exclude men? If we have "choice for women," how about "voice for men"? How about *requiring* women to inform potential fathers of their pregnancies? No, they cannot laugh it off. And how about requiring women to inform biological fathers of their intention to have abortions? How about offering the father the first right of adoption, instead of allowing women to anonymously drop off babies at hospitals and fire stations? Since women can absolve themselves from all responsibility for a child by having an abortion, shouldn't men have the equivalent right to absolve themselves of responsibility within the first trimester? Ouch, equality bites! (See www.choiceformen.com).

How about the right of children to know the true identity of their biological parents? How about enforcement of court-ordered visitation rights? How about restrictions on "move-aways," where the custodial parent maliciously prevents children from having contact with their other parent. How about eliminating draconian divorce and child support laws that result in the financial ruin of men? How about ending debtor's prisons for men who cannot pay?

How about rape shield laws that protect the identities of men as well as women? How about eliminating the assumption of guilt when sexual assault charges are brought against men? How about restitution for male victims of false rape accusations? How about making false accusers face the same jail time as rapists? If we can't punish false accusers for fear of them never recanting, can't we at least give them a criminal record? How about a false accuser registry? These women are sex

The Rantings

offenders as much as rapists. Put that runaway bride on the list. Perhaps a false rape accusation should be considered a hate crime.

How about equal prison sentences for women who break the same laws as men? How about the equal application of statutory rape laws for women who induce underage boys or girls to have sex? How about protecting underage boys from having to pay child support to older women who have seduced them into becoming unwitting sperm donors?

I wonder if women will see their "oppression" in a different light once they are no longer excluded from the draft because of their gender? Being made to register for selective service may be the wake-up call women need. No fair slipping in special exemptions to keep women out of harm's way. Let's make sure women make up half the dead and wounded, at least until we eliminate gender-norming, affirmative action, and all other social engineering programs that benefit women at the expense of men.

How about ending the "assumption of oppression" used to justify the plundering of international relief funds? Feminists have made their way into organizations like Amnesty International, The World Health Organization (WHO), and the United Nations where they have succeeded in diverting financial resources away from programs inclusive of men by dramatizing the needs of women. WHO has multiple women's health programs (http://www.who.int/health_topics/womens_health/en/), but no corresponding men's health programs. The UN's Division for the Advancement of Women (www.un.org/womenwatch/daw/index.html) coordinates the effort to direct funding toward female-specific programs. The UN program UNIFEM (http://www.unifem.org) has the mission to advance feminist goals worldwide, such as focusing resources only on *women* with AIDS. Amnesty International has women-only programs (http://www.amnestyusa.org/women/index.do) supporting asylum and "human rights" for women, but none for men.

Although there are many countries where boys' enrollment in school lags behind girls, UNICEF targets extra funding only where girls' enrollment lags. They have a "Go Girls" program, but no program for boys (www.unicef.org/girlseducation/campaign.html). The humanitarian organization CARE has a similar approach to education. As if plagiarized from Orwell, their website (www.careusa.org/campaigns/childrenpoverty/) proudly proclaims "CARE's education programs emphasize equal access, especially for girls."

Even with the help of international funding, feminists will have a difficult time imposing feminism upon the world. Their pro-lesbian, anti-male "women über alles" agenda is not welcome outside the tolerant West. And most women in the world do not share the feminist goal of the elimination of gender roles. Not even the "oppressed" Muslim women want the feminist version of "liberation."

In fact, the opposite is happening. Instead of the globalization of feminism, we are undergoing a cultural displacement of Western civilization. Those "oppressive" cultures with male dominance and clearly defined gender roles are coming to the West with their value systems intact. Because of the ideological fad called "multiculturalism," we are welcoming masses people who believe women should be obedient to men. They will be the ones redefining Western culture as our own populations implode due to the popularity of abortion, the rise of anti-male culture, and the growing number of women who prioritize success over family. Feminism will have few heirs.

Despite this litany of issues, most men seem unconcerned with the growth of anti-male biases. Men are still waiting around for women to get over themselves, as if male-bashing is going to go out of style. It's not. In fact, it's getting worse. Women have been listening to all the voices telling them they are better and smarter than men. These women are beyond hope. They're possessed. Cut them loose. Let them find their doormat men.

A few women have managed to pry those cucumbers off their eyes. They have that rare ability to see things from a non-female, non-pathological, non-narcissistic perspective. Christine Stolba is one, author of an excellent short exposé on women's studies, *Lying in a Room of One's Own*, downloadable at www.iwf.org/pdf/roomononesown.pdf. Another is Trudy Schuett, who founded an organization to challenge domestic violence myths and misinformation. See www.mediaradar.org.

Female writers like Christina Hoff Sommers, Wendy McElroy, and Daphne Patai have a grasp of what we're up against. As men, we owe them a debt of gratitude. To their credit, they've been ex-communicated by the feminist elite. Perhaps they can help make equality equal again. Though I doubt they can exorcise the demons from feminism, they're welcome to try. Personally, I don't see a baby in that bathwater. I wish they would stop trying to dredge up positives from the sludge. Feminism will never be egalitarianism.

I think the role of truly enlightened women will be to "deconstruct" feminism itself. Put them in charge of the backlash. They've gone through women's studies and read all the books. Not many men have that level of understanding. It's women who dragged us into all this,

What Needs to Happen

so they should help take it down. Will a genuine Joan of Arc emerge from among the heretics? Maybe *that's* the next wave. I'll take up arms, but I certainly don't want to lead the battle against pathological feminism. I'm not trying to turn this into a profession—I'm just a guy trying to figure out how things got so fucked up.

I've noticed the tendency of many men's rights activists to denounce anyone not in complete agreement with them, especially when their identities are concealed on Internet forums. They'll spot one issue of disagreement and launch a scathing attack. It's the "more radical than thou" mentality. It doesn't help us. We should welcome people who support men's rights issues regardless of their political or religious views. Or gender. And yes, we should also welcome gay men into the men's movement — as long as they don't use it as a platform to preach the gay gospel like lesbians have done with feminism. And as long as they haven't betrayed their masculinity by behaving or dressing like girls. Effeminate gay men belong to the feminists and always will. I see the men's rights movement as a spectrum of men and women coming together to repair the damage of feminism. Save the denunciations for those who truly oppose us.

Besides the behemoths like N.O.W. and the Feminist Majority, there are hundreds of women-first groups and "research centers" promoting female-only policies. There are only a handful of small, unfunded men's rights groups, like The National Coalition of Free Men (www.ncfm.org). In spite of the claim by feminists that men control the Internet, there's only a spattering of men's rights forums and websites among an ocean of pro-feminist sites. Here are a few sites I frequent:

www.mensactivism.org—A news and commentary based forum that permits anonymous posters, and rarely censors anything. Very diverse views are found on this apolitical board. It is a valuable source of men's rights issues and opinions from all English-speaking countries. It's a free-for-all that comes under occasional feminist troll attacks.

www.standyourground.com—Men's rights forum with tight monitoring of personal attacks. Extended discussions of all men's rights topics are encouraged.

www.ifeminists.com—Wendy McElroy's information site containing gender-related articles and a discussion forum. The site supports men's rights, but is very acceptant of feminist views as well. It's the Bahai version of feminism. The forum reads like a therapy session.

www.iwf.org—The Independent Women's Forum could probably be called "The Republican Women's Forum." They have a database of articles and a blog. This mostly pro-male site tends to support traditional gender roles while fighting feminist misinformation.

www.mensnewsdaily.com—A listing of gender-related news events and articles along with strong doses of neo-conservative ideology. The heavily moderated forum focuses on discussion of men's rights issues and politics. Watch out for the flashing banners and pop-ups.

www.angryharry.com—An extensive UK anti-feminist site featuring news and lots of entertaining articles.

www.cooltools4men.com—Darren Blacksmith's growing UK anti-feminist site that consists of informational "tools" such as a men's issues forum, essays, and examples of anti-male articles from the print media.

http://www.the-niceguy.com/forum/—An established site with a forum where men unleash their pent-up wrath. This place frequently ventures over the line from anti-feminist to anti-female. However, this also makes it the most brutally honest and intense of the men's forums I have yet seen.

www.mens-rights.net—Good general information site for all aspects of men's rights in the Western world, including the U.S., England, Wales, Scotland, Australia, and New Zealand.

www.askmen.com—This highly commercialized and popular website now has a moderated forum dedicated to men's issues.

www.mensmovieguide.com—A movie website that reviews and rates films according to entertainment value as well as pro- or anti-male content.

www.glennsacks.com—This radio show host has become one of the foremost men's rights advocates. His articles are available on this website. He also uses the site to coordinate activism. You can register for his e-newsletter.

I don't debate feminism with women anymore. I don't put my hand too close to a mad dog's dinner dish either. I can't go out on the feminist blogs without getting a warped view of women in general. That's where the most vile of the man-haters reside. They are way beyond hope. Let them be lesbians. I plan on talking to women who still like men. Yes, there are some. No blog wars for me.

It's futile to discuss anything with professional victimologists trained in women's studies classes. I have no desire to read another 20 or 30 feminist books so that I can refute them. I refuse to dwell on their insanity. Neither will I waste my time listening to them spew their favorite manipulated data about domestic violence and the "wage gap."

What Needs to Happen

You can show them specifically how they are wrong, but it doesn't matter. They are pre-convinced of their own infallibility.

Sometimes I get so sick of hearing the same old oppressor/victim female superiority bullshit that I'm ready to voluntarily go brain dead. Make it stop. How many more years do I have to hear this endless drivel? Will someone just strap me down and stick the needle in my arm, please? I'm sure N.O.W. would gladly post a sign-up sheet for the honor. I'd rather not give them the satisfaction.

I've heard women say unless I lighten up I'll never change anyone's mind. I think this is more about changing laws than changing minds. Besides, I can't recall changing a woman's mind about anything in my entire adult life. Women will have to change their own minds. I prefer to spend my time working with other activists to change policies in government, corporations, and the media.

As interest in men's activism grows, we need to avoid the mistakes of feminism. It's a "men's rights movement," not a "men are always right movement." Just as feminism is full of angry women intent on destroying men, there will be men within the men's movement who display an equivalent ugliness toward women. That is not the equality I have in mind.

Men's activism is not about anger or retribution. It's not about anyone's personal or political agenda. It's not a vendetta. It's not about gay rights. It's not about religion. The men's movement is not married to any political party. It's not about Marxism or capitalism or liberals or conservatives or world politics. It's not about achieving our own preferential treatment. It's about the elimination of legalized double standards. It's about the exposure of feminist lies and hypocrisy. It's about ending the wholesale ravaging of the male gender. It's about the fulfillment and unity of both genders. Women have incredible talents and intelligence if they will only stop squandering their energy on anger. Women need their lives enriched by men, and I want to hear them finally say it.

In the End

For those of you who have skipped ahead to the last chapter looking for some easy kernel of testosterone wisdom, I offer you this: As you go through life, take time to smell the hops. Czech Saaz is as fragrant as any rose. That may be all the real wisdom I have for you. I have no New Age metaphysical inspirational philosophy to heal everyone. But who needs that when you can get a cold Pilsner? That's my herbal remedy. There's something very therapeutic about a bitter brew. I've found a lot of answers at the bottom of a glass. Sometimes there's no place else to look.

Understanding the current mentality of women won't help us get along with them. If that's what you want, it's better to pick up a positive-thinking self-help book and pretend the world is made of flowers and that hope itself solves problems. It's better to tell women they are wiser and smarter because of their intuition. It's better to tell women they are right about everything and to apologize for something every day. Pour me another, please. Better numb than dumb.

Men and women will never fully understand each other. But then, what would life be without unattainable goals? Women will always want to explain their feelings and men our reasons. Maybe these writings simply address why we cannot achieve a complete understanding. It will continue forever. Misunderstanding perpetuates itself. We will continue to fuck up our relationships with each other because we're just so damn good at it. Can't we at least learn to fuck things up in more constructive ways?

Whether or not there is an organized men's rights movement, men need to stand up and stop tolerating the ideological abuse. I don't know if our relationships with women will ever recover from feminism, but we *will* recover our rights. A few years ago I referred to Petra as "mademoiselle." She quickly informed me, *"Kein Mensch sagt das mehr."* Feigning affection, she kissed me and told me to try it again using the word "madam." It was an attempt to enforce her old femspeak on me. I refused. The whole gulag summer came rushing back to me. We dropped the subject. That same day we were watching the French Open and the announcer gave the score for "Mademoiselle" Hingis. "So, *no one says that anymore?*" I packed up my things and walked out on her. She was terribly hurt. Oh well. Yes, I've seen her since then, but femspeak is no longer enforced. I can even use the word "girl" to reference an adult female without being "corrected." It's quite simple. Standing up for yourself gets results.

So what ever happened to Petra? She's a self-righteous feminist single mother who sits around wondering why she has no men in her life. She looks at herself, still attractive in her late 40s. "What is it?" She seems genuinely puzzled. I could tell her I've written an entire book on the subject. It wouldn't do her any good. She'd be horrified, in fact. She keeps raising the possibility of getting back together with me after her daughter has grown up, as if Gabrielle is the one keeping me away. She doesn't understand that Gabrielle is the one who drew me back to her. I'll consider getting back together with Petra after she explains exactly how she earned a living in Montreal, apologizes to that guy she tricked into getting her pregnant, and returns all the child support he paid her. Oh, and I almost forgot—this time she has to read all the books *I assign to her*, repudiate feminism, and become a men's rights activist.

Why did I put up with Petra's destructive misconduct for so long? I think it's because I'd been taught to. For years I held her to a lower standard of responsibility because of her gender. Not any more. Finally I see things for what they are. What I have with Petra is not a relationship—it's a bad habit.

When she's not spewing feminist ideology, Petra is wonderful and warm. She was created with those qualities. The destructive aspects of her personality were all learned. But she'll never be able to unlearn them. She's been in the kiln. She's swallowed the poison. I can't discuss anything of substance with her; she's in denial about so many things. For years I found myself clinging to that youthful sexual image of her back in Spain, when she was passionate, caring, and couldn't speak English.

Petra now spends her time trying to heal people holistically, but she could never figure out how to heal her own relationships. I don't think she's going to find an herb in the rain forest for that one. The pain she inflicts upon others has never been important to her. It turns out Ursula was the sane one of the two girls in my car on that trip to Spain. Ursula never took a single women's studies course. Instead, Ursula became a pediatrician, has a stable marriage with two children, and is perfectly rational. Ursula has done very well without the feminist anger that ate away so much of Petra's life.

During one visit to Munich, I was playing with Petra's daughter who was nine at the time. I was swinging her around and she was riding on my shoulders steering me like a horse when she suddenly said to me, "Hey, you want to be my dad? Come on, it'll be great! You could do it!" Petra intervened, knowing Gabrielle couldn't comprehend the complexities involved. She doesn't understand that we live on different continents. She doesn't understand that her mom and I have nothing in common except a long painful history. She doesn't realize that my relationship with her mom is damaged beyond repair—otherwise, I'd be her dad in a minute. She doesn't realize, that's the nicest thing anyone has ever said to me in my entire life.

Just beneath the surface of civility is an enormous amount of anger I have toward Petra. It's less about whatever she may have done to me than it is about what she's done to her daughter and the man she used to conceive her. How is it I can make my peace with a Panzer driver who certainly killed hundreds of people during his four years in Hitler's army, but I can't seem to forgive Petra? I think part of it is that Petra has never acknowledged her own misdeeds. Her crimes are ongoing. She continues to extract money from Gabrielle's biological father, which further drives him away. It's something I cannot reconcile.

I don't know what will happen to Petra's daughter, but there are consequences to not having a father in her life. I'm sure Gabrielle cannot throw a ball, use power tools, perform basic auto mechanics, play a musical instrument, or use a computer. She showed amazing interest in learning about computers and playing computer games, but it was a struggle to find games that met with Petra's approval. The girl games were too stereotypically female; but the boy games were too violent, even the ones that just shoot down spaceships. The computer I gave them fell into immediate neglect. Petra stacks clothes on it.

So, what was accomplished by Petra's lifetime dedication to feminist ideology? It was the elimination of a father from her family. At least she doesn't have to worry about the terrible effects of the patriarchy on her daughter. Gabrielle craves male attention, and gets almost none. She likes being held by male arms, but has learned to do without. Petra recently told me she wouldn't try it again—raising a

In the End

child without a father. Isn't she the wise one now? Gabrielle will remember the faces of the Hindu women that decorate her bedroom, but
they can't help her achieve anything. They can't walk with her in a
park. They can't help her with math. She can't sit on their laps.

I'm sure Gabrielle will track down her father at some point. He lives
only a few miles away. I imagine Petra dreads the time when they finally meet. What will he say when Gabrielle asks him why he refused
to see her? Will he take the fall as a bad father, or will Petra be forced
to admit that she deliberately deceived him? Will Gabrielle be able to
win her biological father's love even though her mother committed
rape to conceive her? Will Gabrielle think she is the cause of the problem? Gabrielle doesn't even know she has a brother and two sisters.
We have the makings of a very angry young woman. I'm just not sure
where her anger will be directed. It's a time bomb waiting to go off.
But Petra got herself into this. I am not her white knight. I am not her
redeemer. I will not assume the role of an American rushing in to save
someone's world. There is no version of rescue forthcoming. Petra is
on her own. If I ever see her again, it will be to check in on Gabrielle.

It amazes me when I think about how much thought and effort I've
put into the pursuit of females, and how little I've ended up getting out
of it. After years of not being able to tolerate dysfunctional dating, dysfunctional relationships, and dysfunctional women, perhaps I should
reconsider if it's *me* who's dysfunctional. Are women insane, or is it me?
I can hear the collective female scream urgently proclaiming I'm the
one with the problem. And most of my life I would have agreed. I was
not exciting enough. I was not aggressive enough. Not confident
enough. Not controlling enough. Not sensitive enough. Not spiritual
enough. Not successful enough. I wasn't a challenge. I couldn't conform to the female soap opera vision of a man. Finally, I've unburdened
myself of all that. I no longer need their approval. I am a free man.

Maybe someday women will come to realize the damage they inflict on men and relationships. Maybe they will begin to accept us as
we are. Maybe they will look inward for change and abandon their
anger toward men. Maybe they will finally learn to express unam-
biguous appreciation of men. And they'll actually start to listen to us.
And they'll wear shirts that say, "It's all about *You*." And they'll stop
using sex as a weapon. And they'll stop manipulating us in destructive
ways. And they'll apologize to us when they're wrong. And they'll
learn to play electric guitars. And why are there ants crawling all over
me? Why are my sleeves tied behind my back?

It doesn't really matter how many times they've repeated it. In the end, it's women who "just don't get it." Women still have no clue what "equality" means. Women have been insisting on equality for more than a century. That is the standard I now hold them to. But they won't achieve it until they understand it. Equality means eliminating all gender privileges, not just male privilege. Equality means respect for both genders, not just for females. Equality means more responsibility, not less. Men have to be prepared to patiently explain and point out all the hypocrisy and double standards of feminism that have been used to demean us in the name of equality. It will take a while.

Incredibly, I haven't given up on women; however, I may have given up on ever having a relationship. Don't bother telling me I'm wrong about everything. Is there a woman who can step forward and show me I'm wrong? Is romance a two-way street? Is there true love forever? Will there come a time when men and women resolve to inflict only kindness upon each other? Suddenly, all I hear is collective silence.

So how did all those married men out there get together with women? A few of them got lucky and met cooperative sane females. But I think most men have just learned to cope with dysfunctional relationships because they have become the norm. They've gotten used to not having sex. They don't care anymore that the money is always spent. They don't expect any gratitude. They're comfortable being inadequate. They just suck it up whenever they're demeaned. They don't even feel it anymore. They've taken up the challenge of dealing with women who think being psychotic is a form of entertainment. A lot of men just consider it their destiny to remain subservient to emotionally demanding women who can never be satisfied. These men have never known better. I have. I've met women who genuinely love and respect men. I can't tolerate less than that now. If I am to remain forever single, it's because I refuse to be the target of the nebulous anger embraced by women. I can't take the unnecessary drama and unresolvable conflicts. I will not be the emotional whipping boy for a woman who thinks life is just not good enough for her. I'll take my pathetic, peaceful life. I'm not happy; but I'm not unhappy, and that's not bad. I just hope I live long enough to witness the awakening of men.

I still believe in women. I'm not sure why. Maybe it's because I believe nature could not have screwed up that badly. Maybe it's because I keep catching glimpses of incredible women as they struggle to pursue men in a shattered relationship dynamic. Maybe it's because I see more potential in women than they apparently see in themselves. Maybe I believe in women just because I want to so badly. But one thing is for sure—there's no one making me say it.

In the End